D1627096

Seder Talk
The Conversational Haggada

OUPRESS　MAGGID

Erica Brown

SEDER TALK

The Conversational Haggada

Eight Essays for the Eight Days of Pesaḥ

Maggid Books and OU Press

Seder Talk
The Conversational Haggada

First Edition, 2015
Maggid Books
An imprint of Koren Publishers Jerusalem Ltd.

POB 8531, New Milford, CT 06776-8531, USA
& POB 4044, Jerusalem 9104001, Israel
www.korenpub.com

Haggada layout: The Koren Beth Jacob Family Haggada
Cover Image: Le Cantique des Cantiques IV, 1958 / huile sur toile/
50 × 61 cm / Collection Musée national Marc Chagall, Nice
Marc Chagall, Study to Song of Songs IV
and Zippora Sketches © ADAGP, Paris 2015
Shraga Weil, Song of Songs © Shraga Weil
Page from The Golden Haggadah courtesy of The British Library Board
Page from The Prague Haggada courtesy of
the National Library of Israel, Jerusalem
Four Sons Playing Cards © 2014 by David Moss. Used with permission by
www.bet-alpha-editions.com Berkeley California

The publication of this book was made possible
through the generous support of *Torah Education in Israel*.

ISBN 978-965-301-724-5, *hardcover*

A CIP catalogue record for this title is
available from the British Library.

Printed and bound in the United States

Eight Essays for the Eight Days of Pesaḥ

For the full Haggada text, with translation and commentary, turn to the other end of this volume.

Day One

On the wind
in the cool of the evening
I send greetings to a friend.

I ask him only to remember the day
of our parting when we made a covenant
of love by an apple tree.

"Song," Yehuda Halevi
(Translated by Carl Rakosi)

Day One

All Who Are Hungry

After a good dinner one can forgive anybody, even one's own relations.

Oscar Wilde

There is immense joy in hosting others, in gathering together people we love and feeding them. Having others share in our personal abundance seems to multiply what we have, generating a sense of even greater blessing. When we can do that with strangers, we extend ourselves beyond the boundaries of our table and create – for a time – a new, more expansive community. The mitzva of *hakhnasat orḥim* thus transforms both the one who receives our outlay of generosity and the one who gives, by doubling the perception of bounty we have. If you have enough to share, you must indeed have enough.

In a talmudic passage reminiscing about the good deeds of the great sage R. Huna, the scholar Rava plied Rafram bar Papa for information. The great rabbi thought back to his past and observed: "Of his [R. Huna's] childhood I do not recollect anything, but of his old age I do. When he had a meal he would open the door wide and declare, 'Whosoever is in need, let him come and eat'" (Taanit 20b). We know these words. They leap off the first pages of our Haggada, but they first lived in the behavior of a man whose scholarship was balanced by goodness. We open the Seder with our central, symbolic Passover food – the matza, bread of our affliction – and an impassioned appeal: "Let all who are

hungry come in and eat; let all who are in need come and join us for the Pesaḥ."
We raise the matza to be sure that everyone at our table knows that though we
start with poor man's food, we invite all to join us in a magical evening of food,
story, and song, as if to say: no matter how sorry our lot, we are always blessed
enough to share it. No matter how desperate our situation, anyone who is in need
can be assured of a place with us.

And then, in the same sentence, as we extend the invitation, we mention
the Passover sacrifice, letting the needy know that even when we move from the
bread of affliction to the expensive Paschal lamb, they are still welcome to join
us. An invitation any less inclusive would be disingenuous, since we need both
foods to tell the full story. We became a nation through the Passover sacrifice.
How then can we deny it to someone who cannot afford it? This generosity of
spirit was passed down to us from R. Huna. No meal touched his lips without
a sincere offer to share his food with others. He did not merely utter the words.
He first opened the door wide.

OUR JEWISH HOSPITALITY INDUSTRY

Opening the door or sitting by an open door is a behavior we recognize from
long before R. Huna became the subject of talmudic conversation. Hospitality is
the hallmark of Abraham, our patriarch and founder. When the Lord appeared
to Abraham near the great trees of Mamre, "he was sitting at the entrance to his
tent in the heat of the day" (Gen. 18:1). Abraham, who was recuperating from
his circumcision, and may well have been experiencing his own sense of frailty,
was not cooling off in the center of the tent, protecting himself from the midday
sun in its shade. Instead, the verse stresses that he sat at his threshold in Canaan,
seeking out passersby in need.

This may sound like strange behavior, but when it comes to identifying
those who are needy, we have to leave the comfort zone of protected space. Few
people will announce their neediness outright. Those in need may suffer a quiet
alienation, a sense of loneliness that remains unexposed or undisclosed. And in
his own state of vulnerability, Abraham also clues us into how our own fragility
often makes us more cognizant of the vulnerability of others.

I have noticed, living in an observant community, bonded by the cement
of ḥesed, loving-kindness, that there are certain people who are quick to identify
newcomers, who think nothing of approaching strangers with a smiling "hello"
and an offer for Shabbat dinner or lunch. Others remain in their small clusters
of familiarity, the inner circles we create among neighbors, friends, and family.
To an insider, these groups seem like casual cells of laughter, conviviality, and

conversation. To a stranger, these inner circles seem like impenetrable cities; standing on the outside, the guest or stranger feels helpless watching others who know the language and mores, the customs and accepted practices that appear foreign and inaccessible. You do not have to be in a foreign country to experience this personal dissonance. You just have to be in a crowded room where you recognize no one. Rabbi Joseph Soloveitchik captured this impenetrability and its after-effects in a scene he described in his article "The Community":

> Quite often a man finds himself in a crowd of strangers. He feels lonely. No one knows him, no one cares for him, no one is concerned about him. It is an existential experience. He begins to doubt his own ontological worth. This leads to alienation from the crowd surrounding him. Suddenly someone taps him on the shoulder and says, "Aren't you Mr. So-and-so? I have heard so much about you." In a fraction of a second his awareness changes. What brought about the change? The recognition by somebody, the word![1]

There is a moment, often brief and fleeting, when we experience angst in a crowded room because we recognize no one and no one recognizes us. This is not a significant instance of anguish, not enough to merit attention, and yet it makes us feel small and unimportant. If no one knows us does that imply that we are not worth knowing? If no one speaks to us, does that mean we have nothing worthwhile to say? All of this changes with a simple tap on the shoulder. As Rabbi Soloveitchik brings us into this small moment of alienation and then grace, we suddenly understand that our kindness to strangers, our empathy with their feelings of vulnerability, does more than make others feel welcome. It makes them feel whole again. It has restorative properties.

The continuing narrative about Abraham in Genesis 18 imparts a number of other important lessons about hospitality:

> He [Abraham] said, "If I have found favor in your eyes, my Lord, do not pass your servant by. Let a little water be brought, and then you may all wash your feet and rest under this tree. Let me get you something to eat, so you can be refreshed and then go on your way – now that you have

---

1. Joseph Soloveitchik, "The Community," *Tradition* (Spring 1978) vol. 17, no. 2: 16. The essay was first delivered as a talk at the 78th annual meeting of the Conference of Jewish Communal Service in Boston, May 31, 1976.

come to your servant." "Very well," they answered, "do as you say." So Abraham hurried into the tent to Sarah. "Quick," he said, "get three seahs of fine flour and knead it and bake some bread." Then he ran to the herd and selected a choice, tender calf and gave it to a servant, who hurried to prepare it. He then brought some curds and milk and the calf that had been prepared, and set these before them. While they ate, he stood near them under a tree. "Where is your wife Sarah?" they asked him. "There, in the tent," he said. Then the Lord said, "I will surely return to you about this time next year, and Sarah your wife will have a son." Now Sarah was listening at the entrance to the tent, which was behind him.

Abraham had a keen sense of the needs of others, perhaps born of his own experience with alienation. It takes a stranger to recognize a stranger. When Abraham actually saw people on the horizon he hurried in their direction. "Abraham looked up and saw three men standing nearby. When he saw them, he ran toward them from the entrance of his tent to meet them and bowed low to the ground" (Gen. 18:2). The verse stresses the verbs of hospitality: seeing, rushing, meeting, and bowing. It is easy enough to ignore someone in one's peripheral vision. We do it all the time when we don't want the emotional complications that result from eye contact. In a short customer service book by Ari Weinzweig, *Zingerman's Guide to Giving Great Service*, the author outlines a rule for all employees of his restaurant. If a customer is within ten feet, employees must make eye contact. Within four feet, they must approach him. Eye contact and then physical movement minimizes the detachment that can develop if eye contact is avoided and distance is preserved. Before the bar mitzva of one of my boys, a friend asked me if I was practicing the six-month rule: "Don't look anyone you're not planning to invite in the eye for six months before a *simḥa* [a joyous occasion]." I told her it was a ridiculous idea, but as the date neared, I understood perfectly what she meant. By looking at you, I feel obligated to you or experience shame that I have not included you.

Abraham looked up, saw his guests, and then hurried to greet them by prostrating himself low before them. This final action is difficult to understand. Bowing low – to the ground – seems out of place here, especially given Abraham's own weakened constitution. But perhaps Abraham knew that strangers always feel humbled in unfamiliar circumstances. He preempted their sense of alienation with a physical gesture that communicated his own humility, as if to say to them with one deep bow, I am no better than you simply because I am from here and you are not.

Abraham and the Three Angels, James Tissot

The French artist James Tissot (1836–1902) captures the extremity of this encounter in his majestic watercolor "Abraham and the Three Angels." In the composition, the approaching angels are viewed from inside Abraham's tent, which is carpeted by colorful, fringed Oriental rugs and pillows. The tent folds narrow the window of observation, and the tops of the heads of the three approaching strangers in white appear to be cut off to Abraham who, in the painting, is lying on the floor of his tent cutting a sharp diagonal from the right-hand corner of the painting until the middle of the composition. This image of submission demonstrates that Tissot was a careful and literal reader of this Bible story. Abraham's physical position hints to recovery from his circumcision, but also, and more importantly, suggests how he diminished himself in the presence of others. Through intentional contraction, he made space for these strangers and honored them. He let down the defenses that one might typically put up when confronting three unfamiliar men approaching the entrance to one's home.

The text in Genesis 18 emphasizes speed as another aspect of humility, putting someone else's time before one's own. Abraham and Sarah – who themselves did quite a bit of traveling in Genesis – understood that people who are traveling generally have a destination and somewhere they have to be within a time frame. If I hesitate as a host, then I am not really at your service. I am working within my own framework of convenience. With surprising alacrity, emphasized several times in the narrative, Abraham and Sarah offer up a meal both expensive and time-consuming to produce. Roasting meat and kneading bread require time, but they also indicate that the host has indeed put himself out for his guest. In Jewish law, the host is supposed to distribute the portions to his or her guests since he or she will, we presume, be more generous than a guest serving himself.

The mitzva of *hakhnasat orhim*, welcoming guests, is not merely about greeting strangers at the threshold with friendly gestures. The infinitive "*lehakhnis*" means to cause one to enter, to bring one inside. In other words, we are not merely asked, in fulfillment of this commandment, to be welcoming, which is to say a gracious hello and make introductions. We are obligated to bring someone who stands on the outside of our lives into our lives. That movement from outside to inside requires effort, sensitivity, and energy. It mandates us to consider the factors that would constitute being on the outside and minimize them so that strangers can become friends.

EATING WITH STRANGERS

Equalizing the playing field between host and guest also requires intensifying our understanding of the dining experience we offer at the Seder and every Shabbat and holiday. In *Religion for Atheists*, Alain de Botton acknowledges the significance of communal dining as a way that religion teaches people to reach out to others. He bemoans the fact that in modern society, we have more restaurants than ever, "but what is significant is the almost universal lack of venues that help us transform strangers into friends."[2] As an atheist, de Botton suggests the creation of what he calls the Agape Restaurant, from the Greek word for love. It would have an open door and separate families and couples. It would have a guidebook of rules for the meal, much like the Seder has, with prescribed topics to stimulate conversation. In fact, de Botton mentions the Seder as a prime example of a meal that achieves brotherhood. He appreciates the fact that meals taken with strangers force goodwill and, at the very least, minimize suspicion:

> Prejudice and ethnic strife feed off abstraction. However, the proximity required by a meal – something about handing dishes around, unfurling napkins at the same moment, even asking a stranger to pass

---

2. Alain de Botton, *Religion for Atheists* (New York: Pantheon, 2012), 41.

the salt – disrupts our ability to cling to the belief that the outsiders who wear unusual clothes and speak in distinctive accents deserve to be sent home or assaulted.[3]

In this vein, he believes that there are fewer effective means of diminishing distance and promoting tolerance than forcing people to eat supper together. Inviting guests to join us is thus not only an act of compassion toward the other. It is an instruction manual in goodness for ourselves. It helps us overcome the natural prejudices that we develop in the presence of strangers. It is a way we tell ourselves that strangers are really potential friends, and that a shared meal can actualize that potential. Relationships change when we break bread together, when we bring others into our homes and our lives. Isaiah reminds us of our mission, "Is it not to share your bread with the hungry and bring the homeless poor into your house?" (Is. 58:7). Our very purpose is to ensure that others live with us in dignity. To achieve it, we must bring them in.

Many years ago, when I was studying Bible in the class of Professor Nechama Leibowitz, of blessed memory, she suddenly paused with a question reminiscent of Isaiah's words: "There was never a time when Jews did not take in their homeless. When did Jews stop taking in the homeless?" She allowed the weight of this question to sit, thick in the air, as she waited for a response. No one was quite sure what she was getting at. She dismissed the guesses and said simply, "When Jews got wall-to-wall carpeting." When we had nothing, we were happy to split that nothing with others. Sleep on the floor, as long as you have a place to sleep. But as we began the journey to material success, we could not have someone sleep on the floor because it might damage our fine carpeting.

On Passover we don't break bread together, but we do crumble matza as a group. And anticipating de Botton's thinking, the Hebrew Bible stresses that our experience of alienation as slaves must translate into the responsibility to minimize the dislocation or oppression of others: "You shall not wrong a stranger or oppress him, for you were strangers in the land of Egypt" (Ex. 22:20). A variation of this verse appears dozens of times in the Hebrew Bible. Maimonides wrote that anyone who does not share food on a holiday experiences sham happiness: happiness of the stomach, he called it.

When a person eats and drinks [to celebrate a holiday], he is obligated to feed converts, orphans, widows, and those who are poor and needy.

---

3. Ibid. 43.

In contrast, a person who shuts the gates of his courtyard while eating and drinking with his children and wife and does not feed the poor and destitute, is not rejoicing in the joy of the holiday as a mitzva but merely celebrating his stomach. (*Mishneh Torah*, Laws of Holidays 6:18)

Authentic happiness comes not from material pleasure but from emotional generosity. When I share, I am thanking God by telling God that I have more than enough and that I am a steward for the happiness of others.

TO HAVE EQUALLY

A mishna about pre-Passover practice and Seder ritual wants us to think about those outside our household and their needs especially on a holiday, offering a subtle understanding of the intense foreignness that the destitute experience.

The evening of Passover close to the time of the afternoon service, a person should not eat until night falls. Even a member of the Israelite poor should not eat until he reclines, nor should one give him fewer than four cups of wine, even if he is fed through a soup kitchen. (Pesaḥim 10:1)

We want all at the Seder table to look forward to the symbolic meal that accompanies the story of the Exodus and also enjoy the festive meal at its center. This anticipation is regarded in the halakhic category of "*hidur mitzva*," the beautification of a commandment. If a person eats right before the Seder, he or she will not experience the requisite hunger that creates an added layer of holiday anticipation. Maimonides wrote that the sages of old used to refrain from eating on Passover eve to go into the holiday with great appetite (*Mishneh Torah*, Laws of Ḥametz and Matza 6:12). Even if a poor person who is fed through a soup kitchen is presented with food right before the holiday – an opportunity one in such dire straits would hardly pass up – he should refrain from eating so as to experience the same state of anticipation as his better-off neighbor. The mishna adds the detail "until he reclines." Reclining is regarded as the prerogative of the rich at mealtime. Lean back and be served rather than serve. The poor person who is used to sitting rigidly over his food, ready to jump at the call of those with greater power or money – akin to a slave in this regard – must wait to eat until he can do so with the mindset of the free man. He must recline and then eat. The sages understood that the tensions of poverty are well-aligned with the mentality of servitude, and that economic deprivation stands in the way of true freedom. The medieval Talmud commentators add that even were this man to sit on a bench for the Seder, as he is generally accustomed, he must recline and his reclining is still considered the act of a free man even if the fantasy of freedom is not entirely supported by the furniture.[4] The absence of pillows and sofas cannot diminish his role-playing for the evening.

In discussing the four cups of wine that all must drink at the Passover table, the mishna employs a strange circumlocution of language in reference to the poor person. It twists the language in the law, reading: "Do not give him fewer than four cups." Why not write: "Give the poor man four cups," in a positive, declarative way to avoid all ambiguity? The sages of the Mishna understood a great deal about human nature. They knew the human tendency to grab what you can when you can and to give less than is necessary when you can cut corners. We might have thought that for a poor person, three glasses of wine would be more than sufficient or perhaps even one glass would do, since it is one more than he would have had if he is truly needy. And yet, if Passover is to be the great hospitality equalizer, we cannot deny the poor man his due. He must participate in the meal like everyone else. The four cups of wine punctuate and accentuate the story, corresponding with the four expressions of freedom that ring out of the Exodus story itself: "Say to the Israelite people: 'I am the Lord, and I will **bring you out** from under the yoke of the Egyptians. I will **free you** from being slaves to them, and I will **redeem you** with an outstretched arm and with mighty acts of judgment. I will **take you** as My own people and I will be your God'" (Ex. 6:6–7). We partake of the first cup as Kiddush, the opening prayer for all Shabbat and holiday meals. We have the second cup over the reading of the Haggada's core story, the third completes the meal, and the last follows the Hallel phase of the Seder after the meal. The poor person must be part of the trajectory of this experience in its entirety, not partially. And, if those in charge of dispensing charity fail to deliver four cups or the financial equivalent so that the poor person can recite and drink in this story, then he must go to extreme lengths to purchase his freedom, so to speak. The Rashbam, Rashi's grandson, and other later commentators specify that he must go as far as selling his own clothing or indenturing himself in some paying relationship so that he can purchase the wine. If we have failed to make accommodation to bring the most vulnerable into the narrative, then they must bring themselves into it. If they stand on the outside without the requisite tools and feelings, then both they and we will have betrayed the Exodus narrative wholesale.

On the night of the Seder, everyone is a king. Everyone is a free person. Thus, everyone is entitled to experience freedom deeply. For the poor, the

---

4. See *Tosafot* and *Mordekhai* ad loc.

problem standing between himself and the re-enactment of freedom this night is only what money can buy. We use *tzedaka* to make sure that this obstacle does not stand in the way.

CREATING COLLECTIVE CONSCIOUSNESS OF THE STRANGER

As an illustration of this equalizing power, we turn to Emma Lazarus (1849–1887). Her family had settled in the United States in America's colonial days. She wrote a poem whose lines would be immortalized in bronze on the pedestal of the Statue of Liberty, placed there in 1903. She donated the sonnet to an auction to raise funds for the statue's pedestal and was herself an advocate for immigrant rights. "The New Colossus" compares the Statue of Liberty to the ancient Colossus of Rhodes, the largest statue in the ancient world, built to celebrate the Greek victory over Cyprus and once considered among the Seven Wonders of the World. "The New Colossus" commemorated something else, not the collapse of the strong under the more powerful, but the welcoming of the weak and the vulnerable into the sheltering arms of freedom.

> Give me your tired, your poor,
> Your huddled masses yearning to breathe free,
> The wretched refuse of your teeming shore.
> Send these, the homeless, tempest-tost to me,
> I lift my lamp beside the golden door!

It is as if Lazarus herself had invited us through her golden door and into her dining room to participate at the family Seder. And she points to the feeling that the inviter must create for the invited to feel welcome. The poem offers us an embrace; but for some, having guests is an obligation, preceded by a chilly offer that alienates even as it includes. Lazarus's lamp, like Abraham's position at the threshold, represents ways to seek out the stranger rather than reactively attend to his needs when he appears. The lowlier the tempest-tost immigrant, the more home matters, Lazarus suggests.[5] The most vulnerable often become aware of their alienation only after they have been welcomed somewhere. The intake

---

5. One scholar, Daniel Marom, posits that Lazarus's stanzas were not only informed by her Jewish background and understanding of the Jewish immigrant experience but were a direct contrast to the image represented by the statue itself, the Roman goddess Libertas, who holds the Declaration of Liberty in one hand and a torch in the other. In other words, the message on the statue's pedestal undercuts the statue itself, suggesting that the words rather than the image capture what the embrace of the stranger really means.

of kindness makes them aware of how truly hungry they were for warmth, for any crumb of kindness. A friend shared with me that she invited a family with a handicapped son for a Shabbat meal, and the woman broke into tears, she was so grateful. She told the hostess that such offers of company came so infrequently that they precipitated joyful weeping.

ON BEING A BETTER HOST

If we were to take a page out of Abraham's playbook on hosting, we might turn to certain rabbinic laws and customs that emerged as a result of a close reading of Genesis 18. As noted above, the host should offer the portions because the host will always be most generous. We should accompany our guests four cubits from the door (about 6 feet) to show them we are not anxious for them to leave. But most of all, we should be mindful of the rabbinic dictum, inspired by Abraham's narrative, that puts us in the mindset of a good host: "Be happy as you sit at your table and the hungry are enjoying your hospitality" (*Derekh Eretz Zuta* 9). We should experience joy when we open our tables to others. Professor Daniel Sperber in his series *Minhagei Yisrael* (Customs of Israel) mentions a kabbalistic practice reported by the medieval scholar Rabbenu Baḥya ben Asher: those who invested a great deal in hosting the poor and the stranger were buried in coffins made out of their tables as a positive judgment on how they welcomed people to their homes.[6] Your table judges you, and you will leave a legacy based on its availability to the stranger.

Moving from ancient wisdom to contemporary practice, we turn for guidance on making guests feel welcome to New York restaurant entrepreneur Danny Meyer in *Setting the Table*:

> Hospitality is the foundation of my business philosophy. Virtually nothing else is as important as how one is made to feel in any business transaction. Hospitality exists when you believe the other person is on your side. The converse is just as true. Hospitality is present when something happens *for* you. It is absent when something happens *to* you. These two simple prepositions – *for* and *to* – express it all.

Hospitality is measured not by what we are served, but by how we are served, by whether we feel that someone is doing something for us rather than to us. Meyer looks for warmth, enthusiasm, good listening skills, and excellent follow-up in

6. Daniel Sperber, *Minhagei Yisrael,* vol. III (Jerusalem: Mossad HaRav Kook, 1994), 184.

employee hires and evaluates his employees accordingly. Strong interactive skills and emotional intelligence are critical in terms of the atmosphere he tries to create in every eating venue. He aims for what he calls legendary hospitality, the kind of service that makes people remember and talk. He also makes an important distinction between hospitality and service:

> Understanding the distinction between service and hospitality has been at the foundation of our success. Service is the technical delivery of a product. Hospitality is how the delivery of that product makes its recipient *feel*. Service is a *monologue* – we decide how we want to do things and set our own standards for service. Hospitality, on the other hand, is a *dialogue*. To be on a guest's side requires listening to that person with every sense, and following up with a thoughtful, gracious response. It takes both great service and great hospitality to rise to the top.

You might read this and think it's good advice for a business but not really for a private home. There is truth to this. Yet when people make hospitality their business, best practices surface. Imagine that every time we invited guests we aimed for legendary hospitality. Imagine that we set that standard for our institutions, our schools, synagogues, community centers. And think about the messages we could take away and apply in our own homes. We are not yet close enough to that goal.

These hosting behaviors can not only change and deepen our relationships with others, they also model the kind of behavior we should expect in families. In *How to Run a Traditional Jewish Household*, Blu Greenberg writes that

> *Hakhnasat orḥim* [welcoming guests] is a wonderful mitzva for children: a) it is a concrete model from which to learn the art of sharing; b) children have an opportunity to become acquainted with all different kinds of people, including non-Jews; c) it reminds them, periodically, that they are not the center of the universe.[7]

That reminder needs to be made more than periodically to help children acknowledge and embrace others.

---

7. Blu Greenberg, *How to Run a Traditional Jewish Household* (Northvale, NJ: Jason Aronson, 1988).

ON BEING A GOOD GUEST

In our Grace After Meals, we make a point of blessing those who host us: "May the Merciful One bless the heads of this household, their entire family, and all that is theirs." We cannot bless God for a meal only in the abstract sense of divine provision. We must also acknowledge the concrete way in which others have provided for us. This is the other side of the hosting equation, which can prove complex if our expectations are unrealistic or we are mired in entitlement with a dollop of ingratitude. While our Jewish texts remind us to be generous in bringing others into our lives, the Talmud also understood how difficult it is to be a "generous" recipient of the kindness of others:

> What does a good guest say? "How much trouble my host has gone to for me. How much meat he has set before me. How much wine he has given me. How many cakes he has served me. And all this trouble he has gone to for my sake!" But an inconsiderate guest, what does he say? "What kind of effort did the host make for me? I have eaten only one slice of bread. I have eaten only one piece of meat, and I have drunk only one cup of wine! Whatever trouble the host went to was done only for the sake of his wife and children." (Berakhot 58a)

It is hard to understand why anyone would minimize a host's generosity unless we believe that at heart, people are uncomfortable on the receiving end of goodness, which may make them feel dependent or needy.

If we think this behavior never surfaces in such a direct and outright fashion, listen for a moment to the words of Rabbi Joseph Telushkin in *The Book of Jewish Values* on his candid estimation of what often happens at the end of a meal:

> I know that when my wife and I entertain, we spend hours preparing the house and planning the event so that our guests can spend as pleasant an evening as possible. The thought that some of them might afterwards dissect us critically pains me. And I don't think I am being paranoid in suspecting that many of them do so; I realize how often I have acted that way myself.[8]

---

8. Joseph Telushkin, *The Book of Jewish Values* (New York: Crown Publishing, 2011), 307.

We may think that Rabbi Telushkin is being overly sensitive until we catch ourselves doing this as we leave a host's home, critiquing the experience, the décor, the food. We may sense a touch of ingratitude when we host others. I am often struck by how many guests leave my home having no idea what my husband and I do or think about, while we have asked them a myriad of questions about themselves. When curiosity is so one-sided, it makes us wonder how people feel about their experience at our table. Miss Manners, Judith Martin, makes a helpful, tongue-in-cheek suggestion to this end: "It is easy to be the perfect houseguest. All you have to do is to remember everything you've learned in the last few years about being totally honest, in touch with your feelings, able to communicate your needs, and committed to doing what makes you feel comfortable. And then forget it."[9] She continues the point: "The best present a guest can make after he has left and written thanks is his silence. This must consist not only of the wonderful silence that pervades the house when he leaves, but of his own precious silence in refusing to divulge family secrets to others."[10]

Miss Manners reflects the advice from another rabbinic source: "The guest should comply with every request the host makes of him" (*Derekh Eretz Rabba* 6). This refers both to what a host asks specifically of a guest in terms of help preparing or serving, but it may also include the implicit request that guests not criticize their hosts, judge them, or reveal to others inadequacies in their food or their company. We honor those who honored us with an invitation by respecting their privacy and thinking well of them.

BEYOND THE SEDER TABLE

By spilling over the Passover tradition of an open table of physical and spiritual nourishment beyond the Seder night, we honor the message of the holiday and its lessons for our behavior yearlong. Our mandate, having experienced alienation as strangers in a strange land, is to welcome others with a warm embrace, and to remember that we did not learn the art of hospitality from hostility. We learned it from the very first Jews – Abraham and Sarah – who taught us by example the way that strangers become friends and friends become angels.

---

9. Judith Martin, *Miss Manners' Guide to Excruciatingly Correct Behavior* (New York: W.W. Norton and Co., 2005), 274.
10. Ibid. 276.

LIFE HOMEWORK

- What is one behavior or action you can adopt to become more hospitable? Name one way you can be a better guest.
- How can you personally make our synagogues, schools, and Jewish organizations more friendly and open to strangers?
- Think of the most hospitable person you know. What "ingredients" describe his or her character?
- Use Passover and the first Hebrew month of our nationhood as a chance to build a more diverse, compassionate, and engaged community this coming year by inviting unlikely guests to your table once a month. Transform social dining – where we invite our relatives and friends – into the mitzva of *hakhnasat orḥim*.

Day Two

And we shall not get excited. Because a translator
May not get excited. Calmly, we shall pass on
Words from man to son, from one tongue
To others' lips, un-
Knowingly, like a father who passes on
The features of his dead father's face
To his son, and he himself is like neither of them. Merely a mediator.

We shall remember the things we held in our hands
That slipped out.
What I have in my possession and what I do not have in my possession.

We must not get excited.
Calls and their callers drowned. Or, my beloved
Gave me a few words before she left,
To bring up for her.

And no more shall we tell what we were told
To other tellers. Silence as admission. We must not
Get excited.

"And We Shall Not Get Excited," Yehuda Amichai
(Translated by Barbara and Benjamin Harshav)

Day Two

The Four Sons, the Right Question

An infinite question is often destroyed by finite answers.
Madeleine L'Engle

Transmission of knowledge is very tricky. Its difficulty may explain why so much of the Seder is focused on questions rather than answers. Every year, we sit down at the Seder table and ask the same questions, perhaps expecting the same answers. This routine can be tiring until we realize that in life we continuously ask the same questions, recognizing with advancing maturity that the question is a variation of one we asked earlier and that the answers we expect become, hopefully, more sophisticated over time. The large universal questions about love, life, suffering, human nature, and God repeat themselves, mushrooming from the personal to the philosophical and back again. In 1903, the poet Rilke wrote in *Letters to a Young Poet* that we must be slow to find answers and not demand them prematurely:

> Have patience with everything unresolved in your heart and to try to love the questions themselves as if they were locked rooms or books written in a very foreign language. Do not search for the answers, which could not

be given to you now, because you would not be able to live them. And the point is to live everything. Live the questions now. Perhaps then someday far into the future, you will gradually, without even noticing it, live your way into the answer.

The question represents a posture of curiosity and mystery. We may jump at answers that end up being ultimately dissatisfying because of our need for an answer instead of our enduring capacity to live the question that then may – or may not – live a way into an answer.

The Four Sons section of the Haggada offers a framework to entertain the art of the question by pushing the reader to look around the table and register who is there before we start to ask. The scholar Daniel Goldschmidt wrote that the Four Sons segment of the Haggada is "possibly the most difficult portion of all the Haggada; scholars have still not overcome its difficulties."[1] One of these difficulties has to do with the very nature of the Haggada. The mandate to tell the story of the Exodus on Passover would seem best addressed by opening up the Book of Exodus and then reciting and discussing its first fifteen chapters, from oppression to the Song of the Sea. Instead, the Haggada is a strange amalgamation of biblical verses and rabbinic passages cobbled together. One of these rabbinic cobbling acts is the weaving together of biblical verses in response to the questions of the Four Sons. In four separate places, the Bible directs us to tell our children our foundational story:

> **Exodus 12:26–27:** And when your children ask you, "What is this service to you?" you shall say, "It is a Pesaḥ offering for the Lord, for He passed over the houses of the Children of Israel in Egypt while He struck the Egyptians, but saved those in our homes."

> **Exodus 13:8:** And you shall explain to your son on that day, "Because of this the Lord acted for me when I came out of Egypt."

> **Exodus 13:14:** And when, in time to come, your son asks you, saying, "What is this?" you shall say to him, "With a strong hand the Lord brought us out of Egypt, from the grip of slavery."

---

1. Daniel Goldschmidt, *Seder Haggada shel Pesaḥ al pi Minhag Ashkenaz U'Sfarad* (Jerusalem and Tel Aviv: Schocken, 1947).

Deuteronomy 6:20–21: When in time your children ask you, "What are the testimonies, the statutes and laws, that the Lord our God commanded you?" you shall say to your children, "We were slaves to Pharaoh in Egypt and the Lord our God brought us out of there with a strong hand."

The rabbis were troubled by these repeated mentions because they operated according to a hermeneutic theory that there are no unnecessary words in the Torah. This repetition must teach additional laws that are not obvious on first blush. Their conclusion is not that there are four different stories or depths of interpretation but four different recipients, whose learning needs vary. All must be told this story. All must learn it and be able to transmit it.

Transmission is not the same as acquisition. You have to own knowledge in order to pass it on. Ask anyone who has ever taught anything about the difference between learning something to learn it and learning something to teach it. The integration of knowledge is of an entirely different quality. And yet, even with this conclusion, the rabbis had different versions of how this transmission should take place. There are three versions of the Four Sons, the version in our Haggada, the *Mekhilta*, and the Jerusalem Talmud. The version in our Haggada (which is similar, but not identical to the *Mekhilta*) typecasts children into four archetypes:

There are four sons: one wise, one wicked, one simple-natured, and one who does not know how to ask.

1. The wise son – what does he say? "What are the testimonies, the statutes and laws, that the Lord, our God, commanded you?" And you must tell him the laws of Pesah: "After eating the Pesah offering one does not eat anything more (*afikoman*)."
2. The wicked son – what does he say? "What is this work to you?" To "*you*," he says, not to *him*. When he sets himself apart from the community, he denies the very core of our beliefs. And you must set his teeth on edge and tell him, "Because of this the Lord acted for me when I came out of Egypt." "For *me*," and not for *him*; had he been there he would not have been redeemed.
3. The simple-natured son – what does he say? "What is this?" And you must tell him, "With a strong hand the Lord brought us out of Egypt, from the grip of slavery."

4. And the one who does not know how to ask – you must open [the story] for him, as it is said: "You shall tell your son on that very day."[2]

The Jerusalem Talmud has an alternative version of the Four Sons, and although the differences are minor, the meaning of the differences is significant in terms of the larger issue at hand: how can one master a story well enough to share it with very different listeners?

R. Ḥiya teaches: The Torah relates to four types of sons: the wise, the wicked, the stupid, and the one who does not know how to ask.

1. The wise son – what does he say? "What are the testimonies, the statues and laws, that the Lord our God commanded us?" And you must tell him, "With a strong hand the Lord brought us out of Egypt, from the grip of slavery."
2. The wicked son – what does he say? "What is this work to you? What is this work that you burden us with every year?" Since he sets himself apart from the community, you tell him, "Because of this the Lord acted for me." "For *me*"; for this man, He did not do it. Had this man been in Egypt he would never have been worthy to have been redeemed from there.
3. The stupid one – what does he say? "What is this?" And you must teach him the laws of Pesaḥ, that after eating the Pesaḥ offering one does not eat anything more, so that he will not stand in this group and enter another.
4. The son who does not know how to ask – you must open [the story] for him.[3]

One meaningful difference in these two versions is the nature of the work that the wicked son dismisses. "*Avoda*," the Hebrew for work, can imply both physical labor and divine service. In the Haggada and *Mekhilta* versions, work is a function of the latter. Here, *avoda* refers to the Paschal lamb sacrifice which involved intensive labor and effort. The wicked son cares nothing for the sacrifice and belittles its significance. We "set his teeth on edge," a symbolic suggestion that

---

2. *Mekhilta, Parashat Bo* 18.
3. Y. Pesaḥim 10:4.

we quiet his speech, quelling the kind of skepticism that can be contagious if unchecked. In the Jerusalem Talmud, we can see that people of this period were already highly influenced by the rabbinic interpretations of the laws of eliminating leaven and preparing the house for Passover. These, rather than the Paschal lamb sacrifice, represent the *avoda*, the work. They are a burden that is deemed a waste of time by the wicked child. This kind of humdrum preparation is easy to belittle, degrade, and undermine with questions like, "Do you think this is what God wants?" "Is there any purpose to any of this?" "Isn't this expensive?" And we silence this too. These questions are of a different order of magnitude because it is easy to identify with them and the damage is insidious. Cleaning for Passover is hard work. Very few people want to do it.

I remember many years ago teaching a packed room of women who wanted to study about Passover a week or so before the holiday. I must have made a joke about the cleaning and preparation because a woman stood up indignantly in the back of the room. "I am a convert, and I have noticed how many people who are born Jewish and observant make fun of cleaning for Passover. I love cleaning for Passover. I feel holy when I do this mitzva, and I am tired of people taking that away from me with their jokes." I apologized immediately and thought of the high level of piety and perspective she had achieved that I had not.

FOUR DIFFERENT CHILDREN

Returning to our two versions of the Four Sons, one type of wickedness undermines the Bible, another undermines the Talmud. This shift is dramatic and important and comes into play in another difference in the texts. The wise son and the stupid son (the literal translation of the word in the Jerusalem Talmud) ironically reverse places here. Wisdom in the Haggada and *Mekhilta* is regarded as interest in and mastery of law. The more detailed the question, the better the showcase of knowledge. Smart children want to know what to do, goes this thinking. Consequently, the answer cited offers a sliver of ritual practice which only those who are deeply punctilious would stress. This changes in the Jerusalem Talmud rendition, where it is the philosophical underpinnings of the holiday that reflect true wisdom. This is *why* we do what we do. The "stupid" care only about *what* and *how* we do what we do. Ritual details are for those without the capacity for theological inquiry.

This sentiment about the importance of "why" over "how" is echoed about one thousand years later in Maimonides' *Guide for the Perplexed*, in the famous parable of the *armon*, a castle where God "lives." He identifies those who live far and near to the castle, those who encircle it, and those who can enter its innermost chambers:

> Those who desire to arrive at the palace, and to enter it, but have never yet seen it, are the mass of religious people; the multitude that observe the divine commandments but are ignorant. Those who arrive at the palace, but go round about it, are those who devote themselves exclusively to the study of the practical law; they believe traditionally in true principles of faith and learn the practical worship of God, but are not trained in philosophical treatment of the principles of the law, and do not endeavor to establish the truth of their faith by proof.

Mere observance of law gives off the false impression of mastery of a system that is inherently theological in nature. Those who are punctilious in their observance of the law but seek no philosophical reassurances for what they are doing will only really ever look at the castle from the outside, giving themselves the comfort of an image without the acquisition of true wisdom. Maimonides then goes on to describe those who have a better chance of entry:

> Those who undertake to investigate the principles of religion have come into the antechamber; and there is no doubt that these can also be divided into different grades. But those who have succeeded in finding a proof for everything that can be proved, who have a true knowledge of God, so far as a true knowledge can be attained, and are near the truth, wherever an approach to the truth is possible, they have reached the goal, and are in the palace in which the king lives.[4]

The philosopher – and only the philosopher, according to Maimonides – can achieve this intimacy with God. Thus, knowing why God took us out of Egypt is a placeholder for knowledge in the Jerusalem Talmud's version in a way that knowing when to eat the *afikoman* can never be.

The categorization of children and learning styles we see in both versions is echoed in another famous text of roughly the same period. The fifth chapter of *Ethics of the Fathers* contains many different categorizations that apply to spiritual, emotional, and intellectual life. The fact that the sages of the Talmud reflect on learning styles and temperaments is not surprising because as part of

---

4. Maimonides, *Guide for the Perplexed* III:51, trans. M. Friedländer (London: 1904), 384–5.

their learned discourse, they often make observations about how scholars should think, process information, and even how they should dress and with whom they should socialize. The nature of the learning community intrigued them. Consequently, we have three different passages that focus specifically on cataloging student intake and behaviors:

> There are four types of students. One who is quick to understand and quick to forget, his deficiency cancels out his virtue. One who is slow to understand and slow to forget, his virtue cancels out his deficiency. One who is quick to understand and slow to forget, his is a good portion. One who is slow to understand and quick to forget, his is a bad portion. (*Ethics of the Fathers* 5:12)

The sages do not state whether one can change these learning patterns, but each seriously impacts the art of transmission. How can you tell a story every year that you learn but rapidly forget or that you have trouble learning in the first place? This is augmented by a passage in the same chapter about where learning takes place:

> There are four types among those who attend the study hall. One who goes but does nothing has gained only the reward of attendance. One who does [study] but does not go to the study hall has gained the rewards of studying. One who goes and learns is pious. One who neither goes nor studies is wicked. (*Ethics of the Fathers* 5:14)

Here the emphasis is on the importance of study in community, which shapes learning and character and also creates a deeper model of transmission. When you study with others you become more aware of what you must hold onto as a collective, not only what you as an individual prefer or find easy to learn.

Finally, the last passage in the chapter that classifies learning personalities combines place, people, and learning temperaments and emphasizes yet another aspect of knowledge: the capacity to sift and filter what should be retained in learning and what can be dismissed. This is a learning skill that achieves great importance when there is so much to learn and takes on even greater significance when thinking about transmission. Which parts of a narrative are critical to imparting values and the texture of history and possibility, and which are extraneous?

> There are four types among those who sit before the sages: the sponge, the funnel, the strainer, and the sieve. The sponge absorbs everything. The

funnel takes in at one end and lets it out the other end. The strainer rejects the wine and retains the sediment. The sieve rejects the coarse flour and retains the fine flour. (*Ethics of the Fathers* 5:15)

Some people take in learning and then let it go. Just think of how many subjects you have studied or books you have read and think of what you have retained and lost along the way. For many of us, the loss is staggering. We have a vague recollection of a book or course title and that we had some relationship to it, but the memory is murky. This also helps us understand why the sages recorded in the Haggada emphasized that no matter how wise, every person must tell this story again and again. Repetition helps compensate for the loss of memory.

CHILDREN MUST BE NURTURED DIFFERENTLY

All of this reflection and categorization is designed to help people assess themselves and others intellectually and inspire people to move into categories that are more helpful in retaining knowledge and generating wisdom. But there is also something else going on here, something obvious but not articulated, that is critical in our understanding of the inheritance of knowledge. Children are different. They need labels, but they will fight to break out of them even as they are helped or limited by them. When we do not give enough thought to how children learn, we deny them something precious, and we also block the portals of transmission that may sustain our future.

To display these differences, the artist and calligrapher David Moss depicted his four sons in the Moss Haggada as four different playing cards, with the question appearing on each card and the word "blessing" in Hebrew appearing in bold contrast to the other words to communicate that each child is indeed a blessing.

Every child is unique and the Torah embraces them all. The iconography that I've chosen here is based on playing cards. As in a game of chance, we have no control over the children dealt us. It is our task as parents, as educators, to play our hand with the attributes of the children we are given. It is the child, not the parent, who must direct the process. This, I believe, is the intent of the midrash of the four children.[5]

5. David Moss, *The Moss Haggadah, Companion Volume* (Berkeley: Bet Alpha Editions, 2008), 36.

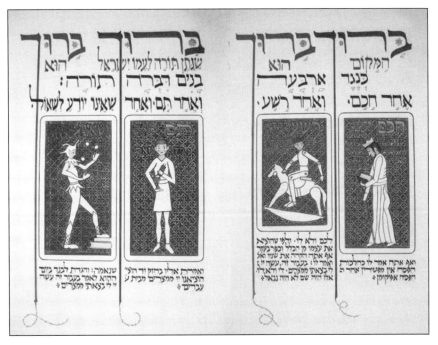

The Four Sons, David Moss

Hundreds of years earlier, Rabbi Samson Raphael Hirsch understood this when he commented on Rebecca's pregnancy and the way that Rebecca and Isaac raised their sons: "There were twins in her womb," states Genesis 25:24. Two verses later, Rabbi Hirsch observed, "The surprising thing was that they were really identical twins. Their only difference was in their constitution." Esau and Jacob looked so alike from the outside – in contrast to the way we usually understand their appearances – that their parents erred in thinking this reflected their insides, too. The parents should have "studied" their differences and paid attention to them. As a result of neglecting this, there were "mistakes in the way they were brought up."

As long as they were little, no attention was paid to the slumbering differences in their natures, both had exactly the same teaching and educational treatment, and the great law of education, "bring up each child in accordance with his own way," was forgotten: That each child must be treated differently, with an eye to the slumbering tendencies of his nature, and out of them, be educated to develop his special characteristics for the one pure human and Jewish life. The great Jewish task in life is basically simple, one and the same for all, but its realization is as complicated and varied as human natures and tendencies are varied.[6]

When we educate to erase difference we betray our own legacy, thinking that we are simply making deposits instead of offering gifts in subtle and highly individualized, customized ways.

KNOWLEDGE IS *NOT* AN INHERITANCE

The realization that knowledge is critical to transmission but not enough for it to take place leads us to a painful conclusion that is also found in *Ethics of the Fathers*: "R. Yossei would say…. Ready yourself for the study of Torah because it is not your inheritance. And all your deeds should be for the sake of Heaven" (*Ethics of the Fathers* 2:12). I cannot assume that just because someone passed down knowledge to me that it is mine. I cannot assume that because I transmit knowledge to you, that it is yours. We would all like to say that we as Jewish parents have done our jobs. We sent our children to Jewish schools. We observed Shabbat and holidays. We taught them to pray. But it is not enough. In his book *Kaddish*, Leon Weiseltier poignantly describes his consternation at this discovery:

> "Ready yourself for the study of Torah because it is not your inheritance." I have pondered this statement for years. It is the most counterintuitive observation about tradition that I have found in tradition. What an estrangement it proposes: the Torah is not my inheritance! How can this be? If I was taught anything, it is that the Torah is my inheritance…
>
> Rabbi Yossei is a realist about continuity. He cautions that in the transmission of tradition there is a moment between the giving and the receiving, a moment when it is no longer the possession of the father and not yet the possession of the son, a moment of jeopardy, like the pause in a beating heart, a moment of discontinuity, a beat skipped, when what has stopped has still to start, and what has been transmitted can slip away or run out. This is the moment for which you must "ready yourself."[7]

Like the passing of the baton in a relay race, the moment of transmission is the most vulnerable, and for this we must ready ourselves. The rabbis of old

---

6. Rabbi Samson Raphael Hirsch, *The Hirsch Chumash* (Philipp Feldheim, 2009), on Genesis 25:27.
7. Leon Weiseltier, *Kaddish* (New York: Knopf, 1998), 259.

understood that our own piety or scholarship was not a guarantee, and for this reason, they discussed a strange and problematic observation in their lives and the lives of their colleagues: many children of scholars were themselves not scholars. Some were actually rebels. They asked – and there is pain in the asking – "Why is it common for Torah scholars to have sons who are not Torah scholars?" (Nedarim 81a).

This was not asked rhetorically but practically. They had to stem the tide of this trend. After all, it was not someone else of whom they spoke. These were *their* children. This was their failed transmission of Torah. In categorizing students, they were not only speaking about other people's children but about their own scholarly community and how they negotiated the anguish of giving but not transmitting learning. They contemplated a variety of answers conveniently summed up here:

- R. Yosef said: "So that they should not say that Torah is an inheritance for them."
- Rav Shisha b. Rav Idi says: "So that they should not lord it over the public."
- Mar Zutra says: "Because they domineer the public."
- Rav Ashi says: "Because they call people donkeys."
- Ravina says: "Because they do not recite the blessing over the Torah first."[8]

Knowledge can create arrogance, authoritarianism, complacency. These were the dangers that lurked in the study hall and that affected the children of scholars. Some blame must be passed from the children back to the parents. It is not only because your child is a funnel and not a sponge. It may be because along with intelligence came superiority when humility would have been more attractive to those you live with and teach.

TRANSMISSION THROUGH THE ART OF THE QUESTION

Questions breed a spirit of humility. Answers tend to foment arrogance. The Seder advances our master narrative through questions that lead to transmission. We sing four questions but, in actuality, so much of the text prompts curiosity. Very little in the Haggada follows any logical sequence. We relay a story in the exposition of several verses that seem disconnected, making it hard to squeeze out any narrative

---

8. Nedarim 81a.

in chronological sequence. All of the evening's oddities provoke questions and force us out of rote learning. The choppy presentation of the Haggada text is full of ellipses that represent the space that questions occupy. This strange style illuminates three interesting scenarios:

- If a child asks a question before the parental prompt, does the parent have to repeat the question?
- If two scholars eat together, must they ask each other questions when they know the Exodus story very well already?
- If someone eats alone, must he or she ask questions?

Although the obligation is on the parent to tell the child the story through asking questions, if the child preempted that process by generating the questions himself, then the Seder leader need not repeat the questions, because the educational desideratum has already been achieved. On the flip side, even if two Torah scholars eat alone and know the laws of Passover intimately and intricately, one scholar must ask the other questions. More curious than either is the recommendation that when conducting a Seder alone, one must pose questions to oneself (Pesaḥim 116a). Asking questions, even or especially of oneself, may stimulate us to look at the same piece of text or ritual with new eyes, the eyes of wonder.

If the child lacks curiosity in the face of the narrative, the leader, says Maimonides, must become a provocateur: "It is a commandment to inform one's children even if they do not ask, as it is stated, 'You shall tell your child' (Ex. 13:8). A father should teach his son according to the child's capacity" (*Mishneh Torah*, Laws of Ḥametz and Matza 7:2). The parent must adapt to the child's learning style and needs because the learning must be integrated into the child's being in order for a master story to accomplish its objectives. In order to achieve this lofty spiritual – rather than purely intellectual – goal, Maimonides advises the parent to engage in behaviors others may view as eccentric:

> He should make changes on this night so that the children will see and be encouraged to ask: "Why is this night different from all other nights?" until he replies to them: "This and this occurred; this and this took place." What changes should take place? He should give them roasted seeds and nuts, the table should be taken away before they eat, matzot should be snatched from each other, and the like. (*Mishneh Torah*, Laws of Ḥametz and Matza 7:3)

The pedagogic style need not conform to any logic or be in itself educational. It is merely an instrument to stimulate a general awareness that the Seder night is distinctive and a specific awareness around particular rituals, making the learning both interesting and entertaining. The associations a child has with the evening should not remind him or her of a tedious school day but of a warm, engaging evening of participation. Knowledge is not only about the handover of information but about the strong emotional associations that accompany the act of learning.

FORCING THE QUESTION

The Seder is essentially the performance of questions in a highly ritualized way that prompts us to ponder the role of questions in daily life. Intellectual life thrives when people learn to ask ever-increasingly detailed, nuanced questions. Cynthia Ozick, in her article "Notes Toward Finding the Right Question," suggests that refining a question helps yield a more potent and compelling answer because "every answer is concealed in the question that elicits it, and what we must strive to do then, is not look for the right answer but attempt rather to discover the right question."

As we enter the universe of the Four Sons, we begin to ponder the role of questions in everyday life and how we might discover the "right questions." Questions within a framework of conversation demonstrate interest and engagement. Certain questions can transform the course of a life:

- Would you think about a career in this field?
- Will you accept this job offer?
- Did you ever think about spending a year abroad?
- Have you thought about the role of God in your life?
- Will you marry me?

The question itself becomes a path marker for personal discovery, particularly when the answer is practically consequential. There are also questions we avoid because we are afraid of the answers or believe that the answers are not within our control:

- Does my life have meaning?
- What will I do if I admit that I hate my job?
- Should I stay in this relationship?
- Should I retire?
- Should I see a doctor about this pervasive health problem?

The question is not only the arbiter of knowledge. It is the door to within, to a place that can cause discomfort and alienation. That discomfort brings the questioner to significant or unwanted change precisely because it is not a statement but an invitation, desired or not. A question waits for an answer with a posture of openness, sometimes with patience, sometimes in agitation, but never in stillness or stagnation.

In the course of a day and in the course of a life, the questions we ask generally fall into three categories.

Rhetorical questions force emotional or spiritual self-confrontation or a confrontation with another. They are not waiting for an answer but serve as comment or provocation or judgment. Most questions in the Bible are rhetorical in nature, usually formulated by God to help the individual being questioned come to terms with sin, alienation, or distance. The three conversations below point to this very encounter. In the first, God tries to get Adam to take ownership of his disobedience by marking where he is physically as a way of forcing self-realization around betrayal. Note that there is not one question but many because rarely is one question enough to accomplish this difficult challenge. Here the questions use a different opening but all aim at the same line of answers: Where? Who? What did you ... ? Why?

> The Lord God called out to the man and said to him, "**Where are you?**" He replied, "I heard the sound of You in the garden, and I was afraid because I was naked, so I hid." Then He asked, "**Who told you that you were naked? Did you eat of the tree from which I had forbidden you to eat?**" The man said, "The woman You put at my side – she gave me of the tree, and I ate." And the Lord God said to the woman, "**What is this you have done?**" The woman replied, "The serpent duped me, and I ate." (Gen. 3:9–13)

Soon after in the biblical text, God confronts Cain before he murders his brother, augmenting the disobedience of his parents. Trying to get Cain to analyze his embittered feelings toward God because God has rejected him, God asks him to think about his dejection, both in its inner and outer manifestation:

> And the Lord said to Cain, "**Why are you distressed, and why is your face fallen?** Surely if you do right, it will be uplifted. But if you do not do right, sin crouches at your door; its urge is toward you. Yet you can be its master." (Gen. 4:6–7)

God here tells Cain a simple message that would take a lifetime to apply. If you act virtuously, you will be uplifted. Your sorrow is caused by your angst and bad feelings. This was too complicated for poor Cain at this stage of his development. Had he answered God's first question honestly – why is your face fallen? – he would have arrived at a conclusion that would have prevented the killing of his brother. I am mad at You, God. You rejected me, and I am in pain as a result. But he did not answer, and silence came with its own costly price.

After murdering his brother, Cain is confronted once again, but this time with a simpler question: Where is your brother? Cain answers with a question often regarded by commentators as rhetorical in itself. But in its context, it is a question that holds a statement: I am not responsible for my brother; I had no idea that I was ever supposed to be responsible for my brother's welfare.

> Cain said to his brother… and when they were in the field, Cain set upon his brother Abel and killed him. The Lord said to Cain, "**Where is your brother Abel?**" And he said, "I do not know. **Am I my brother's keeper?**" Then He said, "**What have you done?** Hark, your brother's blood cries out to Me from the ground." (Gen. 4:6–10)

The last chapter of Jonah also contains questions that are articulated by both God and humans. Jonah told God that he never bought into the divine plan to rescue Nineveh morally, something he claims he had told God initially, though that piece of information was never provided in the text. God did not tangle with details but asked Jonah to look within and, like Cain, examine his own distress.

> But Jonah was greatly displeased and became angry. He prayed to the Lord, "**O Lord, is this not what I said when I was still at home?** That is why I was so quick to flee to Tarshish. I knew that You are a gracious and compassionate God, slow to anger and abounding in love, a God who relents from sending calamity. Now, O Lord, take away my life, for it is better for me to die than to live." But the Lord replied, "**Have you any right to be angry?**" Jonah went out and sat down at a place east of the city. There he made himself a shelter, sat in its shade, and waited to see what would happen to the city. Then the Lord God provided a vine and made it grow up over Jonah to give shade for his head to ease his discomfort, and Jonah was very happy about the vine. But at dawn the next day God provided a worm, which chewed the vine so that it withered. When the sun rose, God provided a scorching east wind, and the sun blazed on Jonah's head

so that he grew faint. He wanted to die, and said, "It would be better for me to die than to live." But God said to Jonah, "**Do you have a right to be angry about the vine?**" "I do," he said. "I am angry enough to die." But the Lord said, "You have been concerned about this vine, though you did not tend it or make it grow. It sprang up overnight and died overnight. But Nineveh has more than 120,000 people who cannot tell their right hand from their left, and many cattle as well. **Should I not be concerned about that great city?**" (Jonah 4:1–11)

The Book of Jonah is the only biblical book to end on a question, perhaps reflecting the ambivalence of Jonah himself and his mission. Jonah, who ran away, recommitted, and then left Nineveh, had to come to terms with his definition of misery. His self-concern was regarded as narcissistic by God, who saw the unevenness of his commitment to self versus his commitment to the other.

Rhetorical questions are not enough in the repertoire of conversation. There must be fact-based questions to establish reality or find out information: "Why do animals behave the way they do?" "Why does the sun shine?" There are questions we ask as children and then, as adults, more detailed variations of these questions prepare us for our work and our lives. We need critical information to function. We learn early on that children who ask good questions get the attention of adults – teachers, potential employers, relatives. We learn the truth of what Voltaire once wrote, "Judge a man by his questions rather than by his answers." We know we are judged so we try to ask a question that impresses. In Yiddish it is the good "*kasha*" that makes you stand out in the study hall. The Yiddish expression "You don't die from a question" protects the questioner, allowing a full range of intellectual motion in thought.

Informational questions also hold requests: we ask something of others. We sometimes think we have made a request when, in actuality, we have only thinly asked a question. We issued a complaint that was really meant to be a question. In these instances, it is best to ascertain what precisely we want from someone else, determining when we need the request satisfied and by whom, and identifying any other conditions that need to be met to achieve satisfaction. Breakdowns in family and professional communications often happen because we think we have completed these steps but they have not been clearly articulated to the listener.

Sometimes the line between a confrontational question and a factual one is hard to determine. In one passage in the Talmud, a sage posits that everyone who knocks on heaven's door will be asked a series of questions at the pearly gates:

When a person [goes to heaven] and faces judgment, he is asked: "Did you deal with integrity in business? Did you set times for study? Did you have children? Did you work on behalf of the world's redemption? Did you engage in the dialectics of wisdom? Did you understand one thing from another?" (Shabbat 31a)

The questions move from the general to the highly specific – about life accomplishments and integrity to personal learning styles. And while they confront on one level, they are also a way to gain information before judgment. If we are honest with ourselves, we will ask how many hours we truly committed to relationships, to redeeming the world, to studying Torah during our lifetime. We will come up with a number – an approximate, of course – because this line of questioning demands hard evidence.

Exploratory questions are, by their nature, open-ended. "Why did you do that?" is an accusatory question, as is "What were you thinking?" Both of these could be exploratory questions with a different intonation, but the wording has come to indicate judgment. A genuinely open question has no ring of judgment:

Powerful open-ended questions often begin with "what"…

Nearly all the questions we ask begin with one of five words: "who," "what," "why," "when," or "how." Although these words help us gather facts and understand each other in conversation, not all of them yield wisdom.

"Why" questions can easily put people on the defensive. They are questions that go backward.

"Who," "when," and "how" fall into the information question category. They also immediately go into problem-solving mode.

"What" helps the brain behave as an efficient search engine. "What" questions force you to be specific in your query and being specific leads to solution and awareness; on the other hand, asking "why?" leaves you with only the question. It is important to recognize the generative power of language through "what" questions.[9]

These are the words of leadership coach Laura Berman Fortgang. Coaching is a process of self-discovery prompted by an outsider's gentle nudge. Framing questions for others requires thinking about the relevancy of the question to the one

9. See Laura Berman Fortgang, "Strategic Questioning: Engaging People's Best Thinking," *The Systems Thinker*, vol. 13, number 9.

who hears it. What is the significance of the question to the life, work, feelings, and personal development of the person to whom I have asked this question? Will it provoke fresh thinking, creativity, or different reflection and behavior?[10] The skill of asking a question which holds up a mirror instead of putting someone on the defensive is a life skill. It is a skill that the Haggada asks us to revisit annually. Will the question I ask or answer inspire new layers of meaning in my life and in the lives of others?

REDEEMING THE CHILDREN/REDEEMING THE PARENTS

Questions lie at the heart of redemption because they allow us to ask about our future and then to change it. One leader, Moses, asked a question about a burning bush and changed all of our lives. He pondered a mystery and the rest became history. Because children are natural questioners, children on Passover become intertwined with the future and with our redemption. The intensity of this truth became apparent to me when I read a passage from *The Carlebach Haggada*. This is what Rabbi Shlomo Carlebach shares about the way we break and then celebrate a piece of matza:

> The Koznitzer Maggid says about *Yaḥatz*: "The world is so broken but our children can make the world whole again. We break the matza; the small piece we keep, and the big piece – the bigger brokenness – our children take away. Then they bring it back to us whole, to serve as the *afikoman* at the end of our Seder." Our children: they are the ones that are taking brokenness away from us.
>
> You know, friends, sometimes I come home from a concert at four o'clock in the morning, and I'm dead tired. After that, if anybody woke me up at five o'clock I would be angry. But if my children wake me up, oh, it's so beautiful! Master of the world, how can I thank you for children? They're so perfect, so good. I don't want them to grow up in a broken world.

Children take away our brokenness. We hide and they seek. And when they bring back the *afikoman*, it does not mean that we can glue that piece of matza back together. It means that in the tumble of learning that takes place on these Passover nights, we fill them with questions and that fills us all with a trust in a better future, one that they are holding onto tightly.

---

10. Ibid.

LIFE HOMEWORK

- Describe rituals and spiritual behaviors you engage in that you hope your children or those who live after you will also practice. Have you made your desire to continue this legacy clear to them?
- If you have children, identify some characteristics that make those children different from each other. Name something you do to accentuate and celebrate those differences.
- Try to make time over Passover to engage in a conversation with a young person in your community or your children individually about how each wants to practice Judaism in his or her own future and about his or her own spiritual aspirations. Too often, we make assumptions rather than check in with our children and then we miss the spiritual journey and struggles they experience in their own paths to and away from faith. Show interest and respect their autonomy, and you may find them more open to conversation on this sensitive subject.

Day Three

How many women have already spotted their first gray hair
in the cold eyes of the mirror?
The dream has ended,
We enter into reality
Or perhaps it's the other way around?
The world becomes clear and white;
the water freezes
a blue shard of ice
becomes our ship.
We stretch out our hands to red horizons –
And just as our sisters
In the ocean depths,
the medusa,
glow bright and light up their own ways –
so shall we here on the surface,
through the nights and days,
glow bright and light up our own ways.

"Before the Mirror," Reyzl Zykhlinsky
(Translated by Miriam Leberstein)

Day Three

Tzippora's Flint

> *Without passion, man is a mere latent force and possibility,*
> *like the flint which awaits the shock of iron before it can*
> *give forth its spark.*
>
> Henri Frederick Amiel

Af hen hayu be'oto hanes – "they, too, were included in the miracle."
This well-known talmudic principle justifies a woman's active participation in a
number of holidays shaped by time-bound mitzvot. Women are usually exempt
from such commandments to free them to engage with other family matters. But
here – specifically at Passover, Ḥanukka, and Purim – a woman's involvement
is not to be overlooked or understated.[1] The medieval commentaries differ in
their understanding of this principle. It may be activated because women were
profoundly impacted by the miracles of these days, though this would be true
for every person on every holiday. It seems that the choice of the word "miracle"
for these days, however, specifically references the military victories in each

---

1. This principle is stated unambiguously in three talmudic tractates: (1) "R. Yehoshua b. Levi said:
   Women are obligated in Megilla reading, for they, too, were included in the miracle" (Megilla 4a);
   (2) "R. Yehoshua b. Levi said: Women are obligated in Ḥanukka candles, for they, too, were
   included in the miracle" (Shabbat 23a); and (3) "R. Yehoshua b. Levi said: Women are obligated
   in these four cups [at the Seder], for they, too, were included in the miracle" (Pesaḥim 108a).

instance. Enemies not only threaten and victimize the general population but present specific threats for women, who often became sexual chattel in times of war. Victory relieves this immense vulnerability. Including women in the observances of such holidays is a way to help Jewish women express their deeply felt natural impulses of relief and gratitude to God and the hand of history for offering a different fate.

Other commentaries believe that this phrase refers to the leadership roles that women took in these confrontations to bring about these miracles. Specifically, they reference Esther in her role as Persian queen, Judith in her decapitating of Holofernes, and the women who brought about Israel's redemption: Miriam, Shifra, Puah, and ordinary slave women who, despite the depressing climate, seduced their husbands to enable childbearing. Pharaoh's unnamed daughter is also an important, if minor, presence in these narratives as the woman who saved Moses. Disobeying her father's strict instructions for all Egyptians to throw male Jewish babies into the Nile, she chose, instead, to rescue one. Disobedience to authority is what unites all these women and redeems them. In the case of the Passover miracles, the involvement of each of these women with babies is also central to understanding their roles as redeemers, who bring about – as the Talmud understands it – more birth because of oppression rather than despite it. Persecution and hardening circumstances only hardened their resolve to become stronger in number and presence to face evil with the force of numbers. If children are the future, then the women who helped bring children into the world are all midwives of redemption (Sota 11b).

These public/private battles can often morph one into another. In Exodus 1:18–19, we learn that the midwives who defied Pharaoh moved to the narrative foreground and challenged the normal boundaries between servant and master.

> The king of Egypt said to the Hebrew midwives, whose names were Shifra and Puah, "When you help the Hebrew women in childbirth and observe them on the delivery stool, if it is a boy, kill him; but if it is a girl, let her live." The midwives, however, feared God and did not do what the king of Egypt had told them to do; they let the boys live. Then the king of Egypt summoned the midwives and asked them, "Why have you done this? Why have you let the boys live?" The midwives answered Pharaoh, "Hebrew women are not like Egyptian women; they are vigorous and give birth before the midwives arrive." So God was kind to the midwives and the people increased and became even more numerous. And because the

midwives feared God, He gave them families of their own. Then Pharaoh charged all his people, saying, "Throw every boy who is born into the river, and the girls let live." (Ex. 1:15–22)

Everything about this passage is strange. It is odd that the king of Egypt would himself have had a conversation with these women and given them instructions on future birthing. It is odd that midwives rebelled in this public fashion and that for it they were not killed but given the opportunity to explain and that Pharaoh would have believed their odd excuse. To these midwives, kindness seems to be understood concretely as an increase in work: more babies were born, pushing these poor women into overtime. Pharaoh also let girls live. In his anger at the midwives' defiance, he might have had the girls killed as well. But he did not. In the Talmud, Shifra and Puah are identified as Yokheved, Moses' mother, and Miriam, Moses' sister, or Elisheva, Aaron's wife. Josephus disagreed with that reading and believed that these women were actually Egyptians.[2] Either version explains the terror of having to confront an angry Pharaoh face-to-face and explain why they challenged his authority. Maurice Samuel explains the midwives' behavior with this justification: "Prophecy is for the prophet and heroism for the hero; for the rest of us there is a halfway morality between martyrdom and damnation."[3]

The curiosities of this text indicate that the dominant norms stereotypically associated with males, especially in tense times, are suspended when women usurp their places. Pharaoh seems almost charmed by these midwives, demonstrating that there are women who dominate the Exodus story with public, almost brazen activities, and those whose work gets done in the shadows. And there are women who were in the shadows who then moved to the forefront – from the background to the narrative cusp, also through an act involving an infant. Like the midwives, Pharaoh's daughter and Miriam also challenged normal boundaries, in their cases between daughter and father and sister and brother. But perhaps no one does this more than Tzippora, a woman often ignored at the Passover table, much as she seems to be slighted in the biblical text.

TZIPPORA – FROM BEHIND THE SCENES TO CENTER STAGE

Tzippora, Yitro's daughter and Moses' wife, does not stand out by name or reputation among her many sisters. She seems arbitrarily chosen to cement the alliance

---

2. Josephus, *Antiquities of the Jews*, Book 11, chapter 9.
3. Maurice Samuel, *Certain People of the Book* (1955; reprint, Ulan Press, 2012).

between Yitro and Moses and is likely the eldest since she seems to be married off first among siblings. No explanation is given for Moses' marriage choice. Yitro was clearly impressed by the kindness to strangers that Moses exhibited. A stranger himself in a strange land, Moses shooed away the shepherds, who obstructed the well and possibly harassed Yitro's daughters when they were there grazing their father's sheep.

> Moses fled from Pharaoh and went to live in Midian, where he sat down by a well. Now a priest of Midian had seven daughters, and they came to draw water and fill the troughs to water their father's flock. Some shepherds came along and drove them away, but Moses got up and came to their rescue and watered their flock. When the girls returned to Reuel their father, he asked them, "Why have you returned so early today?" They answered, "An Egyptian rescued us from the shepherds. He even drew water for us and watered the flock." "And where is he?" he asked his daughters. "Why did you leave him? Invite him to have something to eat." Moses agreed to stay with the man, who gave his daughter Tzippora to Moses in marriage. Tzippora gave birth to a son, and Moses named him Gershom, saying, "I have become an alien in a foreign land." (Ex. 2:15–23)

As in Jacob's meeting at the well with Rachel, it is the man who facilitated access to the well and was the protagonist of kindness.[4] But unlike Jacob and Rachel, Moses did not fall in love with a woman he protected. It is the men in this text who actually bonded. Yitro invited Moses after the women returned home and shared what happened with their father. Moses "agreed to stay with the man," not the woman. Yet marrying into this family that warmly welcomed him, or even having a child with Yitro's daughter, did not ease Moses' experience of alienation. Instead, these experiences, which should have led to a sense of inclusion and contentment, seemed to heighten his isolation and pushed Moses even further into a state of dislocation. How else can we explain the name he gave his son, Gershom, and the explanation he offered for the naming: "I have become an alien in a foreign land"? The articulation of his existential unrest is critical to rolling out the burning bush scene and understanding why Moses was a likely candidate to lead the Israelites out of slavery.

---

4. For a masterful treatment of well scenes in the Hebrew Bible, see Robert Alter, *The Art of Biblical Narrative* (San Francisco: Basic Books, 1981), 55, as part of the entire chapter "Biblical Type-Scenes and the Uses of Convention."

We do not meet Tzippora again until Exodus 4, two chapters later, when Moses asked his father-in-law for permission to return to his *brothers*, "to see how they are faring," almost the exact language that Jacob used when he asked Joseph to go out into the fields to see how his brothers were doing. In both instances, these were invitations to danger. One two-letter root word, *ah*, brother, gives away Moses' inner reasoning. By articulating that he wanted to see his brothers, Moses tied this expedition into his first act of heroism: "Some time after that, when Moses had grown up, he went out to his *brothers* and witnessed their labors. He saw an Egyptian beating a Hebrew, one of his *brothers*" (Ex. 2:11).

Always at some distance from his people, Moses nevertheless had an innate curiosity and connection to them and could not help but defend and protect them, seek out their welfare, and eventually create possibilities for their liberation. Strangely, only after Moses asked for permission from Yitro did God tell him directly to return to Egypt. Before this moment, the calling was described in abstract terms. Moses may have needed the unambiguous mandate to hasten a commitment he accepted reticently. With permission secured, Moses was now directed to address the practical aspects of the journey with assurances for his personal safety: "Go back to Egypt, for all the men who sought to kill you are dead" (Ex. 4:19). Ironically, the fact that the current Pharaoh's predecessor was dead could only assuage one level of worry since the new Pharaoh was in the same position of authority to put an end to Moses' life. Then the text turns to the portrait of this small family, a wife weighed down with two babies and a husband imbued with newfound inspiration about to take on a supreme political power in the ancient Near Eastern world with little more than a staff.

Suddenly the text breaks from this choreographed moment to the danger we as readers have been anticipating. Three biblical verses in Chapter 4 create narrative tension that contains a universe of anxiety and responsibility.

> And it came to pass on the way, in the place where they spent the night, that the Lord met him and sought to kill him. Then Tzippora took a sharp stone and cut off the foreskin of her son and cast it at his feet and said, "Surely you are a bridegroom of blood to me." So He let him go. Then she said, "A bridegroom of blood you are because of the circumcision." (Ex. 4:24–26)

One of the most difficult passages in the Bible also unlocks one of the key themes of the Book of Exodus and the meaning of Passover: personal covenant must be linked to national covenant must be linked to a homeland for the nation so that notions of Jewish peoplehood can take root. These three overarching themes – personal covenant, national covenant, and homeland – come together in a narrative jumble in this three-verse diversion to show how inseparable they are for the Israelites and how inseparable they are for the one who led them. The firstborn in our story (4:25), according to some commentaries, is linked to the firstborn mentioned only verses earlier where God said he was willing to kill Pharaoh's firstborn if His own firstborn were not free to worship Him (4:22). The firstborn here is similarly linked to a later passage where God asked for the firstborn to be sanctified and related this commandment to the death of the firstborn in the plagues (13:11–15). The *mila* in our story (4:24–26) parallels the *mila* mentioned later that permits a person to participate in the Paschal lamb sacrifice (12:43–49). The individual commitment of a family is linked to the larger national destiny. Each event is crucial in and of itself; each event is a propaedeutic for the next link in the larger contextual picture of nationhood. No link can be "passed over" for Passover to be a true holiday of freedom, as this story will teach us.

THE NARRATIVE CONTEXT

Tzippora was not an Egyptian; for her, going to Egypt represented neither homecoming nor ideological partnership with a husband who may have even regarded her company on the journey as an additional unwanted burden. The man identified as an Egyptian at the well where Yitro's daughters first spotted him was reluctantly on his way back with a wife and two babies: "So Moses took his wife and sons, mounted them on a donkey and went back to the land of Egypt; and Moses took the staff of God with him" (Ex. 4:20). We can easily imagine ourselves freighted down by the weight of a journey, packing up our lives for an unknown future that involves pushing ourselves into realms of insecurity and personal inadequacy. This odd scene, like the packing before a long trip, seems a banal, extraneous detail in a momentous story, but it is this very small scene of apparent insignificance that puts the reader into the mindset of the characters.

Taking the staff in hand is the one detail that differs from an ordinary family excursion. And, in midrashic terms, it was no ordinary rod but one created before the world was created, along with nine other ordinary objects that would come to have extraordinary significance.[5] Moses was not told directly to take his staff, but no doubt he was moved by its powers when God transformed

---

5. See Genesis Rabba 92:7 for the full list.

it into the very symbol of Pharaoh. It turned into a *"naḥash,"* snake; elsewhere it turned into a *"tannin,"* crocodile. In Ezekiel 29:3, Pharaoh is called the great crocodile crouching in the river, an epithet that associated the supreme ruler with the supreme strength of Egypt, the Nile River. Thrown on the floor, the rod-turned-snake could only symbolize for Moses the power he would be given to overthrow Pharaoh's rule. God helped transform Moses' own insecurities into tools of leadership by asking Moses, "What is that in your hand?" and helping Moses understand that within his very hand he had the power to change the future of the Israelites (Ex. 4:2). He had to unleash this power, but it was a power within his reach. By taking his staff on the journey, Moses understood that, more than a public symbol of power, it would serve as a reminder that he had been imbued with the divine capacity to triumph.

The journey continued, but in the narration of it in the Bible, comes a sudden urgent pause. First, God told Moses that Pharaoh would lose his firstborn son if he did not permit God's firstborn to worship their deity. Then Moses fell into a sinkhole of unexpected danger where his own firstborn was threatened, according to readings that believe it was Gershom rather than Eliezer who was at risk:

> And the Lord said to Moses, "When you return to Egypt, see that you perform before Pharaoh all the marvels that I have put within your power. I, however, will stiffen his heart so that he will not let the people go. Then you shall say to Pharaoh, 'This says the Lord: Israel is My firstborn son. I have said to you, *Let My son go, that he may worship Me, yet you refuse to let him go. Now I will slay your firstborn son.'"* (Ex. 4:21–23)

Abandoned as a child by one father – as a forced act of pain – and pursued to the death by his next father figure, Moses was told by God in no uncertain terms that *He* was Moses' new father, and that Moses was His firstborn son. On the face of it, this is a reference to all the Israelites who are God's chosen children, but it is not articulated that way. It is articulated as if it were Moses himself who is God's firstborn son. Moses could not have helped but feel he was in God's sheltering arms.

And then another father figure put Moses into life-threatening danger. An angel obstructed Moses' way when he finally assented to his mission. This small digression at a stop along the way back to Egypt is full of enigma. Having fled Pharaoh's murderous anger, Moses was told to now return and take the Jewish people out of bondage. But then God inexplicably placed Moses, or his child according to different commentators, in mortal danger. Tzippora rushed in and circumcised her son, saving the day and allowing this newly formed family to proceed with their journey while leaving us with a host of unanswered questions:

- Why is the story of Moses' son's *brit*, his circumcision, told here and told in this sudden, rather than ceremonial, fashion, as it is recounted in the narratives of Abraham and even in the circumcisions of an entire town in the story of the rape of Dinah (Gen. 34)?
- Why would God possibly want to kill Moses after just instructing him to go confront Pharaoh and telling him what to say?
- Since when is a father of an uncircumcised son punishable by death for the failure to circumcise a son?
- Why did Tzippora suddenly enter this narrative as a main character? What motivated her to grab a flint?
- What does the odd expression "*ḥatan damim*," a bridegroom of blood, mean? Who is the bridegroom of blood? What about the next extended expression, "*ḥatan damim lamulot*," a bridegroom of blood because of the circumcision, which just further obfuscates the meaning?
- Who is the "he" referenced several times? The pronoun/antecedent confusion once again jumbles the meaning.

All who interpret this story are challenged by its thematic and linguistic mysteries. Its verses are choppy and ambiguous, as emphasized by modern Bible scholar Robert Alter:

> This elliptical story is the most enigmatic episode in all of Exodus. It seems unlikely that we will ever resolve the enigmas it poses, but it nevertheless plays a pivotal role in the larger narratives, and it is worth pondering why such a haunting and bewildering story should have been introduced at this juncture.[6]

Some state the case even more radically, believing that these three verses are the oddest in all the Hebrew Bible. Two Hebrew verbs – "*vayifgashehu*" followed by "*vayevakesh*" – to encounter and then to request – seem too formal for the suddenness of the action. God had revealed Himself to Moses multiple times. What need did God have to "encounter" Moses when God spoke with him freely?

---

6. Robert Alter, *The Five Books of Moses* (New York: W.W. Norton and Company, 2004), 330.

The encounter suggests violence, not unlike the way Jacob encountered an angel who wrestled with him. And this story will be about physical violence to Moses or possibly one of his sons. It will be bloody, with one scholar acknowledging that the word *"damim"* in the plural, bloods, suggests a multiplication of just such violence or bloodshed. Like the Jacob story, this one will result in the permanent physical disfigurement of one of its chief characters, an action that seemed necessary for the story to proceed. Like a rite of passage in a novel about adolescence, this story offers a glimpse of suffering and sacrifice on the way to becoming a man or, in this case, a leader. With all of the groundwork God laid for Moses – the burning bush, the persuasive speech, the brother, the rod – God surprised Moses with this test of faith, a last ring of fire to leap through to show readiness for the challenges ahead. Tzippora became an unexpected supporting actress in the drama, taking on the role of heroine as she tried desperately to save her family.

TZIPPORA'S ONE GREAT ACT

We do not know of Eliezer's birth until Exodus 4:20, and his name is not yet mentioned. As if the introduction of Moses' new role was not enough, we learn that Tzippora gave birth during the trip's preparations. It is this detail that fuels Rashi's explanation of the narrative context. Because they were about to move their family, Moses and Tzippora delayed the *brit*, following the Jewish law that circumcision can be delayed on a journey to circumvent danger to the child. Physical movement at this sensitive and vulnerable time can bring harm to a newborn and can, therefore, be postponed in Jewish law.

Rashi bases his commentary on a swath of Talmud that analyzes these biblical verses, providing flourish and detail to fill in the narrative gaps of the text itself (Nedarim 31b–32a). The Talmud records a dispute between R. Yehoshua b. Karha, who believes that Moses was punished for his apathy to circumcision, and R. Yossei, who explains that Moses was not ignoring a his son's *brit*, but was attempting to balance two imperatives, his own family responsibility and the need for national survival. In prioritizing the two tasks before him, Moses initially placed God's revealed command at the head of his list, and failed to strike the right balance between God's revealed command and his own family obligations. R. Yossei tells us that Moses learned in an alarming way how poor this judgment was.

Tzippora seemed to understand that Moses was being punished for not circumcising their son, but it was not female intuition that led her to this conclusion. According to Rashi, an angel who took the form of a serpent had swallowed Moses up until his groin. This was an immediate giveaway to Tzippora that postponement of *brit* was the cause. Tzippora, in this reading, was angry at her newborn son, believing that because of him her bridegroom's very life was compromised. She stood to lose her husband and was prepared to fight for his life since he was incapacitated and could not fight for his own life. The next "he" in verse 26 – "he let him go" – is a reference to the angel who let Moses go from the serpent's grip once Tzippora attended to the responsibility of *mila*, which explains her exclamation after the circumcision, "You are a bridegroom of blood because of the circumcision."

Rashi, in trying to solve numerous exegetical problems, created a host of other problems that are predominantly theological in nature. According to R. Yossei in the Talmud, Moses was not being punished with near death for neglecting to circumcise his son but merely for delaying the *brit*, a sharp response in light of their sojourn, since this makes the "sin" even smaller in scale. The serpent explains why Tzippora entered the scene with such verve and helps us understand the nature of the confrontation and the error. But must we go that far? Must we introduce to the text a new "character," let alone a fantastical leg-eating beast, in order to resolve the difficulties in the passage? Rashi also fails to explain why Tzippora made her observation twice about the bridegroom of blood. The first may be a statement of the problem. Looking at Moses she called him a bridegroom of blood; her husband of only a few years was suddenly a bloody mess. Once the serpent departed, affirming that her intuition was correct, she then called out that Moses was a bridegroom of blood because of circumcision. She figured it out on her own. It was this failure to act before the trip that endangered Moses, and now she could finally put a name to the problem.

The Talmud introduces this bizarre explanation by saying how great a mitzva *mila* is (Nedarim 31b) and concluding that despite all of Moses' fine qualities and service to the Lord, he would have been punished thoroughly for failure to carry out this command. His leadership did not grant him a pass. If anything, his future position in the community absolutely necessitated that he set the standard. Interestingly, Abraham ibn Ezra, the twelfth-century exegete, believes that it was Moses' son who was the bridegroom of blood, blamed for his father's near death over not bringing him properly into the covenant. This reading also explains why Tzippora may have been referring to her own son as the murderer when she called him "a bridegroom of blood because of the circumcision." Her uncircumcised son, after all, compromised her bridegroom, Moses.

THE POWER OF AMBIGUITY

The difficulty of this imaginative reading is occasioned by the ambiguities in the biblical text itself. The lack of clarity of pronouns and word meanings allows for great variance in interpretation. The fact that numerous commentators weighed in on the exegetical difficulties with answers radically different from each other suggests that there was not a clear, accepted tradition in reading this story that all or most could subscribe to with a unified approach. Although widespread agreement of meaning is rare, this much disagreement among classic commentators is also unusual. The sensitive Bible student can only wonder how unclear this passage looked to scholars if they varied so greatly in their reading. Their confusion becomes our confusion.

In the Talmud, R. Shimon b. Gamliel maintains that Eliezer's life, not Moses', was at risk as the narrative unfolds. This makes sense in answering the question of why God would give Moses a task and then immediately put his life in danger. It was not his life that was in danger. This differs from another ancient approach, cited in the Targum attributed to Yonatan b. Uziel. This view maintains that Moses was the person in danger, and it was on account of his firstborn son, Gershom, not his recently born son, Eliezer. In the *Mekhilta* (*Parashat Yitro* 1), R. Eliezer HaModa'i says that Yitro was only willing to give over Tzippora, his daughter, in marriage to Moses if he would refrain from the commandment of *mila*, a distasteful and alien custom to the Midianites. Yitro was, after all, a Midianite priest and represented his faith and his people as an exemplar. Consequently, Gershom was to remain an idol worshipper, following in the tradition of his mother and her family. In this view, Moses' life was in danger not only because of the lack of *mila* for his children but because he permitted them to worship idols, even at such a tender age.

A later view expands this explanation. Rabbi Samson Raphael Hirsch believes that it was not only Yitro's condition but Tzippora's own will that their children not be circumcised. When the circumcision finally took place, it is she who said, "You are a bridegroom of blood *to me*" to signify that it was on her account that Moses almost died. You are a bridegroom of blood *because of me*. Rabbi Samson Raphael Hirsch adds that while Moses was in Midian he was willing to live by her cultural norms and agreed-upon family arrangement, but when they were on their way back to Egypt, it became apparent that Moses could not take on a leadership role for the Israelites without having his own sons enter the covenant. His tormented naming of Gershom explains why he felt so dislocated after being welcomed so warmly into Yitro's home and reflects the angst of, "I am not allowed to circumcise my son in this land. I am so alien here."

Tzippora's act was her way of accepting this change and her own role in Jewish life. The moment Moses left Midian, this responsibility of *brit mila* devolved upon him, and in avoiding it, even for a moment, he was putting his own life at risk. Tzippora needed to demonstrate that this was her covenant, too.

Commentators also struggle with another small but significant detail in the story, the ambiguous pronoun in the clause "cut off the foreskin of her son and cast it at **his** feet." She may have thrown the foreskin at the angel's feet as if to say in the most visceral and violent way possible that she had done what needed to be done to free her husband and allow him to continue on his mission, and the angel needed to stop the punishment. The deal had been brokered and was done. In essence, the foreskin was a *korban*, a sacrifice intended to mollify the angel's anger. In the Book of Judges, both Gideon and Manoah offer sacrifices to angels out of fear, in hopes of changing what they anticipate are circumstances beyond their control.

Alternatively, Tzippora threw the foreskin at Moses as an act of protection, believing that the blood of this act would be some kind of compensatory measure to release Moses of his own sudden incapacity. This symbolic act of inoculation – using the blood that could have signaled death to renew life – was a way to suggest that the blood of one already joined to the people by covenant would rid the blood of the other who was initially denied the act of entering the covenant. We can only imagine an exhausted young mother, hands bloodied and taut, holding the flint and pleading that her husband be free to rejoin the family in preparation for the task ahead. Ḥizkuni's third possibility is that Tzippora threw the cut foreskin at the child himself, throwing at him her anger at the situation or as a way of acknowledging that whatever had been neglected up to this point had now been dealt with appropriately. The Hebrew "*raglav*" does not mean only "leg"; many scholars believe it is also a reference to the male genitalia. This would render the casting of the foreskin a ritual act rather than an impulsive throw of revulsion or a debt paid. She touched the circumcised foreskin to her son's genitalia making note of the act and the fact that her son was now in his total body a full-fledged member of the Jewish people.

The scene forces tensions in the Exodus story to the surface. The choice of a non-slave to lead this radical movement, a man who lived in Midian, married to a Midianite rather than an Israelite woman, only lightly touches on the ambiguities present in the narrative. The yeoman's task of single-handedly running a revolution with unwilling partners against a man of godlike power, assigned by a God who refused to reveal Himself other than through the past and the future – "I am the God of your forefathers and I will be what I will be" – makes the task at hand seem impossible and unlikely. Moses required neither past nor future. He required a God of the present.

WHO IS THIS MAN MOSES?

In *Like unto Moses*, James Nohrnberg compares Moses' early story to elements of several Genesis narratives. Moses achieved notoriety only after he left Pharaoh's house, unlike Joseph who achieved fame *in* Pharaoh's house.[7] Moses took himself out of reach of Pharaoh just as Jacob took himself out of reach of Esau's juris-diction. And, in another strange connection to Genesis, Moses landed in the house of Yitro, whose pedigree traces back to the fourth son of Keturah (Gen. 25:2), linking Moses back to Abraham. Not insignificantly, when God appeared to Moses at the burning bush in Exodus 3:6, He introduced Himself as "the God of your father, the God of Abraham, the God of Isaac, and the God of Jacob," jumping from Moses' own father all the way back to the first father and thus cementing Moses' personal story within the larger covenantal context of his people.

As the story progresses, Moses' travel back to Egypt is contingent upon the two patriarchal figures in his life letting go of their hold in some way, enabling him to come into his own as a hero. Pharaoh died, an event recorded only verses before Moses' encounter at the bush, and Moses asked permission from his father-in-law to leave Midian in pursuit of this larger mission: "Moses went back to his father-in-law Yitro and said to him, 'Let me go back to my kinsmen in Egypt and see how they are faring.' And Yitro said to Moses, 'Go in peace'" (Ex. 4:18). The fugitive with seemingly no connection to his past is suddenly linked to kinsmen.

If we secure identity in part by defining ourselves relative to those around us, Moses' own identity issues were heightened by the fact that God was unwilling to identify Himself, and Tzippora, mother of his progeny, appeared as a link to a momentary refuge in his past life but not as a part of his future life. Who are you if you do not have continuous links to others?

THE LARGER PICTURE

Given the oddity of these verses and the difficulty of their explication, it would not be a stretch to believe that these verses were a later interpolation or a mis-taken addition, appearing sandwiched between texts of greater import and sig-nificance. But careful examination of linguistic and thematic similarities shows that these verses both parallel larger themes and add new and important details to the story's ultimate meaning.

Like the story of Noah and Ham in Genesis 9 that sets a small family interaction against the much larger postdiluvian narratives of reconstruction and further destruction, this brief encounter is meant to reveal a larger motif at a critical juncture in Israelite history. Our verses seem to be a direct and logical continuation of what happens before them in the Book of Exodus:

---

7. James Nohrnberg, *Like unto Moses: The Constituting of an Interruption* (Bloomington, IN: Indiana University Press, 1995), 154.

And Moses took his wife and sons and set them upon a donkey and he returned them to the land of Egypt. And Moses took the rod of God in his hand. And the Lord said to Moses: "When you return to Egypt, see that you do before Pharaoh all the wonders which I have put into your hand; but I will harden his heart that he shall not let the people go. And you shall say to Pharaoh: "Thus says the Lord: 'Israel is My son, My firstborn. And I say to you, Let My son go that he may serve Me. And if you refuse to let him go, behold, I will slay your son, your firstborn.'" (Ex. 4:20–23)

Immediately after this, our verses appear. They appear in the context of firstborn children and death. One cannot but wonder if this foreshadowing of what was to come in Egypt was also a warning to Moses to understand the full power of God's might. God could instantly change the known universe. Pharaoh's power was nothing compared to God's capacity to locate and destroy Pharaoh at his point of greatest vulnerability, his first issue, his pride, his heir, and his legacy. God could paralyze Egypt simply by cutting off the legacy of the current Pharaoh so that there would be no next apparent Pharaoh.

Linguistic similarities connect our few verses with those that precede and follow them. The idea that one seeks the death of another appears in our passage in 4:24 and also immediately before that in 4:19. "*Encountered him*" appears in 4:24 and also in 4:27, the verse following our narrative. This linguistic glue discourages the reader from looking at our brief encounter atomistically, disconnected from that which comes before or after it.

There are also much larger structural parallels that cannot be ignored. Moses' return to Egypt in 4:20 is bookended by his call to leave in 12:31. Circumcision is mentioned as a prerequisite to partaking of the Pesah sacrifice in Exodus 12:43–49 and then later in Joshua 5:7–10, as a requirement for eating the Pesah once the Israelites had crossed the Jordan. The connection affirms the notion that only once one enters the personal covenant represented by circumcision can one then enter the national covenant represented by the Paschal lamb.

These verses all point to an unarticulated tremor that appears beneath the surface of this story and Tzippora's act. There is a meaningful connection between *brit*, Passover, and Israel in these verses. It is the story of history as a continuum: entering the covenant as an individual, partaking of the Paschal lamb sacrifice at Passover as part of the national commitment, and then entering Israel to demonstrate that national commitment in our homeland. History takes place in this order. Moses could not possibly have threatened Pharaoh's children, left for Israel, and served as the leader of the people of the covenant if his own children were not part and parcel of that Israelite covenant.

Our narrative was not only a statement of Tzippora's commitment; it was also a statement of Moses' recommitment. Moses, too, had been remote from Israelite life. Removed from slavery, raised in Pharaoh's palace and then in Yitro's home in Midian, he needed to affirm his own commitment before asking for the commitment of others. He needed to join his destiny with the fate of the larger Jewish historical picture. That picture begins with the individual and then manifests itself in a larger commitment to national goals symbolized by the Passover sacrifice and joined to a sacred land central to the covenant. The beginning of this ladder commitment was first imprinted in Abraham's very body through *mila*, then entrusted to a people consuming a sacrifice in clusters of community, and finally bequeathed as a whole national entity to a people entering the Land of Israel. We see this framing clearly in Joshua 5. Before Passover, there was a mass circumcision so that those not formally bound by the covenant could enter and partake of the Passover sacrifice. After healing, they would cross the Jordan River into the Land of Israel, imprinting this clear and affirmed connection in the hearts of the whole nation.

At that time the Lord said to Joshua, "Make flint knives and circumcise the Israelites again." *So Joshua made flint knives and circumcised the Israelites* at Givat HaAralot. Now this is why he did so: All those who came out of Egypt – all the men of military age – died in the desert on the way after leaving Egypt. All the people that came out had been circumcised, but all the people born in the desert during the journey from Egypt had not…. And after the whole nation had been circumcised, they remained where they were in camp until they were healed. Then the Lord said to Joshua, "Today I have rolled away the reproach of Egypt from you." So the place has been called Gilgal to this day. On the evening of the fourteenth day of the month, while camped at Gilgal on the plains of Jericho, *the Israelites celebrated the Passover.* The day after the Passover, that very day, they ate some of the produce of the land: unleavened bread and roasted grain. The manna stopped the day after *they ate this food from the land*; there was no longer any manna for the Israelites, but that year they ate of the produce of Canaan. (Josh. 5:2–12)

Like Moses before them, the people needed to ready and prepare themselves spiritually for the larger, demanding commitments ahead. There came a time in the life of a man and his family and then subsequently in the life of a nation when commitment to a cause had to be sealed in the flesh.

The pairing of this festival with personal covenant is so crucial to understanding the nature of Passover and the story of Tzippora's flint that we find the

Talmud emphasizing that the narrative in Joshua 5 follows, as the *haftara*, our public Torah reading on the first day of Passover:

> The sages taught in a *baraita*:[8] On the first day of Passover, the congregation reads from the portion of the Festivals [Lev. 22:26, 23:44] and they read as the *haftara* the account of the Passover celebrated at Gilgal [Josh. 5:2–14].[9]

Readiness for the holiday and the entrance into the Holy Land itself was dependent on the mitzva of circumcision. Without it, there would be – to borrow from Wallace Stegner – no crossing to safety.

TZIPPORA'S FUTURE

Tzippora's early proactive leap into the covenant through circumcision takes an unusual and disturbing turn. After this momentous scene, we expect to see more of this first lady of Exodus, yet she falls into the shadows, reappearing in Exodus 18 and then disappearing from the Pentateuch altogether, referenced only obliquely – if at all – in Numbers 12. Until we hear about her return to Moses with their young sons and her father Yitro in Exodus 18, we have no idea that the couple had ever spent time apart. Yet in this scene, Tzippora appears painfully alone and neglected, a woman who has had a crowning moment that marked the end rather than the beginning of her story.

> Now Yitro, the priest of Midian and father-in-law of Moses, heard of everything God had done for Moses and for his people Israel, and how the Lord had brought Israel out of Egypt. After Moses had sent away his wife Tzippora, his father-in-law Yitro received her and her two sons. One son was named Gershom, for Moses said, "I have become an alien in a foreign land"; and the other was named Eliezer, for he said, "My father's God was my helper; He saved me from the sword of Pharaoh." Yitro, Moses' father-in-law, together with Moses' sons and wife, came to him in the desert, where he was camped near the mountain of God. Yitro had sent word to him, "I, your father-in-law Yitro, am coming to you with your wife and *her two sons*." So Moses went out to meet his father-in-law and bowed down and kissed him. They greeted each other and then went into

---

8. A *baraita* is a passage of Talmud that was not included within the mishnaic canon, but because of its important and authoritative status is used to compare to and contrast with existent *mishnayot* as part of Talmud study.

9. Megilla 30b, *Koren Talmud Bavli* translation, Noé edition (Jerusalem: 2014).

the tent. Moses told his father-in-law about everything the Lord had done to Pharaoh and the Egyptians for Israel's sake and about all the hardships they had met along the way and how the Lord had saved them. (Ex. 18:1–8)

Yitro had to reintroduce Tzippora to her husband. He introduced the children, as one mystical reading points out, as her sons rather than his or theirs. Two black and white depictions of this scene are rendered by the artist Marc Chagall; both communicate deep family fractures. In one, Moses bows low to the ground upon the arrival of these distinguished guests. And they are guests. They have not been part of the immense dramas that shaped the early life of this nation. Yitro was told what happened to them because he did not experience the miracles himself. Neither did Tzippora. In the drawing, we find a tent in the left upper corner with an opening that Moses and Yitro will utilize when the two relocate inside, while Moses' wife and sons stand outside in retreat. Yitro does not look happy with his son-in-law. His eyes look downward. His hands cradle each other, not reaching out to this distant man who took his daughter to wed. Tzippora is also taciturn. Hers is a figure bloated with child-bearing, a woman who nurses alone. Her sons, held by a helper, also look at this stranger – their father – with wonder. The youngest is ensconced in the arms of an unnamed supporter but the older child looks disfigured. He has only one eye, large and strange. His head is bent. Like his mother and grandfather, this child's right arm sweeps around his side, protecting himself from the man before him who is,

Zippora Sketches, Marc Chagall

ironically, his father. Chagall, like the text's ellipses, has offered us a family portrait of estrangement and pain.

Tzippora came out of anonymity with her flint, ready to join forces in the making of a new chapter of our history. She enabled Moses to continue his journey to leadership while her own light receded. Her utility for the story spent, she became a quiet character who disappeared into the larger story. As Jacques Mallet du Pan wrote in an essay in 1793 about the French Revolution, "the Revolution devours its children." She was swallowed whole by the crusade of her husband, disappearing into the ether of larger national issues. In the making of a master story, there are heroes and there are those who have heroic moments. Both made us a nation.

LIFE HOMEWORK

- Contemplate a large sacrifice you made for your faith or belief. Was it worth it and if so, why? Think of someone who made a significant sacrifice for you and make sure to use Passover as a time to thank them profoundly for it.

- Ever feel swept up in a moment of history? Describe it and what gave it that eternal, transcendent feeling.

- This Passover, use Tzippora's glorious moment to help others think about the bigger picture of commitment, a larger life purpose that feels grand and majestic.

Day Four

He stands, stamps a little in his boots,
Rubs his hands. He's cold in the morning breeze:
a diligent angel, who has worked hard for his promotions.
Suddenly he thinks he's made a mistake: all eyes,
he counts again in the open notebook
all the bodies waiting for him in the square,
camp within camp: only I
am not there, am a mistake,
turn off my eyes, quickly, erase my shadow.
I shall not want. The sum will be in order
without me: here for eternity.

"The Roll Call," Dan Pagis
(Translated by Stephen Mitchell)

Day Four

The Plagues, Hard Hearts, and Free Will

When the heart speaks, the mind finds it indecent to object.
Milan Kundera

The heart beats billions of times in the average lifespan of a human being, about seventy-two beats per minute. In order to hear the heart, our minds have to be very quiet. At these times, our deepest emotions guide our intellect. The heart speaks. It speaks a language without words. In our ineffable moments, laughter and tears are its language. In our withdrawal or anger, the heart speaks the language of self-diminishment or aggrandizement. The heart gives us away when words try to hide what we really mean. When our hearts are touched, and we are moved to feel profoundly, our feelings often inspire goodness or compassion or allow access to our greatest insecurities. When we allow our hearts to speak, our weaknesses and mistakes become vehicles for deeper understanding, empathy, and learning.

Dr. Brene Brown describes the paradox of this kind of vulnerability in her book *Daring Greatly*, a phrase taken from Theodore Roosevelt's speech "Citizenship in a Republic," where he advises his listeners to take risks and do great things by daring greatly. In Brown's words, "Our willingness to own and engage with our vulnerability determines the depth of our courage and the clarity of our purpose; the level to which we protect ourselves from being vulnerable is a measure of our fear and disconnection."[1]

---

1. Brene Brown, *Daring Greatly* (New York: Gotham Books, 2012), 2.

The heart speaks the language of vulnerability.

In the Hebrew Bible, the heart was the seat of both the emotions *and* the intellect. This perception, shared by most of the ancient world at the time, probably developed from the knowledge that the ever-pumping heart distributed blood to all parts of the body; none remained untouched by the heart's work. In Homeric Greek, Chinese, and Sanskrit, the word for heart incorporates the understanding that it is both a physical organ and a metaphysical center of human consciousness akin to the soul. Blood in the ancient world was, understandably, a sign of life, as we find in Leviticus, "The life (*nefesh*) of the flesh is in the blood" (Lev. 17:11). In Jewish law, we must not drink blood, spill blood, or leave spilled blood uncovered. Leaving blood uncovered indicates disrespect for the sanctity of human life, because blood is regarded as the very soul of human life. If blood is the soul, then the heart moves the soul. It is the command center, so to speak, for human drive, ambition, and intimacy.

The biblical heart is one that has the capacity to hold many complex feelings – ranging from joy to desperation – together. Those entrusted to build the *Mishkan* – the portable Tabernacle – had to be "*ḥakhmei lev*," wise of heart.[2] Those who donated generously to the *Mishkan* were called "*nedivei lev*," giving of heart.[3] God blessed Solomon with a "*lev ḥakham venavon*," a wise and discerning heart, because he asked for the capacity to judge carefully instead of requesting wealth and a long life (1 Kings 3:12). The curses in Deuteronomy remind us that if we forgo a life of commandedness, we will find no peace and have a "*lev rogez*," an anguished or broken heart (Deut. 28:65). Isaiah mentions "*simḥei lev*," the happy-hearted (Is. 24:7), and also tells those who are "*nimharei lev*," of anxious heart, to be strong and unafraid (Is. 35:4). This understanding of the biblical heart begs us to allow and experience a wide emotional range.

In order for the biblical heart to be moved, we must, as we are told at the end of the Book of Deuteronomy (30:6), do something: "The Lord your God *will open up* your heart and the hearts of your offspring to love the Lord your God with all your heart and soul in order that you may live." In Hebrew, the term "open" is unusually rendered as "*umal*," which we would translate literally as God circumcising our hearts. In order for us to experience the heart's range of possible emotions, we need to create a small opening in the heart, a release valve, which enables us to lose the "air" within and create lightness and humility, which enables us to lose the density within and fills the heart with possibility. The thin membrane or covering of the heart – much like the translucent skin of an egg – has to

---

2. For example, see Exodus 28:3, 35:10, and 36:1, 2, 8.
3. See Exodus 35:22.

be peeled back and exposed for the heart to do its most critical work. When we do this, the hearts of our offspring will also have greater emotional accessibility; the outcome is not merely so that we can love. We ask God to open our hearts so that we and those who come after us may "live." A life worth living must include the capacity to feel deeply. An open, vulnerable heart is the only way to achieve an honest and authentic life. Charles Dickens reminds us of this with the character of Estella in *Great Expectations*, who says, "Suffering has been stronger than all other teaching, and has taught me to understand what your heart used to be. I have been bent and broken, but – I hope – into a better shape." A broken heart can bend into a better shape. We serve God and others best when we recognize the brokenness, and potential to mend, within us all.

This understanding of heart imagery in the Hebrew Bible helps us put Pharaoh's hard-heartedness within its proper context. The open heart will live. The closed heart will not. Because of the heart's importance in the Hebrew Bible as a vehicle of intimacy and empathy, we realize that Pharaoh's closed heart will be the source of his own unraveling. The closed heart cannot make itself vulnerable. It cannot feel anguish. It cannot generate compassion. It cannot learn. It feels nothing. If it feels nothing, it can do nothing. No acts of goodness, no moments of mercy, no promotion of justice will come of a closed heart.

THE EGYPTIAN HEART

As in other ancient traditions, the heart was central to Egyptian life and lore as the seat of thought, imagination, and emotion. It powered the mind and was the locus of decision-making. The heart could expand or contract to reflect the temperament or mood of its possessor. The heart, or *ib*, was mythically formed from one drop of the mother's heart at the time of conception but lived on beyond the corporeal life of the human being as the central organ that passed into the afterlife and served as a witness to the life of the person it had occupied.

In ancient Egyptian culture, the pursuit of grace in this life paved the way for a dignified afterlife. Pharaohs stockpiled their futures into pyramids with the belief that they would have the appropriate furniture, food, and accessories to live a grand life of luxury after their time on earth was done. But achieving the afterlife was no easy accomplishment. It required a light heart, a heart as light as a feather. The god who determined the weight of one's heart was Anubis, represented in ancient hieroglyphics as a human with a dog- or jackal-shaped head. In the papyrus of Hu-nefer, Anubis placed the heart on a scale balanced against a feather. If your heart, weighted down by sin and malice, tipped the scales out of your favor, you would be judged a sinner. Your heavy heart would fall to the ground, soon to be consumed by a little dog, Amenit the Devouress, poised at the scale's base. The door to the afterlife would then remain closed. If, however, your heart was equal in weight to the feather or lighter, you earned a good afterlife.[4]

> Egyptians, particularly those in senior positions of leadership who were worshipped as gods, were supposed to be pure of heart, which would, in their case, be feather-light.[5]

If, on the other hand, their hearts were weighed down with callousness and stubbornness, they were doomed. Ultimately, no matter how punitive and harsh one's action to others, a hard heart hurt its owner most of all.

THE CHRONOLOGY OF THE PLAGUES AND PHARAOH'S STUBBORN RESPONSE

In Exodus, the heart-hardening process appears most frequently with Pharaoh's reaction to each plague. Like a critic at the theater, Pharaoh proclaimed his response to each plague, most often to dismiss its significance or devastation or to suggest that he could easily imitate it. Few plagues impressed him; they intensified his stubbornness and confirmed his opinion of the Israelites and their God. The plagues induced Pharaoh into a competition with God, a game he readily played with skill and disdain, until he was himself humiliated. This seduction had to take place incrementally and gradually to work. Pharaoh had to regard himself as a winner for the early duration of the power contest so that he would keep going. Abrabanel, the great medieval questioner, asked why Pharaoh would be interested in "Jewish" magic at all (Abrabanel on Ex. 7:9). Indeed, Pharaoh was not in the least impressed. One midrash has Pharaoh amused at the gall of amateur leaders, explaining to Moses and Aaron the puzzling words that were attributed to him: "*Tenu lakhem mofeit*" – perform a marvel for *yourselves* – only yourselves, because these tricks do nothing to move me.

It is not surprising then that Moses began the contest in its initial stages with a miracle easy to best – a staff turned into a snake. Everyone in Pharaoh's court was able to mimic the trick with ease, creating the illusion that the rest of the skirmish would be equally easy. That Aaron's snake swallowed their snakes before turning back into a staff was impressive, but only in the manner of a trick that you imagine you could do if you could figure out its secret. It is at this point that Pharaoh's heart first hardened, and we can almost visualize it: "And each cast

---

4. See John E. Currid, "Why Did God Harden Pharaoh's Heart?," *Bible Review*, 9[6] (1993): 46–5; John Oswalt, "*kabed*," *Theological Wordbook of the Old Testament*, ed. R.L. Harris, G.L. Archer, Jr., and B.K. Waltke (Chicago: Moody, 1980), 1:426–428; and James Pritchard, *The Ancient Near East: An Anthology of Texts and Pictures* (Princeton, NJ: Princeton University Press, 1958).

5. *The Book of the Dead* XXXB as seen in translation in Currid, 50.

down his rod and they turned into serpents, but Aaron's rod swallowed their rods. *Yet Pharaoh's heart stiffened, and he did not heed them,* as the Lord said" (Ex. 7:12, 13).

Gustav Dore, in his engraving "Moses and Aaron Before Pharaoh," creates the visual portrait of a callous leader that Exodus, and its commentaries, do with words. In the picture, Pharaoh stands on a highly ornate portico, distinguished from the crowd of courtiers and onlookers that surround him by his headdress and embellished collar, and by the light that Dore draws to his tunic. This ruler of an ancient, powerful empire looks down at Moses and Aaron, and the coiled snake at their feet, from above, with utter disdain and a disgust that suggests they are wasting his time with their childish demonstration. One onlooker points to the snake with some interest, but the others seem bored by the whole affair; a woman leans against an ornate pillar decorated in hieroglyphics with the look of

Moses and Aaron Before Pharaoh, Gustave Dore

someone who is not entertained. Another rests his head on his folded arms over the balustrade and takes a nap. If these are the best signs and wonders Moses and Aaron can muster, then the Israelite God stands to lose the contest of the mighty before it even begins. You can almost watch Pharaoh's heart hardening as we wait for him to turn around and leave, dismissing these two frauds with a wave of the hand. Moses faces Pharaoh – perhaps the artist's way of communicating stubborn tenacity for confrontation that foreshadows Moses' eventual success – while Aaron looks down. We suffer his humiliation with him.

The same attitude held true for the first plague of blood. Impressive as it was to turn a deity into a death warrant, the Nile's new and alarming color did little to tamper with Pharaoh's confidence. He had his magicians replicate the trick and walk away, giving little heed to the Canaanite pests that were Egypt's slave labor force: "And the soothsayers of Egypt did thus with their spells, and Pharaoh's heart *toughened* and he did not heed them, just as the Lord had spoken. And Pharaoh turned and came into his house, and this too *he did not take to heart*" (Ex. 7:22–23). Pharaoh followed the course God had initially predicted. He was indifferent. His magicians could also do such magic. According to one midrash, Pharaoh not only called in his magicians to replicate the plague, he called in schoolchildren, going on to declare, "Even my wife can do this!" (Exodus Rabba 9:14). Pharaoh, before he turned away in disgust, tried to impart a lesson to Moses and Aaron, which forms the backbone of the Exodus narratives: "This is a land of magic. Everyone here can do magic." Moses and Aaron apparently brought an amateur production to sophisticated professionals.

In the biblical narrative, time passed, and God sent Moses back to Pharaoh to inform him that a scourge of frogs was on its way, ramping up the intensity of the plagues, and hinting at a reptilian revenge that takes us all the way back to the first chapter of Genesis. In Genesis, the earth swarmed with a new species of creepy-crawly reptiles. In Exodus 1, this same language was used to describe the sudden population growth among the Jews in Egypt. They did not just give birth. They swarmed, growing so rapidly that the small family of seventy Jews introduced at the beginning of the book quickly turned into a number beyond count. The plague of frogs symbolized what had happened to the Jews physically: they expanded rapidly in Egypt with a plague-like ferocity. Once again, Pharaoh's magicians imitated the plague, and Pharaoh's heart remained frozen.

Lice became a challenge. The magicians' spells did nothing, and they turned to Pharaoh and proclaimed: "This is the finger of God!" (Ex. 8:15). Paradoxically, they referred to the finger of God, in contrast to the outstretched arm that will be the Israelite reference point for God's power. Pharaoh, however, would still not budge.

After the next three plagues, Moses was told to seek out Pharaoh early in the morning and pronounce that the next punishment would be wrought with a new level of intensity.

> This time I will send all My plagues upon your person and your courtiers and your people, in order that you may know that there is none like Me in the entire world. I could have stretched forth My hand and stricken you and your people with pestilence, and you would have been effaced from the earth. Nevertheless I have spared you for this purpose: in order to show you My power, and in order that My fame resound throughout the world. (Ex. 9:14–16)

The hardening of Pharaoh's heart took place incrementally, with every plague building up another impermeable layer. Up to this point in the narrative, each plague took place beneath the ground, on the ground, or within reach of humans and animals upon the earth. But when the windows of heaven began to pour out their wrath with the plague of hail, Pharaoh could not imitate the miracle, just as he and his conjurers were hopeless to counter the plague of lice, confirming their growing ineptitude. The plague went beyond any hailstorm the Egyptians had experienced to date, as we read in Exodus: "And there was very heavy hail, with fire flashing in the midst of the hail, the likes of which had not been in all the land of Egypt from the time it became a nation" (Ex. 9:24). This may have led to an escalation of concern among Egyptian commoners that perhaps Pharaoh was not as powerful as he made himself out to be. In the words of one scholar, "The God of the Egyptians was serving as the judge of Pharaoh … Pharaoh was simply judged to be a sinner and worthy of condemnation. This is in striking contrast to the Egyptian belief in Pharaoh's perfection."[6] The God of the Hebrews, in judging Pharaoh, was also asserting divine supremacy. God even "controlled Pharaoh's heart; He could harden it. This demonstrated that only the God of the Hebrews was the true sovereign of the universe."[7]

The contest was over. The hail itself was magnificent, a miracle within a miracle to demonstrate God's great might. Pharaoh finally sent for Moses and Aaron, who had been shamed repeatedly by him. This time a different message awaited. Only when the plagues came from the sky, demonstrating a level of ability that Pharaoh's own magicians could not conjure, did Pharaoh seem even remotely moved to action. Yet despite the slight crack in Pharaoh's hard shell – "This time

---

6. Currid, 51.
7. Ibid.

I have sinned…. The Lord is in the right, and I and my people are in the wrong" (Ex. 9:27) – his confession of inadequacy was quickly revoked: "When Pharaoh saw that the rain and hail and thunder had stopped, he sinned again and hardened his heart, he and his officials" (Ex. 9:34). The heart encased itself further with every layer of built-up hardening.

In the very next chapter – chapter 10 – after the plague of locusts and the devastation of Egypt's farmlands, and right before Egypt was submerged in thick, inky darkness, Pharaoh quickly summoned Moses and Aaron and said, "I stand guilty before the Lord your God and before you. Forgive my offense just this once, and plead with the Lord your God that He remove this death from me" (Ex. 10:16). But after Moses pleaded with God and a strong wind blew the locusts away, the temporary change of conditions brought back Pharaoh's predictable stubbornness. "But the Lord stiffened Pharaoh's heart and he would not let the Israelites go" (Ex. 10:20). The moment of self-reflection lapsed, and the exposure of his weak self made Pharaoh even more dogmatic in his pursuit of the Israelites.

LATER IN THE HEBREW BIBLE

The plagues were such an impressive battle of wits and might that they are lyrically mentioned in two psalms, 78 and 105, that stress the impact of the plagues as a competition. Psalm 78 makes God into a warrior:

> His fury was sent down upon them, great anger, rage, and distress, a company of messengers of destruction. He cleared a path for His anger; He did not stop short of slaying them, but gave them over to pestilence. He struck every firstborn in Egypt, the first fruits of their vigor in the tents of Ham. (Ps. 78:49–51)

This psalm makes no mention of darkness and covers only seven of the ten plagues, but it is clear that each and every plague afflicted the Egyptian people, impacting the land and animals in different, troubling ways.

In Psalm 105, darkness is mentioned first instead of ninth, and locusts immediately come before the death of the firstborn, but the verses together communicate escalating fear followed by relief:

> He struck their vines and fig tree, broke down the trees of their country. Locusts came at His command, grasshoppers without number. They devoured every green thing in the land; they consumed the produce of

the soil. He struck down every firstborn in the land, the first fruit of their vigor. ... Egypt rejoiced when they left, for dread of Israel had fallen upon them. (Ps. 105:33–36, 38)

Because of the onslaught of large-scale problems one after another, the Egyptians could not regard them as sporadic and random occurrences that reflected simple bad fortune. And, if Pharaoh continued to believe that all was random or coincidental, the last plague had to prove without a doubt that this was not the case. According to Nahum Sarna, this is why the last plague had to be "wholly outside of human experience, and must defy any rational explanation. It must be clear to all, and beyond the possibility of misinterpretation, that what took place can only have emanated from a divine source."[8]

Pharaoh ultimately lost his battle with God for authority. In the process, his hubris cost him his son's life in the last plague, the dénouement of an ego-ridden scrimmage. Pharaoh also lost his slave labor force. And when that was all over, he lost his own afterlife because his heart was not pure. It is little wonder that he ran after the Israelites into the wilderness after giving them permission to leave. This was the only loss he thought he could recoup. He could not beat God's dominance. He could not bring back his son. His afterlife was gone. At this point, his only display of power was with those under his subordination, the vestigial reminder of his kingship. Pharaoh chased after the Israelites because he had nothing else to lose.

PHARAOH'S HARD HEART

Without an understanding of the heart-hardening process and its personal consequences, we miss the overall message of the plague narratives. As with the plagues, the hardening of Pharaoh's heart is a gradual process of resistance and recognition. The path to victory over Pharaoh was not linear, but rather a circuitous route of self-confidence that turned to self-criticism and back again. Pharaoh's checkered route to stubbornness is captured by the Hebrew verbs used to tell the story. We begin with the term "*leḥazek*" as part of God's explanation to Moses of what he could expect in his leadership mission: "When you return to Egypt, see that you perform before Pharaoh all the marvels that I have put within your power. I, however, will stiffen his heart so that he will not let the people go" (Ex. 4:21). On the surface, this reading should only have terrified

---

8. Nahum M. Sarna, *Exploring Exodus: The Heritage of Biblical Israel* (New York: Schocken Books, 1986), 78.

Moses, who already doubted his own capabilities. But God's hardening of Pharaoh's heart takes on a whole other meaning. Moses, who lived in Pharaoh's home and was likely well-versed in Egyptian culture and religion, understood that by hardening Pharaoh's heart God was actually assisting Moses. Would Pharaoh be willing to put his own afterlife at stake for the sake of a free work force? After all, with every move Pharaoh enacted to worsen conditions for his slaves, he injured himself beyond redemption.

Pharaoh miscalculated the risks to himself in his equation of how and why to keep the Israelites under the arm of oppression. Initially, his heart hardened and he enslaved the Israelites to minimize their growing number, to quell the population explosion. But Pharaoh's original motivation – his kernel of suspicion about Israelite loyalty to his people – grew over time into a full-blown perception of personal threat to his dominance as a god of Egypt.

Pharaoh's dogged enslavement and chase after the Israelites became encapsulated in the strange expression, "hardening of the heart." It appears no fewer than twenty-two times in Exodus. Half of these appearances are attributed to Pharaoh's human character flaws. The other half are predetermined by God. The obvious and looming theological question is how Pharaoh can ever be punished for having a hard heart when it was God who hardened it so often for him, effectively ridding him of his free will and the ability to have a change of heart. After the first five plagues, motivated by Pharaoh's competitive stance and stubbornness, Pharaoh's heart was turned over to God who stiffened it, making it less pliable for transformation. Causally speaking, the more Pharaoh behaved in a particular way, the less he could later behave in any other way. In Nahum Sarna's words: "This is the biblical way of asserting that the king's intransigence has by then become habitual and irreversible; his character has become his destiny. He is deprived of the possibility of relenting and is irresistibly impelled to his self-wrought doom."[9] Pharaoh could not have engaged the world any other way. His "moral atrophy" and the "numbing of his soul" were choices he made that tumbled into a place where other choices could not but be made that followed the same immoral direction.[10] Pharaoh got in his own way by deepening a path that eventually became irreversible. Moments of hesitation may have led to eventual redemption had he used them to open a cranny into his heart. But his heart closed too rapidly for a sliver of compassion to grow.

---

9. Ibid. 64.
10. Ibid.

LEADERSHIP AND CALLOUSNESS

In *The Art of Possibility*, Rosemund Stone Zander and Benjamin Zander discuss what they call the creation of the calculating self – the part of us that is "concerned for its survival in a world of scarcity."[11] When our perception of the world around us narrows, we find ourselves in a calculating modality, worried constantly about retaining our place in a world of change and threat. *The Art of Possibility* presents this self as emerging in infancy. The cry of the baby and its demands all say, "Take note of me." Developmentally, this attitude in some never morphs much beyond this need for attention and centrality, evolving into unbearable narcissism:

> A child comes to think of himself as the personality he gets recognition for or, in other words, as the set of patterns of actions and habits of thought that get him out of childhood in one piece. That set, raised to adulthood, is what we are calling the *calculating self*. The prolonged nature of human childhood may contribute to the persistence of these habits long after their usefulness has passed. No matter how confident or well-positioned this adult-self appears, underneath the surface it is weak and sees itself as marginal, at risk of losing everything.[12]

Pharaoh's calculating self changed as the narrative developed. What enhanced his status in chapter 1 ruined him several chapters later. As such, he changed his strategy in managing the Israelites to accommodate his own ego needs, usually ignoring the acute despair of his own people. What began as Pharaoh's defensive calculation to protect the welfare of Egyptian society devolved into promoting his power at the expense of his subjects. The calculating self must constantly exculpate itself in order to save itself.

Paying close attention to language, we find a new development midway through the Exodus narrative. Before the first plague, God promised Moses an unusual status:

> See, *I place you in the role of God to Pharaoh*, with your brother Aaron as your prophet. You shall repeat all that I command you, and your brother Aaron shall speak to Pharaoh to let the Israelites depart from his land. But

---

11. Rosamund Stone Zander and Benjamin Zander, *The Art of Possibility* (New York: Penguin, 2000), 81–2.

12. Ibid.

I will harden Pharaoh's heart that I may multiply My signs and marvels in the land of Egypt." (Ex. 7:1–3)

Moses was likened to God because he would have power to determine Pharaoh's future by identifying Pharaoh's ego weakness and causing Pharaoh's heart to toughen. The Hebrew here is not *"aḥazek"* but *"akshe,"* from the root *k-sh-e,* to toughen. The hardening process is subtle. The Israelites began to dominate Pharaoh's thoughts and stratagems. Anger and resistance gradually turned into self-righteous indignation. The heart is a soft organ. It only hardens when blood stops flowing through it. This takes time. According to Robert Alter, in order for the Israelites to eventually triumph in the face of adversity, Pharaoh had to stay stubbornly callous:

> Whatever the theological difficulties, the general aim of God's allowing, or here causing, Pharaoh to persist in his harshness is made clear: without Pharaoh's resistance, God would not have the opportunity to deploy His great wonders and so demonstrate His insuperable power in history and the emptiness of power attributed to the gods of Egypt.[13]

Egypt was to be a battlefield of wits for the gain of power. The question was not whether the plagues were an impressive bout of showmanship or whether they were convincing. They were a test of authority and knowledge of God. Pharaoh initially rejected any request presented by Moses because he did not acknowledge God's rulership: "Who is the Lord, that I should heed His voice to send off Israel? I do not know the Lord, nor will I send off Israel" (Ex. 5:2). The plagues were God's pedagogic tool that would lead Pharaoh to know Him.

The term *"vayeḥazek"* is used as part of the stiffening process in the rest of the story, with one exception.[14] Before the final group of plagues, we find a breaking point introduced by yet another verb change to the root *"kaved,"* heavy:

> Then the Lord said to Moses, "Go to Pharaoh. For I have hardened his heart and the hearts of his courtiers in order that I may display these My signs among them and that you may recount in the hearing of your son and your son's sons how I made a mockery of the Egyptians and how

---

13. Alter, 345.
14. See Exodus 4:21; 9:12; 10:20, 27; 14:4, 8.

I displayed My signs among them – in order that you may know that I am
the Lord." (Ex. 10:1–2)

This time, it is not only Pharaoh's heart that becomes intransigent but those of
his advisors as well. He will be unmoved and because his advisors are similarly
unmoved, they will not persuade him to change his mind, as they might have
done before. Not surprisingly, this occurs shortly before the plague of darkness,
emblematic of the condition that Pharaoh found himself in at this time. His
universe was dimming. Ra, the sun god associated with Pharaoh, was losing his
light and capacity to shine. Pharaoh's world shrank. As he tried to narrow the
possibilities for Israelite freedom, his own possibilities diminished until, slowly,
they disappeared. The obsessiveness with which he demonstrated his might eventually obstructed his view. And that is why the text uses the term "*kaved*." The
shell around his heart had stiffened and hardened to the point where it became
irreparably heavy. The scales would never tip in his favor. His heart would literally go to the dogs.

The last references to Pharaoh's hardening heart occur twice in rapid succession in Exodus 14 after Pharaoh had finally given the Israelites permission to
leave: "When the king of Egypt was told that the people had fled, Pharaoh and
his courtiers *had a change of heart* about the people and said, 'What is this we
have done, releasing Israel from our service?' He ordered his chariot and took
his men with him…. *The Lord stiffened the heart of Pharaoh.*" First Pharaoh's heart
changes or reverses its intention (*vayehafekh*) and then it is hardened once again.
At this point, Pharaoh could have relinquished his death hold on his slaves. He
had already freed them, and they had already fled. They were not there as a physical presence to remind him of his anger. But their absence broadcast his weakness to his people, and in contemplating his inadequacy, his heart again did its
dirty work. If the heart is the seat of both the emotions and intelligence, Pharaoh
ran out of both.

In her book *Bad Leadership*, Barbara Kellerman identifies callousness as one
of the chief behaviors that cause leaders to suffer a bad reputation and contribute
to their eventual downfall. Kellerman defines callous leadership as being uncaring
or unkind: "Ignored or discounted are the needs, wants, and wishes of most members of the group or organization, especially subordinates."[15] Initially regarded as
authoritative, this behavior soon spirals into authoritarian and followers begin to
move away from outcomes and begin to question process and trust. Kellerman cites

---

15. Barbara Kellerman, *Bad Leadership* (Boston: Harvard Business School Press, 2004), 119.

Joseph Rost in *Leadership for the Twenty-First Century* who writes that in a perfect world, leadership "is an influence relationship among leaders and followers who intend real changes that reflect their mutual purposes."[16] Kellerman contends that "this definition implies that the exchange is based on influence rather than coercion and that it is multidirectional, with followers influencing leaders and vice versa. It further implies that the mutual purposes are arrived at through negotiation."[17] Yet, in the imperfect world we occupy, many leaders opt for coercion because it is easier for a leader to hear his or her voice than to navigate a path through disparate voices. The very idea that a leader has a choice of behaviors is quite modern. Pharaoh believed himself to be a god and was treated as one. Gods don't need to negotiate.

Contrast Kellerman's discussion of callousness with an observation made by two contemporary leadership writers about the nature of the heart in leading others:

> The most difficult work of leadership involves learning to experience distress without numbing yourself. The virtue of a sacred heart lies in the courage to maintain your innocence and wonder, your doubt and curiosity, and your compassion and love even through your darkest, most difficult moments. Leading with an open heart means you could be at your lowest point, abandoned by your people and entirely powerless, yet remain receptive to the full range of human emotions without going numb, striking back, or engaging in some other defense.... A sacred heart allows you to feel, hear, and diagnose, even in the midst of your mission, so that you can accurately gauge different situations and respond appropriately.[18]

THE LAST BEAT OF A HEAVY HEART

A sacred heart is a pure heart – one that lives on beyond the beating heart. Pharaoh was not to meet such a glorious end. Driven by anger, Pharaoh himself chased the Israelites to the banks of the Reed Sea. The Israelites were petrified of his oncoming approach until God created an additional, final plague that is never listed as a plague: He opened the sea waters for those worth saving and closed them for those driven by evil. Where Pharaoh stood out from all of his court in the preceding chapters, in death, he was not a god but merely a human

---

16. Joseph Rost, *Leadership for the Twenty-First Century* (New York: Praeger, 1991), 102.
17. Kellerman, 119.
18. Ronald Heifetz and Marty Linsky, *Leadership on the Line* (Boston: Harvard Business School Press, 2002), 227–8.

of flesh and blood indistinguishable from any of his warriors: "Thus the Lord delivered Israel that day from the Egyptians. Israel saw *the Egyptians* dead on the shore of the sea" (Ex. 14:30). Pharaoh lived as a god but died an ordinary man. His individual death is not even recorded; the Bible reader must but assume that his body, together with his huge Egyptian force, was left to decompose on the banks of a sea that finally engulfed his calculating self. He is not mentioned again in Exodus. There is always a last beat to a hardened heart, the beat that ends in self-destruction. Pharaoh could have kept his heart soft and open. He would have saved his people and earned his afterlife. There was a great deal at stake nationally and personally. But his hard heart tipped the scales out of his favor and, ultimately and gratefully, in ours.

LIFE HOMEWORK

- Think of a person or a situation that hardens your heart to a place of rigidity and a point of little compassion. What can you do this Passover to soften your heart a little?

- Name a personal negative character trait you carry that has gotten worse because you failed to deal with it earlier. What can you do to revisit the damage and reverse it?

- Use this Passover as a time to pay attention to your own capacity to remain open and vulnerable. Notice rigidity or closedness in your body language and in your words. Monitor your communication with others for signs of compassion versus signs of harshness.

Day Five

So what did we have?
The sweet scent of jasmine,
the painted orange sun
discovered suddenly
while cutting the persimmon in half
at the first volley of light.
The chicory flowers'
morning blue,
the entire meadow,
a cluster of snails
on top of a sea onion stalk
and there was also the word "wagtail."
What else was there?
The cicada requiem,
pink sheep in the sloping sky,
and the soft, much-kissed down
on the bottom of the cat's ear
and that's it, I think
that's what we had
today.

"Monday," Agi Mishol
(Translated by Lisa Katz)

—

Day Five

The Love Song of
Our Redemption

I love you without knowing how, or when, or from where.
I love you simply...

Pablo Neruda

The verses in Song of Songs, the Bible's love prose, tease the reader with their hide-and-seek rhythm. The lovers elude each other, search out each other, and, in the absence of the other, create wonderful metaphors of love. The Talmud attributes the text to the pen of wise King Solomon, claiming that he composed this romantic book in his youth, when he presumably experienced the new delights of temptation, companionship, and love.[1] Throughout the ages, Song of Songs has always been understood in rabbinic literature as a physical representation of the love between God and human beings: intense, intimate, and cyclical.[2] Love's engulfing spirit, its playfulness, its bruising rejection, and its unpredictability manifest the ebb and flow of the soul as we search for a God sometimes

---

1. Song of Songs Rabba 1:10. This midrash further states that Solomon wrote Proverbs in his middle age and Ecclesiastes as an old man, attributing to him maturity in his middle years and cynicism before his death.

2. On the holiness of the book in rabbinic literature see, for example, Sanhedrin 101a.

"hidden in the cliff," sometimes the "seal upon heart and hand." Above all, the text cries out with a plea for closeness: "My dove, in the cranny of the rocks, hidden by the cliff, let me see your face, let me hear your voice, for your voice is sweet and your face is exquisite" (Song. 2:14).

There is a backdrop for love throughout Song of Songs: the garden, a place of sensuality and pleasure, friendship and romance. Gardens are a popular image in literature and art, and we are not surprised to find the garden as the stage where intimate relationships bloom in Song of Songs. According to one art historian, the image of the garden is "the embodiment of life and growth,"[3] the physical space that encapsulates paradise, the landscape of perfection, arcadia. The *Oxford English Dictionary* defines "arcadia" as an "ideal region of rural felicity." While it is true that the garden in fine arts has been depicted as "heaven on earth," a place of worldly pleasure or religious reward, it can also be the place of shadowy, mystical, or erotic encounters and cruel temptation.[4] The garden has served as a backdrop for Eden scenes of Adam and Eve in naive discovery as well as crestfallen banishment. In his study of the impact of landscape upon human imagination, British historian Simon Schama observes that arcadia is "a dark grove of desire, but also a labyrinth of madness and death."[5] Notions of arcadia as wild and bucolic gave way, over time, to the manicured garden, a place of highly refined beauty and order. As Schama describes it, "Arcadia redesigned, then, was a product of the orderly mind rather than the playground of the unchained senses."[6] The garden represented an escape from progress, a cultivated piece of wilderness or aristocratic decadence, in the case of opulent personal gardens. Later, Impressionism and Post-Impressionism used the garden motif to experiment with light and color.[7] The garden is a manipulated space, a nexus of man and nature. Man plants, prunes, weeds, and watches his garden grow, determining the limits of the natural world as it enters the human domain.

---

3. Roxanne Marcoci, *Celebrations in Art: Gardens in Bloom* (New York: MetroBooks, 1995), introduction.

4. Compare, for example, the erotic but somewhat frightening panel painting "Garden of Delights" (1505) by Hieronymus Bosch with the idyllic calm of Claude Monet's "Gladioli" (1876) or John Singer Sargent's famous large canvas of children lighting garden lanterns, "Carnation, Lily, Lily Rose" (1886).

5. Simon Schama, *Landscape and Memory* (New York: Knopf, 1995), 522.

6. Ibid. 530.

7. This is somewhat parodied in Pierre-Auguste Renoir's painting "Monet Working in His Garden in Argenteuil" (1873), where the artist captures another artist engaged in garden painting using the "latest" Impressionist techniques.

Schama's polarities of arcadia encapsulate the elasticity and tension of love in Song of Songs. The garden is where love is sought, lost, and found again, where human beings step into the wild of emotions and try to trim and train those emotions in the pursuit of excitement and companionship. Contemporary Jewish artists of the twentieth century tried to capture what went on in Solomon's garden, giving insight into the nature of romance.

In "Study to Song of Songs IV," the fourth of five panels on Song of Songs that hangs in the Musée National Message Biblique Marc Chagall in Nice, Marc Chagall paints a garden that is hardly a garden at all. It is an urban landscape filled with people and buildings, religious objects, and a large blue tree. The painting seems more a reflection of King Solomon, the builder of cities, the Temple, and a stately palace, than King Solomon the youthful lover. Chagall swathes his lovers in a background of blood reds, reflecting the intensity of their passion. Many of the images most prominent in Chagall's work generally – the embracing couple, the imaginative animals, the strong blocks of color, and the crowded activity on

Study to Song of Songs IV, Marc Chagall

the sides – also appear here. The profundity of Chagall's work is often misunder-stood because of these curiosities.[8]

In "Study to Song of Songs IV," the groom, adorned in a marital crown (perhaps hinting at King Solomon), and the bride in a flowing white veil, reflect the text's reference to the lovers: "O maidens of Zion, go forth and gaze upon King Solomon *wearing the crown* that his mother gave him on his wedding day, on his day of bliss" (Song. 3:11). The woman is also described in terms of mar-riage: "You have captured my heart, my own, my bride" (Song. 4:9). Chagall's white veil, which unravels in the painting's center, depicts the verse: "Behind your veil, your hair is like a flock of goats streaming down Mount Gilead" (Song. 4:1). Seen from a distance, a flock of goats descending down a steep mountain must resemble the uneven flow of a bride's veil.[9]

The blue tree in the painting's bottom right-hand corner may refer to verse 5, chapter 8: "Under the apple tree I roused you; it was there your mother conceived you, there she who bore you conceived you." The apple tree is a tra-ditional place of romance. Love of this intensity returns the woman to her own place of origin, the place where she herself was conceived when her own parents were young lovers. The upside down turtledove is, no doubt, a link to the many verses that compare the young woman to the dove. In 4:1, her eyes have a dove-like wideness and intensity. In 2:14, the dove takes flight and disappears, mirror-ing the lover, alone and seeking. The fact that the bird is upside down should not trouble us. It is no more imaginative than the flying horse that carries our couple or any of the other unusual animal depictions found in Chagall's work. Love inverts everything. As one midrash expresses it, love upsets the natural order (Genesis Rabba 55). A blue tree rises out of a city skyline and a half-blue dove

---

8. It was a depth his Russian family failed to appreciate or understand. They did not cultivate his artistic imagination, and in condemnation, Chagall describes a moment when his grandfather turned away from a sketch of a nude woman: "And then I understood that my grandfather, as well as my wrinkled little grandmother, thought nothing of my art (what an art, that does not even convey a likeness) and set a very high value on meat." Meat came before art. One could under-stand a piece of meat. When he told his mother he wanted to be an artist, she said (according to him): "What? A painter? You're mad. Let me put my bread in the oven; don't get in my way. My bread's there." Vitebsk was not a place for art. It was for meat and bread. Chagall developed his unique style in Russia and Paris and spent his last years in New York. Although he was born into the poor circumstances of untutored Jews in the Pale of Settlement, by his life's end he received some of the highest artistic honors across the globe.

9. Yair Zakovitch discusses the possibility of viewing Song of Songs as wedding poems read during the week following marriage. See his introduction to his commentary on Song of Songs, *Mikra LeYisrael* (Jerusalem: Magnes, 1992), 6.

hangs upside down not far from a blue-maned horse. The three natural images in the painting share blocks of the same color and the same, lyrical, absurd positioning. Love helps the animals levitate and transcend the bounds of convention.

Chagall uses natural images rather sparingly here and instead creates a sea of people, some holding ritual items like a menora or a prayer book against the city of Jerusalem. All of the other characters and scenes that frame our couple may be predictive of their future narrative together. If we travel rightward, in the direction of the bride's veil, we come to the tree and then to a man and woman kissing beneath its boughs. As we move to the left we encounter dancers and holidays, and prayers and children. Then we move up the left-hand side in the direction of the horn-blowing angel/man. On the way there is a harp, a baby in the arms of its mother, and another person with an arm outstretched to the oblivious lovers. It is as if we were reading a graphic strip of the couple's future. It begins with ecstatic, levitating love that is formed in passion and then grounded in the spiral of the Jewish calendar and life cycle of events. It is a life encircled by people and song and ritual. Chagall gives our couple a rich future and much happiness.

Alternatively, we may read the surrounding images as the world that this couple has left behind. The pair kissing under the tree, with their faces drawn as connected puzzle pieces, share passion but are hardly a match for the emotional ecstasy displayed by the bride and groom on their mythical, winged horse. Chagall has chosen to highlight the other maidens of Jerusalem who are mentioned repeatedly in the text, as well as others who occupy a this-worldly existence. Whether engaged in acts of love or acts of religious observance, they cannot achieve the height of feeling that carries our lovers aloft; even prayer seems to stop short of love's intensity, as the man with an open prayer book gets lost in the tumble of characters. The sides of the painting are imprinted with people entertaining the lovers with musical instruments but, wrapped in felicity, they seem not to hear anything. All of these peripheral images do not encroach upon the two central figures who are entranced by each other and cannot be distracted.

Chagall dedicated this series of paintings to his wife, Bella, whom he married in 1915 and who died in 1944. The way he describes his personal feelings of love is reminiscent of the "floating" quality of the painting: "I had only to open my bedroom window and blue air, love, and flowers entered with her."[10] There is buoyancy in this description – that of being carried away with love and its

10. From Chagall's *My Life* as seen in Gill Polonsky, *Chagall* (London: Phaidon Press Limited, 1998), 5.

ethereal pleasures – that matches the flying horse. Love lifts its "victims" high above the banality of everyday life. Nothing ordinary can touch them or spoil their intimacy.

LOVE'S INSECURITIES

Chagall's image of Song of Songs does not let in any of the unhappiness of the text, the insecurity of love, and its unshared expectations. The desire for intimacy, eloquently expressed in Song of Songs, is difficult to satisfy. The lovers in Song of Songs keep missing each other, and not only physically. They are often emotionally distant from each other, even as they express strong desire. This is most intensely and painfully communicated in the midsection of the book in a well-known description of presence and absence.

> I have come into my garden, my sister, my bride; I have gathered my myrrh with my spice. I have eaten my honeycomb and my honey; I have drunk my wine and my milk. Eat, O friends, and drink; drink your fill, O lovers. I slept but my heart was awake. Listen! My lover is knocking: "Open to me, my sister, my darling, my dove, my flawless one. My head is drenched with dew, my hair with the dampness of the night." I have taken off my robe – must I put it on again? I have washed my feet – must I soil them again? My lover thrust his hand through the latch-opening; my heart began to pound for him. I arose to open for my lover, and my hands dripped with myrrh, my fingers with flowing myrrh, on the handles of the lock. I opened for my lover, but my lover had left; he was gone. My heart sank at his departure. I looked for him but did not find him. I called him but he did not answer. The watchmen found me as they made their rounds in the city. They beat me, they bruised me; they took away my cloak, those watchmen of the walls! O daughters of Jerusalem, I charge you – if you find my lover, what will you tell him? Tell him I am faint with love. (Song. 5:1–8)

This passage is a celebration of the senses. It is full of tastes and smells and sights. It draws us into the garden where we find the lover who has had her aromatic fill of myrrh and spices and eaten her honeycomb with milk and wine. Nothing is better after a meal than a nice rest. She takes one, yet her heart stays awake, and in the blurry state between sleep and wakefulness, she hears a knock. She hesitates. It is her beloved, but she has just changed and prepared for bed. It seems like such a hassle to get up, to soil her feet. By the time she gets to the door, he is gone. And she becomes instantaneously overwhelmed with panic. Now the text

And Jacob Loved Rachel, Abel Pann

accelerates in pace and urgency, as though to compensate for her sluggishness in changing her mood. She rushes out to find him and practically knocks over the watchmen who ensure that no intruders bother the town's occupants. But they have not seen him. She is distraught.

The artist Abel Pann (1883–1963) does not wait until the middle of the book to portray the love tensions of mood and timing. He captures the way that couples can be in and out of each other's lives while still in physical proximity with a pastel depiction of the very second verse of Song of Songs: "Let him kiss me with the kisses of his mouth – for your love is more delightful than wine."[11]

11. Pann left Europe for Israel in 1913. In the 1920s, he created a number of lithographs of the Bible, beginning with the Book of Genesis. He spent decades experimenting with pastels to realistically capture the landscapes in which the Bible was conceived and its characters as they likely lived.

The people in verse 2 surface a grammatical dilemma: "Let *him* kiss *me* with the kisses of his mouth – for *your* love is more delightful than wine." Is the lover speaking to others about her beloved or is she actually speaking to him? This tension plays out in the entire book. The maidens of Jerusalem and the male friends in the book are like a companionship chorus who serve in a listening capacity. They are deluged with descriptions of the beloved and requests to help find and secure him. They help us understand what each wants in the other because the lovers are so besotted they cannot stop speaking praise. The woman here wants to kiss and be kissed in a way that is all-consuming. She tells this to someone and then turns to her beloved and tells him that his kisses are more delightful than wine, a beverage savored slowly for its rich and distinctive flavors. This opening throws us deeply and uncomfortably into the eros of the text. It is not easy to be party to someone else's intimate moments; it creates awkwardness.

Pann mines this outside point of observation. We stumble upon the scene of two lovers, Jacob and Rachel, almost emerging from the leaves of a tree, grasping for a private moment. These verses of love are spun around an autumnal landscape, creating a tightly woven interaction of humans and nature in a leafy surround of fiery hues. The garden imagery in Song of Songs generally reflects internal passion in a mirror of natural beauty from the spring rain to the apple tree, the blossoms to the turtledove. Animals, fruit trees, hillocks, and lilies all serve as symbols of the burgeoning love of a young couple. The simple, stable imagery of nature also serves as a contrast to the complexity of the human love relationship. Here, the artist did not choose the emerging pinks of spring or the wine reds of summer. The love in this painting has not reached that level of maturity, even though the garments of the lovers intertwine as if into one piece of fabric. Pann's passionate reds, yellows, and oranges in the tree and the young lovers' skin tones, clothing, and jewels help weave the visual images into the text. The beloved's hat matches the gold of the vegetation and the muted colors of the couple's clothing blend into the background. Although in the biblical verse the woman cries out for romantic attention, in Pann's picture the woman is frightened by the intensity of the male attention focused on her, and she focuses on us, the onlookers. She looks like she is asking us for help or at least a little distraction. And she is no woman. She is a girl who looks all the younger for her older, more mature partner. Hers is the fear of the unknown.

Here, the embrace is at the center of the composition. The lover's eyes are tightly closed as he kisses his beloved on the cheek with utmost concentration. But his beloved looks out at us and not at him, her arm does not reciprocate his embrace, and her eyes are wide open and a bit fearful. If you look carefully at the shadows the artist creates with his manipulation of light, you catch the subtlest

Song of Songs 1:8, Shraga Weil

space between her hand and his chest. He is grasping her by the elbow, trapping her with his desire. She, on the other hand, is not even touching him. She gives only the illusion of interest. Her mouth is tightly closed. She does not return his affections. Why should she? It is only the first chapter of the book. This romance will bloom only when both share the same feelings at the same time, and that will take many chapters. Authentic love is one where the intensity of feelings is not always mutual all of the time. We are not sure here, in Pann's rendering, if it will ever be mutual.

The almost inseparable connection of man and nature and the paradoxical tension between man and woman is well-captured by the Israeli artist Shraga Weil.[12] Weil illustrated Song of Songs with black and white drawings. His *Song of Songs* was published by the Worker's Book Guild of HaShomer HaTzair, a socialist Zionist movement started in Europe that was often anti-religious in orientation. Yet Weil believed that biblical texts were still foundational as the literature of the Jewish people and worthy of his artistic attention. His depictions capture the erotic tensions present in many love relationships. On the verse, "If you know not, O you fairest among women, go your way forth by the footsteps of

_____

12. Shraga Weil was born in 1918. He studied art in Prague with a focus on graphics and spent World War II as a prisoner. He moved to Israel – to a kibbutz – in 1947, right before the founding of the State, and stayed there until his death in 2009.

the flock and feed your kid beside the shepherd's tents" (Song. 1:8), Weil shows a man and woman separated by a flock of sheep. The curves of the human figures match those of the sheep and those of the small grove of trees in the background of the composition. If one closes one's eyes slightly, the woman appears to be yet another tree in the scene, the man another sheep.

The images of man, plant, and animal meld into a harmonious picture of nature. Yet, unlike the casually dispersed placement of sheep – also divided into two distinct groups – the woman and man are set at quite a distance from each other. They are on two separate corners of the page. Unlike the sheep who seem absorbed in grazing and are ignoring each other, the man and woman appear posed and deliberate, very much aware of the presence and the distance of the other. The woman's legs are tensed, her left elbow is boldly swung back in a stance that calls out for attention. The man lies outstretched on the ground adopting a carelessly relaxed position, but his amorous anticipation is not easily disguised. A fiery sun seems to touch the ground, sending its burning rays in all directions. Footprints or markings lead from the woman to the oddly placed sun. The heat and light connect the two. Weil has subtly depicted both the harmony and the tension of man and woman in the garden. Man and nature are drawn in swift, simple, and symmetrical blocks placed almost randomly on the page. But man and woman with their parallel jutting elbows and large, rounded thighs are tensed and ready for the unpredictable games of love.

The Jewish artists of the twentieth century who appear in this study – Marc Chagall, Abel Pann, and Shraga Weil – were themselves not observant Jews, but they returned to sacred texts to capture what they felt were the works of Jewish literature that had shaped a people and a culture. The emotions communicated by all three on canvas tell us that love is both delightful and wretched. This duality of emotion in Song of Songs is symbolized in the animal most frequently referred to in the text, the gazelle, and in its mating behavior. The first mention of the gazelle occurs in the second chapter:

> I adjure you, O maidens of Jerusalem, by gazelles or by hinds of the field: do not wake or rouse love until it please. Hark! My beloved! There he comes, leaping over mountains, bounding over hills. My beloved is like a gazelle or like a young stag. There he stands behind our wall, gazing through the window, peering over the lattice. (Song. 2:7–9)

Some confusion has been created in these verses, signifying hesitation in this love scene. The maidens, likened to gazelles, are adjured to be patient with love; it will come in due time and cannot be forced. Yet the next image is of a bounding gazelle, anxious for his beloved, willing and able to scale any obstruction. This is followed immediately by reluctance on the part of the same animal, who stops leaping and stands at a distance, separated by a wall. This strange behavior reappears at the very end of the book when we close Song of Songs: "O you who linger in the garden, a lover is listening; let me hear your voice. Hurry, my beloved, swift as a gazelle or a young stag, to the hills of spices" (Song. 8:14). The gazelles desire to be together, but even at the book's very last verse they are still separated. Love is a powerful magnet, but it has not totally worked its magic yet.

With this last verse we are left with the question of whether there was a happy ending, whether the relationship of the lovers was ever consummated. If the lover is truly lingering in the garden and close enough to listen to the goings-on of his beloved, there would be no need to call out for swiftness or for a far-off destination. Our text has ended, and we are still unsure of the romantic outcome.

In his book *Song of Songs: Nature, Epic and Allegory*, Rabbi Yehuda Feliks, who was a professor of biblical and talmudic botany, writes that the seasons that are described vividly in the text correspond to the behavior of gazelles, who do not mate during any particular season but pursue each other throughout the year. Once they mate, however, they do so for life.

> At first, the sexes are reciprocally indifferent and avoid each other (a period of estrangement), but, when the mating season comes around, the hart [the male gazelle] woos the hinds by alternately chasing and fleeing from them. This maneuver is rehearsed by the hinds. Each then goes in search of the selected mate and eventually they couple.[13]

Feliks continues to describe the gazelle pattern of search and chase that is so well-depicted in Song of Songs. There is temptation, flirtation, and expectation but the *realization* of love only happens when both the hart and the hind express mutual desire. Feliks concludes from this choice of species that the book is trying to convey that a true and natural love never runs smoothly. "Nay, at no time is it free of anguish and struggle, of search and disappearance, and only in the end is 'the love that pleaseth thee' to be found."[14]

---

13. Yehuda Feliks, *Song of Songs: Nature Epic and Allegory* (Jerusalem: Israel Society for Biblical Research, 1983), 12.
14. Ibid. 16.

This theme of closeness and distance, intimacy and rejection, and the smooth, but shaggy, surface of love is the theme song of Song of Songs. As a religious metaphor, it encompasses both the faltering and the ecstatic moments of spiritual connection between man and God. Although the young hart and hind ultimately find the right season and the right apple tree and move their love from the garden to the fragrant hill of spices, there will be many emotional undulations. The garden wall will be too high to clamber, the door will be locked, the lover will be late or lost, the maidens will be jealous, or the passion not yet fully mutual. Chagall's couple transports us to heaven on earth, the arcadia of love. Weil and Pann ground us in reality. The garden's vegetation intertwines with the humans in it, but the natural imagery is uncomplicated, showing off all the complexity of human love. Love, like spirituality, is about joy coupled with struggle, fascination and hesitation, rejection and union.

SONG OF SONGS AND PASSOVER

That love is a game of advancement and regression ties into Passover in a powerful way and helps us understand why this book of Scripture precedes our Torah reading on the Shabbat of Passover every year. The Exodus story is, on one level, a national romance. An enslaved people find a protector and love in a God who redeems them from their misery and creates the conditions for redemption in a new covenantal love together. So far, our Exodus is like the Chagall painting. We levitate above our surroundings, carried by God's affection and an outstretched arm far above the skylines of Egypt to our freedom. In the clasp of eagle's wings, as Exodus 19 describes God's redemption of us, we fly like Chagall's couple above the world, embraced by a loving God. Mired in the dishwater and the unhappiness of slave life, we saw only drudgery until God lifted us above the anguish and carried us to higher ground: to Sinai, to the Tabernacle, to a homeland. We languish in the image of Chagall's couple, who leave all behind, who have forgotten their everyday concerns and who sigh as only lovers can.

But love is never linear. Reading Exodus 1–15, we find the back and forth movement of those afraid to risk all for freedom. Trust in God and Moses buds and then quickly collapses under the weight of Pharaoh's command to intensify the workload. Even after the people muster the courage to offer the Paschal lamb and rush out of Goshen under Moses' lead, they find their faith once again toppled by Pharaoh's quick pursuit of them into the wilderness. The romance is littered with obstacles. Song of Songs is read on Passover to illustrate the non-linear path to a relationship of love and meaning. We read a text that describes an uncertain romance, in Oscar Wilde's language. Love is a risk, one that many refuse to take, because though it can be wonderful, the feeling of lack of control can be deeply frightening. Love is immersive, preoccupying, and bewildering. Not everyone desires that leap into the unknown, the Chagall flight of transcendence, as it were, that lifts two people high above their world, all their responsibilities dissipating into each other's eyes.

We have all refused love or been rejected. We have all feared the unknown and the risks. When we sit at the Seder table, it becomes our national anniversary dinner, when we celebrate how we finally overcame our ancient fears and hesitations and fell in love with God. On this night, we recline on the floor and tell the story of how we met. We drink wine and feel the sweet buzz of hopefulness. We sing. We talk. We look around the room and see all the people who were brought to life and brought together by our romance, just as we might at an anniversary dinner with family. We eat the *ḥaroset*, often thought of as the cement that glued the bricks of slavery together. Perhaps in light of our romantic understanding of Passover, we might look at it instead as the paste of love, the aphrodisiac of freedom. All of the ingredients of *ḥaroset* are found in Song of Songs.[15] One smell or taste and we know that this food should not be associated with hard work and drudgery only, but with sensual pleasure. The apples, wine, dates, nuts, and spices come together to arouse the scent of love and redemption.

Rabbi Elazar ben Moses Azkiri, a sixteenth-century scholar and mystic, relied heavily upon imagery from Song of Songs – which is read every Friday night by some – in his poem *"Yedid Nefesh."* This composition is also sung by many congregations to welcome Shabbat and help us step out of the week into our abiding romance with our Creator:

> Beloved of the soul, compassionate Father,
> Draw Your servant to Your will.
> Then Your servant will hurry like a hart to bow before Your majesty.
> To him Your friendship will be sweeter than the dripping of the honeycomb and all taste.
> Majestic, beautiful, radiance of the universe
> *My soul is sick for Your love.*
> Please, God, heal her now by showing her the pleasantness of Your radiance.
> Then she will be strengthened and healed and eternal gladness will be hers.

---

15. See *Tosafot* Pesaḥim 116a. I am grateful to my friend Rabbi Aryeh Ben David for pointing this out and helping me see the Seder itself in an entirely different light.

The poetry in *Yedid Nefesh* encapsulates the central themes of Song of Songs and helps us understand that redemption relies on love to do its hardest work. Not only the mystics spoke of this love. Maimonides, the medieval legalist and philosopher, questions how we are to love God at all:

> How is one to love God appropriately such that one loves God with a great and impassioned love, such that one's very soul is tied up in that love of God, such that one is constantly preoccupied, as if one was actually suffering lovesickness, as if his mind were not free of this love, just as if he were in love with a woman and thinks of her constantly, when he sits down and when he gets up, when he eats and drinks? Even more than this should be the love of God. (*Mishneh Torah*, Laws of Repentance 10:3)

Maimonides wrote this in the last chapter of his Laws of Repentance in trying to create a framework for what a relationship with God looks like in its ideal state. Unlike the focus on sin in his earlier chapters, Maimonides wants us to understand what we are returning to when we return in an act of penitence. We are returning to a state of love: an obsessive, preoccupying mindset of lovesickness. When we are in that state, we take all kinds of risks to secure and preserve it. We are willing to leave a place of familiarity on eagle's wings. We are willing to endure lapses of feeling to return to the ecstatic emotion of true intimacy. Redemption happens with trust, with submission to a higher calling, with a love-struck commitment to a cause and a relationship.

LIFE HOMEWORK

- If we think of Passover as the wedding anniversary between God and the Jewish people, how can you use this holiday to rekindle or to strengthen the romance in your own relationship with God?
- Do something small, unexpected, and unusually loving for a partner, friend, or someone in your family this Passover. A little unconditional love goes a long way.
- Like the gazelles of Song of Songs, you may feel loving and open when your life partner is moody and temperamental. What can you do this Passover to align your moods with greater synchronicity?

Day Six

Officially You may refuse. I know. I'm
approaching You in English this once.
But, please, be kind,

be attentive to the heart.
Even if it's pointless,
tasteless. Please accept an offering
from me this time.

I'm pleading with You,
please understand,
don't be offended,

even if
when I approach
I seem to You
to cross myself.

"Approaching You in English," Admiel Kosman
(Translated by Lisa Katz)

Day Six

Slave Wealth

I'd like to live as a poor man with lots of money.
Pablo Picasso

The Golden Haggada – written and illuminated in Northern Spain in the early fourteenth century – is one of the few medieval manuscripts to depict the verse, "And they [the Israelites] despoiled the Egyptians" (Ex. 12:36). In this small portrait of a morally troubling scene, four Israelite slaves prepare to leave Egypt.[1] The one on the furthermost left carries a chest on his back, but at such an odd angle it seems like it may slip at any moment. His eyes look toward the future. The other three face the opposite direction. They are busy lifting gold chalices – similar to those used in medieval churches – out of what looks like a cupboard but is strangely the second story of an Egyptian home. The picture is not drawn to scale, and emphasis is placed on the dominant themes in the biblical narrative. Overly long arms reach for the gold. The chalices are about two-thirds the size of the humans, perhaps representing how significant this bounty was for these slaves and also foreshadowing the gold they would need in the wilderness to build their own portable sanctuary for worship, the *Mishkan*. Their size may also represent the large and looming temptation to ravage the wealth of those who "owned" them for so long.

---

1. Folio 3r, d, #65a as seen in Bezalel Narkiss, *The Golden Haggada* (London: The British Library, 1997), 45.

The Golden Haggadah

Each of the four men wears a different colored tunic – navy, orange, red, and light blue – which look resplendent against the gold background. Two have beards while two are clean-shaven. We know that they are slaves because their tunics are simple, their feet unshod. One already has a goblet in hand and observes as the other two slaves reach for the remaining goblets at the same time. These are slaves who work in haste, who understand that as quickly as a moment presents itself, it will close in on itself. They must take advantage. There are no Egyptians handing the slaves the goods in gratitude. The slaves are helping themselves to what they may have regarded as recompense for so many centuries of unpaid labor coupled with excessive abuse. But there is no glee on their faces, no sense of relief. Their lips look pursed and understandably anxious. And when we read today the verses that speak of despoiling the Egyptians, we often feel the same complex mixture of justice muddled with discomfort. Why not leave this place of peril clean, untouched by any moral detritus, free of any guilt or impropriety?

The Golden Haggada answers this question in an unusual way. This rich document is among the treasures of the British Library's collection of Hebrew manuscripts. It illustrates many of the historic episodes shared in the Haggada that form the core of the "*Maggid*" section. In the passage that begins, "Blessed is the One who has kept His promise to Israel," the Genesis covenant to Abraham is mentioned to suggest that God kept His promises to our patriarch: "Know that your descendants will be strangers in a land not their own, and they will be enslaved and oppressed for four hundred years; but know that I shall judge the nation that enslaves them, and then they will leave with great wealth" (Gen. 15:13–14). It can take a long time to fulfill a promise, but be assured, the Haggada reminds us, God will keep covenantal promises. Our slave picture then, depicts not a heist but the consummation of an oath to make one person into a nation of faith, with all of the spiritual and material grounding required. At the time this covenant was made, Abraham was still trying to have one child so that he could begin nation-building with an heir. It is hard to know what comfort he would have found in the knowledge that centuries after his death, his people would be numerous but also enslaved and oppressed. Leaving with great wealth would hardly be compensation for centuries of anguish. Knowledge of the Jewish future would not, in his case, offer any opportunity to shape that future differently. God had set the wheels in motion; Abraham was merely informed of a distant path, hardly imaginable. And yet for a man of faith who would be told on multiple occasions that his people would become as numerous as grains of sand and stars in the sky, deepening the description of that future may have inspired Abraham to overcome the fertility problem immediately ahead of him in favor of a long-term future yet unseen.

At the same time, the accumulation of wealth was not insignificant in the Abraham narrative and may parallel, on an individual level, the activities of nation-building on a large scale. Abraham amassed cattle and land and was given generous gifts by Pharaoh – "sheep, oxen, donkeys, male and female slaves, mules and camels" (Gen. 12:16). A few verses later we are told that, "Abram was very rich in cattle, silver, and gold" (Gen. 13:2). Later, Avimelekh gave Abraham additional gifts (Gen. 20:14–16), and Abraham paid Ephron a princely sum for a burial place for Sarah (Gen. 23:15–16). Without financial security, it is hard to build a people so that they can survive and flourish. Making covenants and winning wars bulked up personal coffers that could then be used to enable the building of national infrastructures.

Rashi adds a postscript for closure to the early prediction to Abraham. The text emphasizes the notion of "*rekhush gadol*" – great wealth – to stress the positive. Not only will the promise of affliction be fulfilled but God will also make good on the commitment to bring a blessed and abundant redemption. The Talmud ironically relays God's fear of the patriarchs who will hold Him responsible for promises made once upon a time that must come to fruition. It is not only the negative aspects of prophecy that come true; positive affirmations must also be actualized for God and the Israelites to partner in an enduring relationship of covenantal trust (Berakhot 9a).

THE BIBLE SPEAKS

With this larger biblical context set, we turn to Exodus and Deuteronomy to understand, both in their legal and narrative portions and through their subtle differences, what was involved in despoiling the Egyptians:

> **Exodus 3:21–22:** And I will give this people favor in the sight of Egypt. And it shall come to pass that when you go, you shall not go empty, but every woman shall ask of her neighbor and of her that sojourns in her house, jewels of silver and jewels of gold and garments, and you shall put them on your sons and on your daughters and you shall despoil Egypt.

> **Exodus 11:2–3:** Speak now in the ears of the people and let every man ask of his neighbor and every woman of her neighbor, jewels of silver and jewels of gold. And the Lord gave the people favor in the sight of Egypt; moreover, the man Moses was very great in the land of Egypt, in the sight of Pharaoh's servants and in the sight of the people.

> **Exodus 12:35–36:** And the Children of Israel did according to the word of Moses. And they asked of Egypt jewels of silver and jewels of gold and garments. And the Lord gave the people favor in the sight of Egypt so that they gave them such things as they required. And they despoiled Egypt.

God's demand ignores the logistic and ethical dilemmas the reader immediately senses. Simply ask the Egyptians and they will give you silver and gold, dresses and ornaments. There is no sense that the idea of this exchange will be rejected or problematic in the eyes of the Egyptians; a "self-conscious" Israelite reflection of how this will look does not feature in any Exodus narrative. But it does appear elsewhere. In the Book of Joshua, the Jews are told that they should refrain from pillaging towns and taking their loot. Simeon and Levi are chastised by their father Jacob for pillaging the town of Shekhem. Jacob's words are resounding and unambiguous in their rebuke: "You have brought trouble on me to make me odious to the inhabitants of the land...and I being few in number, they shall gather together and slay me, and I shall be destroyed, I and my house" (Gen. 34:30). Both Jacob's sense of right and wrong and his awareness of his family's small size make him cautious about his reputation in the eyes of others. Jacob's sons get the last word in the chapter, trumping Jacob's concern for his status and reputation with the vulnerability of their sister. But Jacob's words echo through our narratives in Exodus: "You have brought trouble on me to make me odious to the inhabitants of the land." Leaving Egypt was a drawn-out process of fits and starts. The Israelites would perhaps have been wise to leave without this additional burden and delay. Go forth and take nothing. Just go.

A VIEW FROM THE COMMENTATORS

The complicated medley of interpretations around these biblical verses displays a level of discomfort or a need to defend on the part of classical exegetes. Abraham ibn Ezra compounds our dilemma in his comments on Exodus 3:21 by questioning why the Egyptians would have had to pacify the Israelites and why silver, gold, and clothing would have been adequate recompense for so many years of slavery. It was not enough. Many of the exegetical difficulties revolve around the Hebrew word "*she'ela*," which loosely means "to borrow." The sixteenth-century Italian exegete, Rabbi Ovadiah Seforno, translates the word in exactly this way. Originally, the Israelites borrowed Egyptian wealth to facilitate their exit and would have returned it. When Pharaoh pursued the Jews in Exodus 14, a veritable war broke out, vitiating the need to return the spoils; peaceable leave-taking was replaced by the conditions of war. Other commentators moved away from the complex notion of appropriations. The Rashbam, Rabbi Samuel ben Meir, understood the Israelite request for material goods as a "complete and unambiguous gift," ignoring the usual denotation of the word, which is "to ask," a suggestion that all that needs to be done is to ask Egyptian neighbors for their wealth and they will happily and willingly offer it, as Rashi observes, simply to get the Israelites and their God out of Egypt.

Differences in the language of these three verses from Exodus leave us wondering who is doing the asking. In our first verse, the women were commanded to ask their Egyptian hosts. Later, in 12:35, both men and women were to ask for jewels and garments. Abraham ibn Ezra claims that it is the way of women to ask for such items from neighbors, perhaps reflecting a custom in his own day in Spain. As to the moral conundrum presented in this transaction, Ibn Ezra is not troubled: "And this is not problematic since it is all His." If all riches belong to God in an ultimate sense, then God can determine who gets what and when and how. God, with Robin Hood-like prowess and judgment, redistributed wealth to fit in with a new social order.

In addition to the switch from women to men and women, Moses was singled out as one such man who himself should specifically ask for wealth: "And the Lord gave the people favor in the sight of Egypt; moreover, the man Moses was very great in the land of Egypt, in the sight of Pharaoh's servants and in the sight of the people." In this collective gathering, it is odd that Moses stood out, himself never a slave and not in need of personal recompense for years of unpaid labor. And yet perhaps there is a subtle message being offered in the text about how the confidence that people have in their leader may be influenced by external behaviors, namely how the leader embraces the trappings of success. Wealth was to help Moses look like a leader. Wealth was to help the Israelites look like a nation.

The French commentator *Hizkuni*, Rabbi Hezekiah ben Manoah, explores many of the mysteries of the verses themselves. On Exodus 11:2, he points out the unusual use of the word *"re'ehu,"* friend, a term of endearment not previously used to describe the relations between Israelites and their Egyptian masters. After each plague and the incremental empowerment of the slaves, Egyptians became increasingly friendly with the Israelites and the normal socio-economic boundaries that divided the two populations became blurred. With this lessening of differences, the Israelites were in a better position to help relieve Egyptians of their personal items. The modern Bible scholar, Robert Alter, confirms *Hizkuni's* reading by suggesting an understanding of why women were specifically at the center of these requests: "…women constitute the porous boundary between adjacent ethnic communities: Borrowers of the proverbial cup of sugar, sharers of gossip and women's lore."[2]

---

2. Alter, 324.

The Israelites also had property in Egypt. We know from the Joseph story that when his family relocated from Canaan, the Jews were given the best of Egypt's land in Goshen. They would be leaving property and much chattel behind. Taking Egyptian objects was effectively a self-driven exchange or barter system. It was not a matter of self-determined wages but an upfront transaction to level the financial playing field, reparations taken ahead of time, if you will. The Egyptians would benefit from all that their slaves left behind. The least they could do was balance out the resources with a monetary exchange that would not even cover the Israelite loss.

Seforno joins *Ḥizkuni* in an additional sentiment. Despoiling the Egyptians was not a form of payment; it was a provocative act to foment tensions so that the Egyptians would follow the Israelites to regain their goods. Not unlike God hardening Pharaoh's heart, this reading emphasizes the lack of free will. The Israelites were tasked with being part of the redemptive process, each in his or her respective home of oppression. Resentment would build toward this lowly slave force who not only were leaving, but were also taking the Egyptians' personal items and assets, to the point where the Egyptians would pursue them unto their own deaths.

Rabbi Samson Raphael Hirsch offers an interesting twist. During the three days of predicted darkness of the ninth plague, the Israelites could have taken anything they wanted from the Egyptians with good cover. They refrained. This raised their esteem in the eyes of the Egyptians. This did not, however, mean that they were to leave in abject poverty. By asking their Egyptian masters and neighbors for material support, they were acting with transparency about their forthcoming exit and their long-unaddressed needs.

If this is the case, how are we to understand the repeated mention of this demand? If God predicted it early in Genesis and then made it clear in Exodus, there would be little need to reaffirm the charge three times. This may reflect hesitation on the Israelites' part. Moses had to convince them to take what they deserved and was rightly theirs. The late medieval Spanish exegete and statesman, Don Joseph Abrabanel, thinks that the Israelites did not want to augment Egyptian hatred. By acting forthrightly and with a high hand, they found favor in the eyes of the Egyptians, a notion that is emphasized in multiple verses. The Egyptians respected brute force and power. As the Israelites asserted their power and their new sense of authority, they heightened the respect given to them by the Egyptians and also intensified the respect accorded to Moses. Self-respect translated into respect for others, an acute issue for a humiliated slave population.

MODERN SENSIBILITIES

Many of us read these verses and the accompanying commentary with an understandable lack of ease. While ancient slaves unquestionably deserved compensation for their efforts, the notion that we despoiled the Egyptians at God's command does not sit easy with our general attitude about entitlement or theft. In fact, Nahmanides (Ketubot 19a) mentions a view that one must give up one's life rather than commit the sin of stealing, although this view was never accepted. Stealing is clearly an intolerable transgressive behavior. In the motherly logic of "two wrongs don't make a right," we are not sure what to make of this permission to loot freely from the Egyptians. In Alter's words: "Some readers have felt discomfort at the act of exploitation recorded here. The most common line of defense is that this is restitution for the unpaid labor extracted from the Hebrew slaves."[3]

We can wrap our arms around the notion of fair recompense. We understand cognitively that nation-building requires capital. Without wealth, even the most moral of nations will not be able to create or sustain a homeland. The costly materials involved in the construction of the Tabernacle and then later in the creation of a golden calf suggest that this wealth was put to use. How else can we explain the appearance of so much gold and other luxury items in the arid wilderness?

That is why the text goes out of its way to emphasize that this was not taking without license but asking outright, one person to his neighbor. The verb used in all three instances is from the root of "lish'ol," which means "to ask." There was no thievery but a mass campaign to assist the Israelites in shaping their independence from people who recognized that it was their time to leave. The very presence of the Israelites became punishing and intolerable to the Egyptians. "Borrowing" is not an accurate or nuanced enough translation of the verb. The Israelites were not stealing; they were demanding. They did so on a person-to-person basis. Their demand was not about filling up a national coffer but about a prevalent obligation to an individual in the ancient Near Eastern world that devolved upon the master to take care of the slave at the time of his or her departure. Nations have often convinced themselves and justified the practice of slavery. It is much harder to do that in personal relationships when exploitation reigns and can be pointed to with lashes on the skin or stories of abuse. The act of asking that fell upon each individual was a form of assertiveness training, a lesson in asking for one's due. Even if it did not result in any monetary gain, making demands for

---

3. Ibid.

restitution and support had the secondary effect of empowering each person to attend to his or her freedom. With each rejection came a fiercer version of an Israelite, someone more resentful of injustice, more prepared to leave, and more prepared to fight. While so many exegetes concentrated on the outcome – the loot and the permissibility of it all – the verbs beg us to think of the act of asking as ultimately more important than the result of taking.

REFLECTIONS ON LEAVE-TAKING

Our financed exodus is also referenced much later in Psalms as a foundational rather than accidental part of the divine strategy for the Israelites, but this time without mentioning the source of the money. It is a lyrical way to reflect on our last moments of slavery:

> And He smote every firstborn in their land, the beginning of all their strength. And He brought them out with silver and gold, and there were none who faltered among His tribes. Egypt rejoiced at their departure, for their fear had fallen upon them. (Ps. 105:36–38)

Egypt's emotional decimation is followed by Israel's triumph. Egypt's relief at getting rid of the threat in their midst is also punctuated with this small, hardly noteworthy fact: "He brought them out with silver and gold." Instead of feeling angry and indignant, the Egyptians were jubilant to pay this price to remove the scourge that had become so punitive for them. The triumph of the Israelites also translated into fear of them in another famous biblical narrative, at the end of chapter 8 of the Book of Esther:

> For the Jews it was a time of happiness and joy, gladness and honor. In every province and in every city, wherever the edict of the king went, there was joy and gladness among the Jews, with feasting and celebrating. And many people of other nationalities became Jews *because fear of the Jews had seized them.* (Est. 8:16–17)

If you cannot beat them, join them, goes the saying and the sentiment. Fear of reprisals may have motivated the conversion of some, but others may have witnessed the survival and flourishing of this people under duress and decided to throw their lot in with the Jews, come what may. A passage of Talmud corroborating a midrash mentions that in the Exodus narrative, even Batya, Pharaoh's daughter, converts, which explains her compassion for Moses. The Nile, in this embellishment of the text, is her ritual bath where she emerges and cleanses herself of Egypt's ways and its politics.[4]

Yet in the depiction of the Exodus in Genesis 15 and Psalm 105, we are not told that the Jews acquired wealth specifically from the Egyptians as part of their package of salvation. It could have come as a heavenly gift; manna of a different order. Rabbi Elchanan Samet observes that this feature of the Exodus narrative is not lost on the close reader of the text:

> The fact that it appears in the brief notice transmitted to Abraham hundreds of years before the event, and its inclusion in the description of the psalmist hundreds of years thereafter, indicates its importance…. We have the impression not of a frenzied flight of slaves escaping from their masters, but rather a respectable and just exodus of a nation that is lawfully leaving its slavery behind, while punishment is meted out to the slave-masters. The Exodus of the Children of Israel from Egypt necessitated great wealth, for if one leaves naked and penniless then his freedom is not complete.[5]

The wealth the Israelites were to enjoy was integrally tied into the remission of slaves and directs us to Deuteronomy 15, where Israelites are specifically enjoined to give generous recompense to a slave when he or she achieves freedom: "And when you send him out, do not let him go away empty. You should furnish him liberally with your flock and out of your threshing floor and out of your winepress. Of that which the Lord has blessed you shall you give" (Deut. 15:14–15). This obligation stems directly from our historical experience of servitude in Egypt: "And you should remember that you were a slave in the land of Egypt and the Lord redeemed you; therefore, I command you to do this thing today" (Deut. 15:16). Resonances of the past shape behavior in the present. As former slaves, you must ensure that those who work for you leave with goods from wherever you have benefited from their labor, from your fields to your vats. In every corner of your material life, you must find what you can share with those who worked for you because they must also benefit, in part, from their own labor. From the time of Adam and the curse that "from the sweat of your brow, you shall break bread" (Gen. 3:19), there is a notion that work should yield results, and there is

---

4. See Sota 12b and Exodus Rabba 1:23.
5. Rabbi Elchanan Samet, "The 'Borrowing' of Vessels from the Egyptians," The Israel Koschitzky Virtual Beit Midrash, Yeshivat Har Etzion, Parashat Bo, http://www.vbm-torah.org/parsha.63/15bo.htm.

pride in the causal relationship of effort and product. One of the great emotional challenges of slavery is that the slave can never lay claim to the fruit of his or her labor. He does not own the time; he does not own the result.

That this law was a profound expression of compassion and concern is intimated in a text that highlights the opposite. When Hagar, Sarah's slave in Genesis 16, was finally banished in Genesis 21, Abraham sent her and Ishmael out with scant offerings: "And Abraham rose up early in the morning and took bread and a bottle of water and gave it to Hagar, putting it on her shoulder and the child and sent her away." As the two got lost in the desert, the water ran out. Abraham had only given her enough to fit on her shoulder.

Hagar was given to Abraham as a second wife by his own wife. Had she not been adequately equipped for the journey ahead by virtue of being married to Abraham and mother of his first son, she surely should have been entitled to better remuneration as a slave. Two Hebrew terms of servitude are used to describe her: *ama* and *shifha*, the first indicating a higher status.[6] Over time – as Isaac grew older and through Sarah's harsh treatment – Hagar became more and more demeaned. Arguably, the laws to provide materially for the slave upon his or her departure are offered several books later and did not inform Abraham's behavior. And yet, we can sense from the angst of several commentators, mostly medieval, that Abraham's treatment of Hagar was deemed frugal and unkind, particularly in relation to his generosity to strangers in Genesis 18. One exegete mentions that the water and bread are only *some* of the provisions actually given; the text had no need to go into greater detail. Implicit in such explanations is the shame we experience upon reading that Abraham would treat the woman who carried his firstborn son this way. Hagar and Ishmael left their home bundled with hardly more than resentment to carry into an uncertain future. The compensation that was her due was not forthcoming.

This story also reminds us of yet another reason that a master must be generous with a slave who leaves. The transition from slavery to freedom is a rough emotional climb. Freedom can be as terrifying as it can be thrilling. To go from not determining the way that any of your time is spent to determining how all of it is spent can create paralysis. Add to that the financial stresses of freedom, and the slave may have every inclination to fight for his own oppression back. In the Bible, an indentured Hebrew slave who wants to stay with his master has his ear pierced with an awl at a doorpost, leaving a permanent mark of shame upon him

---

6. See Genesis 16:1 versus Genesis 21:10 to see the change of status through this identification that turns into disdain.

because he reneged on his freedom.[7] The ancient slave owner had to ease the slave into a place where freedom was not a daunting proposition and often push the slave out of slavery when he became too attached.

Michael Walzer in *Exodus and Revolution* affirms this need, tying it into the Exodus narratives: "It was also part of the oppressiveness of Egyptian slavery that the Israelites were not, in their own view, legitimately slaves at all. They had not been captured in any way, and they had never sold themselves into bondage."[8] The Egyptians never officially regarded them as slaves, which would have para-doxically entitled them to certain benefits of slavery. Nevertheless, the Israelites adapted themselves to harsher and harsher conditions. They needed an incentive to leave that they could understand and appreciate. Money was that motivation and inducement for the Jews to leave Egypt, unlike the promises of freedom – the higher expectations – in whose achievement Moses and Aaron invested their very lives. Walzer describes the promise of leaving Egypt as double-sided. It was one of both spiritual and financial proportions: "The people, dreaming of milk and honey, are materialists; Moses and the Levites, dreaming of holiness, are idealists."[9] Later, Walzer argues that in the history of popular struggles, these two goals are often conflated and interwoven: "The carnal and the spiritual are not so easily separated."[10] If the material aspects of the promise to the Israelites were diminished, the result would have been disappointment:

> The door of hope opens on a larger vision, not simply of more and more of whatever good things are available but enough for everyone. Then every-one will be secure in his possessions, and there won't be any tyrants in the land. "They shall sit every man under his vine and under his fig tree; and none shall make them afraid" (Mic. 4:4).[11]

PROTECTION FOR THE JOURNEY

What else did the Israelites take with them when they left Egypt, in addition to this unexpected abundance of Egyptian goods? In Exodus 13:18, we learn that they left "*ḥamushim*," indicating that they left Egypt with something beyond the spoils they asked of their neighbors. The question is what. Technically, the term

---

7. See Exodus 21:5–6 and Deuteronomy 15:16–17.
8. Michael Walzer, *Exodus and Revolution* (New York: Basic Books, 1995), 29.
9. Ibid. 103.
10. Ibid. 105.
11. Ibid. 107.

generally refers to arms, and it makes sense that they left well-protected because of the anxiety they experienced at Pharaoh's change of heart and the anticipated antipathy of their Egyptian neighbors. Rashi supports this view, understanding that the Israelites would also fear the potential enemies they would encounter along the way and in their conquest of an already occupied land. It is best to leave prepared for all possible situations. In a different spirit, the *Kli Yakar,* a sixteenth-century Polish commentator, believes that they took the ark with them; physical protection without spiritual reinforcement would have implied an empty freedom.[12]

One commentary believes that leaving *"hamushim"* implies that they took food rations along the way. No trip is complete without appropriate provisions for the trek, and these fledgling Israelites had no idea that manna was on its way. They knew they were heading into a land without adequate water and that hunting enough food to feed a nation of their size would be near impossible, so they took appropriate rations.

Rabbi Larry Hoffman offers a different understanding of this term that comes from a subtle translation of the word as "laden down." In addition to whatever they took with them of a material nature, they were laden down with the weight of their anxieties about freedom. It is best to travel light because even a pack of medium weight can become heavy and cumbersome over time. We often take more than we need because we anticipate every possible situation where we might possibly need something. In Hoffman's words:

> Laden can easily become laden down. We take what we take, after all, because we believe it will be useful. It is only one short step to the faulty conclusion that if we do not use it completely, we have failed our responsibility…. We do not need all the weapons of war in the world, or even food for the entire trip. We need only bring what we can, do what is reasonable, and trust God to keep us going the rest of the way.[13]

When we travel, we all take things with us that we will not use. We take them because we are unsure of the weather or the conditions. We are not sure of what we will be doing in terms of activities, or we fear enemies. It is not a failure, Hoffman suggests, if we do not use all of our travel resources, since many are

---

12. See Rabbi Ephraim Lunshits, the *Kli Yakar,* on Exodus 13:18.
13. Lawrence Hoffman, "Don't Leave Egypt Without It," *The New York Jewish Week,* January 1, 2011, http://www.thejewishweek.com/editorial-opinion/sabbath-week/dont-leave-egypt-without-it.

brought on thin hypothetical assumptions that may not bear up. A trek of the enormity the Israelites undertook could only stimulate additional worries that may be addressed through the bringing of something else. What was really necessary, however, was not any "thing" at all. Things can be easy substitutes for inner resources and resilience while not actually providing the security they promise us mentally when we pack them. Even the notion of a security blanket is strange. No piece of cloth, no matter the emotional attachments woven into its fibers, can offer true protection other than mental solace.

This idea of holding onto a piece of the past as we walk into a dubious future may also explain the commandment to the Israelites to take something of Egyptian value along with them. Perhaps they needed to believe that they had not cut themselves off totally. Maybe Egyptian gold and silver and clothing – which would hardly be necessary in a desert where water is valued and little else matters – were taken not merely to strip the Egyptians, but also to provide the Israelites with physical reminders of their past, of the wealth that they enhanced without enjoying, of the slavish submission they nursed for centuries, of the imbalance of power in the master/servant relationship. As they matured into a nation, it would be easy enough to forget where they came from. It would be much harder to forget when a little Egyptian trinket took up space in their packets or clinked with their own coins in a pocket.

We find that later, midpoint in the Book of Numbers, the Israelites suffer amnesia precisely regarding this problem. Strangely, they remember an Egypt where food was plentiful and easy to obtain. They remember the fleshpots – some mysterious, seductive, and sexual approach or attitude of the Egyptians in contrast to their chaste, monotonous existence.[14] The odd collection of various pungent foods – the leeks, onions, garlic, melons, and cucumbers – they remember eating freely in Numbers 11 are yet another reminder of an Egypt they desire. But only the trinkets really communicated the truth. They were a talisman of a tortured past. They did not allow the Israelites the comfort of denying or reshaping their suffering because Egyptian wealth was made largely on their backs.

When you hold an object that tells someone else's story woven into your own, you hold the key not only to your past but to theirs as well. It is not something you can segment and easily dismiss. This payment for past labors became a down payment on their future – their homeland and a Temple to adorn it – redeeming the work and its ultimate ownership.

---

14. See Numbers 11.

THE RESTITUTION BACKLASH

Thousands of years later, a group of Egyptians keen to revise the moral problems of ancient history wanted to sue "all worldwide Jews" for the money they took when they left Egypt during the Exodus. In a special dispatch translated from the Arabic, the world learned that Egyptian jurists sought compensation for "trillions of tons of gold" allegedly stolen by Hebrew slaves on their way out of the country in ancient biblical days. The lawsuit was led by Dr. Nabil Hilmi, dean of the faculty of law at the University of Al-Zaqaziq:

> The Egyptian Pharaoh was surprised one day to discover thousands of Egyptian women crying under the palace balcony, asking for help and complaining that the Jews stole their clothing and jewels, in the greatest collective fraud history has ever known. The theft was not limited to gold alone. The thieves stole everything imaginable. They emptied the Egyptian homes of cooking utensils.[15]

In a gross revision of history, Hilmi claimed that this alleged theft was indefensible given the fair and welcoming treatment the ancient Hebrews received at the hands of the Egyptians:

> A police investigation revealed that Moses and Aaron, peace be upon them, understood that it was impossible to live in Egypt, despite its pleasures and even though the Egyptians included them in every activity, due to the Jews' perverse nature, to which the Egyptians had reconciled themselves, though with obvious unwillingness. Therefore, an order was issued by the Jewish rabbis to flee the country, and that the exodus should be secret and under cover of darkness and with the largest possible amount of loot. The code word was "At midnight."

When asked for evidence from the Bible to support this, Hilmi directed his audience to verses from Exodus to substantiate the claim. Wondering if the prosecution could reach a compromise, Hilmi proposed rescheduling the debt payment for a period of one thousand years, including cumulative interest.

Hilmi's classic anti-Semitic statements were right about one thing. As we've seen, there are several biblical references to taking Egyptian wealth. It is

---

15. See the following post for referencing the debate: http://www.freerepublic.com/focus/news/968584/posts.

unclear how much it amounted to, if it was given willingly, and if there was ever any documentation to substantiate the Egyptian claim. With global talk about compensation for war crimes, stolen museum objects, and art works plundered by Nazi hands, it is not surprising that someone would make such a claim. It is difficult to get clarity on what wealth the Jews leaving Egypt had and how it was used.[16] Hilmi, of course, only told one side of the story and ignored the reparations that Jews could claim for centuries of forced and unpaid labor. Class-action suits based on this sacred text can go both ways. Every story holds multiple stories.

This is our story. Our ancient struggle to give the slave what the slave is owed is not a celebration of the institution of slavery but a sad recognition that power over others must be framed by responsibility. In Deuteronomy, we are specifically warned not to mistreat the slave: "You shall not oppress a hired servant who is poor and needy, whether he be from among your brethren or of the stranger in your land…. For you should remember that you were a slave in Egypt" (Deut. 24:14–18). We cannot let go of the memory of injustice – whether it be emotional, spiritual, intellectual, or financial. In Jewish life and law, these memories translate almost immediately into obligations, to respect those who serve us, to treat them with compassion, and when they are ready, to help them achieve independence.

LIFE HOMEWORK

- Think of someone who serves you in some way or works for you. Name one behavior you can commit to undertaking that shows even greater respect for this individual.
- Spend some time thinking of the role that money and autonomy play in your own life and when you have experienced the freedom that comes with paying your own way.
- Consider a personal moment of exploitation and name it. Use three adjectives to describe your feelings. What will you do this Passover to prevent others from being or feeling exploited?

---

16. Ibid.

Day Seven

... And the land will grow still
Crimson skies dimming, misting
Slowly paling again
Over smoking frontiers

As the nation stands up
Torn at heart but existing
To receive its first wonder
In two thousand years

As the moment draws near
It will rise, darkness facing
Stand straight in the moonlight
In terror and joy

...When across from it step out
Toward it slowly pacing
In plain sight of all
A young girl and a boy

Dressed in battle gear, dirty
Shoes heavy with grime
On the path they will climb up
While their lips remain sealed

To change garb, to wipe brow
They have not yet found time
Still bone-weary from days
And from nights in the field

Full of endless fatigue
And all drained of emotion
Yet the dew of their youth
Is still seen on their head

Thus like statues they stand
Stiff and still with no motion
And no sign that will show
If they live or are dead

Then a nation in tears
And amazed at this matter
Will ask: who are you?
And the two will then say

With soft voice: We–
Are the silver platter
On which the Jews' state
Was presented today

Then they fall back in darkness
As the dazed nation looks
And the rest can be found
In the history books.

"The Silver Platter," Natan Alterman
(Translated by David P. Stern)

Day Seven

The Paschal Lamb and Impossible Possibilities

Nothing is more imminent than the impossible...
Victor Hugo

In *The American Heritage Haggada,* David Geffen describes the exuberance of the Jewish community in response to the hundredth anniversary of George Washington's presidential inauguration, in April 1889, which coincided with Passover. A special prayer was composed by the chief rabbi of New York, Rabbi Jacob Joseph, to be read in American synagogues, and many synagogue buildings were draped in red, white, and blue bunting. "A month before Passover it was announced in New York that a free picture of George Washington would be given with every ten pounds of matza purchased," writes Geffen."[1] Many homes prominently displayed depictions of George Washington near the front door so that when Elijah arrived, he would be greeted by this great American leader.

This is happy exile – a glimpse into an American Jewish life that sought to integrate two universes of concern into a passionate mosaic of pleasurable and proud commitments. Israel as refuge and homeland was a far-off dream and for some it was only a metaphor, not an actual possibility. This was logical from

---

1. David Geffen, *The American Heritage Haggada* (Jerusalem: Gefen, 1992), xix.

the vantage of a mainstream American Seder in the late nineteenth century. A metaphor is not even a dream to be actualized. It is a symbolic figment of the imagination. But it is only through risks of the imagination and an embrace of the improbable that we as a nation survived.

It is likely that many of the Jews in ancient Egypt were similarly inclined. The primacy and superiority of exile in the mind of many Jews gives meaning to the rabbinic belief that only twenty percent of the Jews in Egypt vacated when they had the opportunity.[2] A full eighty percent, the majority of the slave population, opted to stay in Egypt. This midrashic opinion has deep roots in the traditional Jewish mindset of Exodus. Rashi, basing himself on midrashic readings, twice notes in his commentary on Exodus that there were Jews who did not want to leave Egypt for fear of the unknown. When thick darkness descended on Egypt for three days and no person could see another, Pharaoh called to Moses and told him to leave Egypt and remove the darkness. Rashi comments on verse 22 in Exodus 10 that the darkness concealed not only the Egyptians but also the Israelites who wanted to stay. They were punished with death during these three days so the Egyptians would not see their punishment. Later, on Exodus 13:18, Rashi engages in a play on words found in a midrash on the word "*hamushim*." Rashi comments that the word, alternatively explained as being armed with weapons, may also indicate that only one-fifth of the Jews actually left when they could, referring once again to their punishment during the three-day plague of darkness, "because they were unworthy of being delivered."[3]

If you fail to take risks for future freedoms, there may be severe consequences. No one in the ancient world was doing a statistical analysis and knew for certain how many people stayed in Egypt and how many people left. The sages were simply observing that the majority of people given the opportunity to transform their lives radically will not take it. They will resist with every fiber of their being. They will doubt and linger and then, if and when they have a slight change of heart and explore the possibility, it may be too late. The door may be closed. We turn back to those Jews of the last century who considered leaving Europe when political tides were turning. Others around them saw the red flags of warning and left, while some ignored the signs or denied them. Instead, they looked for affirmations of their worldview, validation for their decision to stay, which they bolstered with defenses and excuses. When those no longer worked and they tried to leave, the doors of immigration violently

---

2. See the *Mekhilta* and Rashi on Exodus 13:18.
3. *Mekhilta* 13:18.

closed before them. Opportunity knocked once and knocked twice but then the door closed. Perhaps to get into this mindset, we have to create a few doors to push open.

In a remarkable rendition of Exodus 12 called "The Origin of the Paschal Lamb," the German artist Julius Schnorr von Carolsfeld captures the tensions of possibility in his depiction of the Paschal lamb preparation in a slave home. Schnorr (1794–1872), who designed some of the stained glass windows for St. Paul's Cathedral in London, created a series of two hundred woodcuts of the Bible. As a Lutheran who trained as a draftsman within a monastery that functioned as an art colony, Schnorr was a careful and close reader of biblical text. This is reflected in a scene not often painted by those artists intrigued by biblical stories. In the drawing, eight slaves, engaged in different activities, occupy a small and cramped residence. On the right side of the composition, a man sits beside a tray upon which lies an emaciated sheep, its insides spliced open. The artist does not spare us the gore; he directs our gaze to the man holding up the sheep's

The Origin of the Paschal Lamb, Julius Schnorr von Carolsfeld

innards dripping blood in fulfillment of the biblical command to the Israelites to take a sheep, keep it in the house for four days, and then slaughter it:

> Tell the whole community of Israel that on the tenth day of this month each man is to take a lamb for his family, one for each household. If any household is too small for a whole lamb, they must share one with their nearest neighbor, having taken into account the number of people there are. You are to determine the amount of lamb needed in accordance with what each person will eat. The animals you choose must be year-old males without defect, and you may take them from the sheep or the goats. Take care of them until the fourteenth day of the month, when all the people of the community of Israel must slaughter them at twilight. Then they are to take some of the blood and put it on the sides and tops of the doorframes of the houses where they eat the lambs. That same night they are to eat the meat roasted over the fire, along with bitter herbs, and bread made without yeast. Do not eat the meat raw or cooked in water, but roast it over the fire – head, legs, and inner parts. Do not leave any of it till morning; if some is left till morning, you must burn it. This is how you are to eat it: with your loins girded, your sandals on your feet, and your staff in your hand. Eat it in haste; it is the Lord's Passover. (Ex. 12:1–11)

But the text, and the artist after it, do not focus on the technical details of the sacrifice alone. They also elucidate the significance of the Paschal sacrifice as a critical step in the judgment of Egypt and the deliverance of Israel.

> On that same night, I will pass through Egypt and strike down every firstborn – both men and animals – and I will bring judgment on all the gods of Egypt. I am the Lord. The blood will be a sign for you on the houses where you are; and when I see the blood, I will pass over you. No destructive plague will touch you when I strike Egypt. And this day shall be to you for a memorial, and you shall keep it as a feast to the Lord, throughout your generations shall you keep it a feast by ordinance forever. (Ex. 12:12–14)

Schnorr renders God's sweeping passage through Egypt with the depiction of an angel passing across the window. It is easy to imagine that the Israelites would have been anxious to get the blood from the sheep ready to make sure that their houses were passed over. Some would have felt blessed and grateful to be spared. Others may not have believed but were willing to go through the motions or may have been forced by parents or elders to follow directions. Schnorr captures this range of emotions beautifully in his composition. Only three of the eight slaves in his depiction look at the angel with longing and anticipation. The angel looks back with eyes that signal redemption for those who look at him. The other slaves look distraught. A man with a staff sits on the floor with his ankles crossed. He leans his chin on the staff with resignation. A woman with her empty water jug lying on the floor looks like she has no intention of picking it up and fleeing. She looks frightened to the point of paralysis. Two young children look despondent as one holds a round bread, perhaps a matza. A woman's arm, possibly their mother's, hovers over the plate of matza, staying the hands of the children, who are obviously hungry, signaling them to wait for the magical journey ahead. The light of a lamp shines brightly on her right shoulder and makes her whole head glow with an almost halo effect. She carries water jugs on her shoulders and her eyes stare at the angel outside the window, passing over the house. She awaits this moment of possibility. She sees in it what the others could not, reflecting the talmudic statement above that only twenty percent of the Jews left Egypt when given the chance. We miss so many defining moments through disbelief, despair, or our own negativity.

The artist clearly realized the significance of this scene. Where others depicted the plagues in all their gruesome majesty and ignored the Paschal lamb commandment, Schnorr understood that more than any other aspect of the Exodus, there was something about this commandment that undergirded it all, even if some slaves would respond to it with diffidence or fright. Exodus 12 begins with the mandate to view the new year as starting in this very month, the Hebrew month of Nisan, which suggests that the very beginning of time as the ancient Israelites understood it was to begin with the nascence of their peoplehood. On the tenth of the month they had to acquire a lamb and then on the fourteenth at twilight, it was to be slaughtered and its blood painted on lintels and doorposts with a hyssop branch, whose twig would serve as able paintbrush. Having a lamb in one's house for four days before it was slaughtered would build up anticipation and readiness for the momentous break with Egypt that lay ahead. The notion that it was to be a perfect year-old lamb meant that it retained the features that would make it cute and endearing. Keeping it in one's home for several days may have created a temporary sense of attachment to be violently altered with the lamb's slaughter, much the way that the Jews needed to urgently detach themselves from the deep bonds with Egypt, its people, and its culture. Housing a lamb was an act of insurrection, and with each noise it made, the lamb focused compassion upon itself. "Do not become too attached" was the message from above. This lamb which means so much to Egyptian practice means very little to you. It can be gotten rid of quickly and completely by you. You must reject the outside culture.

The bleating lamb had to be silenced so as not to garner too much attention because sheep were holy in Egypt. They were not to be slaughtered. They were to be revered. Once a person slaughtered a lamb, a sacred animal in Egyptian culture that was to be worshipped, there was no going back. The Israelites who prepared the Paschal lamb were essentially terminating any long-term relationship with the Egyptians because decimating an object of worship was a powerful and irreversible way of rejecting their culture. It was an ultimate display of disrespect. Ḥizkuni, a thirteenth-century French exegete, captures this in his explanation of the four-day waiting period: "So that the Egyptians would see their gods tied shamefully and disgracefully in the homes of the Israelites and would hear all the sheep squealing with no one to save them" (Ḥizkuni on Ex. 12:6).

The lamb in one's home was a way to prepare both the Jews who were about to leave and the Egyptians who were about to lose their labor force.

> R. Natan says [that the blood was applied] on the inside [of the houses] ... as is stated, "And the blood on the houses where you are staying shall be a sign for you" (12:13) – A sign for you but not a sign for others. R. Yitzḥak says [that the blood was applied] on the outside [of the houses] so that the Egyptians would see [the blood] and their intestines would fail [they would be horrified].[4]

The divergence of opinion here need not confuse us. The blood of the lamb upon Israelite houses served a dual function. It was an internal sign, preparing the Israelites mentally for the difficulties to come and signaling that they should put their personal faith commitments in order. It was also an external sign, communicating a rejection of the Egyptians' most treasured beliefs and the message that more danger was to come their way.

THE TIME OF FREEDOM

This commandment was also to be performed at a specific time of day to reinforce the same message in chapter 12: "Take care of it until the fourteenth day of the month, when all the people of the community of Israel must slaughter them *at twilight*" (Ex. 12:6). Ḥizkuni stresses on this verse that twilight was the time when people would be returning to their homes after the workday, congregating

---

4. See the *Mekhilta* on 12:13.

in various places, and therefore a more public time to hear the bleating of the sheep and feel the violation of one's most deeply held beliefs. Days and days of this noise would have made an impact on those living in the house and those passing by, culminating in the disposal of the animal through ritual slaughter.

Twilight is the metaphoric time equivalent of the doorpost. These are in-between times and spaces that signify transition. When we enter this time or space, we are aware that we will not stay in it for long. We cannot. The day will soon change to night. Twilight will not last forever. No one stands at the threshold of a door for long. Time advances. We advance. These symbolic domains help us understand the urgency of a moment of decision; the sliver of temporal opportunity forces decision-making. Redemption may present itself, but not for too long. The Paschal lamb sacrifice reinforced that message because it was unlike a typical sacrifice offered in the Temple by a priest who represents the community and acts as intermediary. There is not one sacrifice offered on behalf of all; everyone must participate in the Paschal lamb ritual. Those whose family nucleus was too small to offer a lamb are commanded to join with another family, compensating that family for their inclusion so that they are entitled to partake with everyone else. In Exodus 12, it is the family that makes the sacrifice. The lamb was an expensive food item, and one not ordinarily eaten by slaves. It also had to be a lamb without blemish, requiring the family to engage in a search for an excellent and worthy specimen.

INTENSIFYING COMMITMENT

The Israelites would leave after the tenth plague. This last plague, the killing of the firstborn, was devastating in its body count of animate life. As the intensity and significance of the plagues escalated, God asked that the Israelites also intensify their commitment, even to the point of violence. Freedom is never free. A high bar was raised around the ritual of the Paschal lamb sacrifice, demanding that slaves who may have made do with mediocrity during their detested service had to now reframe their understanding of service as relating to their own God, a God who demanded the best of them, who wanted the Israelites to see themselves as capable of aspiring to and achieving greatness. God desired a perfect lamb, the symbol of perfect worship.

In his philosophical masterwork, *Guide for the Perplexed*, Maimonides emphasized the insurrection of this act of sacrifice and what it would mean in terms of worship for the Israelites:

The Egyptians used to worship the sign of Aries, and they therefore forbade the slaughter of sheep and abominated shepherds. For it says,

"Lo if we shall sacrifice the abomination of the Egyptians," and it says, "For every shepherd is an abomination unto the Egyptians." Similarly certain sects of the Sabians worshipped the jinn and believed that they assumed the outward forms of goats and therefore called the jinn goats.[5]

Maimonides mentions the Indian practice of worshipping cows to illustrate his point. In the pagan universe, that which is worshipped can never be sacrificed. Maimonides then addresses the Paschal lamb ritual specifically:

> We have been commanded to slaughter the Paschal lamb and to sprinkle with its blood in Egypt the gates from the outside, so that we should manifest our rejection of these opinions, proclaim what is contrary to them, and bring forth the belief that the act, which they deemed to be a cause of destruction, saves from destruction: "And the Lord will pass over the door, and will not suffer the destroyer to come in unto your houses to smite." This is in recompense of their manifestation of obedience and their having to put an end to absurd things done by the idolaters.[6]

An act which was punishable by death in Egypt was the cornerstone to freedom and new life for the Israelites. In this act of slaughter and fire, there was something absolute about the rejection of Egyptian belief. Nothing destroys more efficiently and completely than fire. Its destructive capacity reduces beauty and history to ash, sometimes within a matter of minutes. The Israelites needed a fast-acting method but also one which would signal to themselves and to their host country that their presence in Egypt was soon to permanently end.

The Paschal lamb as a home-based sacrifice was essentially the way that Israelite families accepted upon themselves both a deep commitment to God and an understanding that this sacrifice would be viewed as a rebellious act of war by the Egyptians. Up until this point the plagues were performed around them and for them, to initiate their release. With this final plague, God was asking each family – one lamb per household – "Are you in?" Do you have the courage, bravery, brazenness, and boldness to partner with Me in your own redemption? This must be a family decision even though, as Schnorr's depiction reveals, not

---

5. Maimonides, *Guide for the Perplexed*, trans. Shlomo Pines, III:46 (Chicago: University of Chicago Press: 1963), 581.
6. Ibid. 582.

every family member would acquiesce willingly to the plan. Once a decision was made, it would require every member to commit. Unlike sacrifices in the Temple, where a holy representative served as the intermediary between God and an individual petitioner, this sacrifice required complete commitment from the household. Like the Seder that reenacts this defining moment in Exodus, the religious activity is home-based rather than performed in a sanctuary. The home aspect highlights another aspect of this sacrifice. The "*korban*" or central offering was not given to God in the typical way in which a sacrifice might be presented. In essence, the person who was offering it was making his home into a sanctuary and himself into a possible soldier.

We know that there are glimmerings of battle intimated in the text because of the language used to advise the Israelites how the lamb was to be eaten: "This is how you are to eat it: with your loins girded, your sandals on your feet, and your staff in your hand. Eat it in haste; it is the Lord's Passover" (Ex. 12:11). Before eating the Paschal lamb, every participant had to be ready to leave with staff in hand and sandals on feet. But "loins girded" creates a different biblical image in each slave house. Be ready for war. The decimation of so many sheep sacred to the Egyptians at the same time could only mean one thing. Prepare for battle. Know that with this sacrifice comes jeopardy.

Ordering that the Paschal lamb sacrifice, incumbent upon every family, be sacrificed on the same day and at the same time must have had a remarkable impact on both the Israelites and the Egyptians simultaneously. While a lamb could be hidden for several days inside a home, the smell of thousands of lambs roasting would waft high above the Israelites' dwellings. In addition, there was a specific method of preparation that was delineated: "That same night they are to eat the meat roasted over the fire," and it was to be served with bitter herbs and matza, making a satisfying, symbolic meal. The Talmud is very specific in emphasizing this cooking technique and mentions punishments for those who tried to boil it or cook it in any other fashion.[7] The aromatic aspect of spreading the fervor was critical in creating a community of both worshippers and rebels. Freedom has a taste. Freedom has a smell.

The excitement must have been palpable; small children dressed with haste. Mothers and fathers packed their few belongings and prepared the lamb. So many small clusters of anxiety and possibility created both a tense and contagious atmosphere that would have challenged doubters and skeptics to

---

7. The debate appears in Pesaḥim 41a–b.

reconsider. Imagine the scene in ancient Goshen. The physical handling of the sheep, the aromatic smell of the burning meat, the sight of the blood on the lintels, the taste of a filling meal typical of masters not slaves, the sound of young bleating sheep, and the cacophony of people milling about – all of these made freedom a totally sensual and immersive experience everywhere the ancient Israelites dwelled. You could not help but ingest the hopeful taste of your future, a taste both ostensibly impossible because of the cost of the sacrifice for a slave and because of the hazards inherent in the radicalism of the act and its inherent liberation. Everyone around you was participating. In that magical twilight hour, all seemed possible. Every door was open, limned in blood and waiting to be crossed. Although the name Passover refers to God's passing over of Israelite homes to save us, it also reminds us that we, too, had to pass over the threshold to our freedom.

BLOCKING THE DOOR TO FREEDOM

One of the obstacles to realizing any type of redemption, either big or small, is the recognition that someone or something is standing in our way, and the obstruction, at times, can seem too menacing to overcome. It brings to mind an important image in biblical literature that may hold the key to pushing through what stands in the way of actualizing that which can save us. In Hebrew, the word "petaḥ" means a threshold or an opening. A threshold is a space at the bottom of a door that represents the physical place that the door occupies. It has also become a metaphor for a boundary that has to be crossed in the actualization of goals. It is not a finish line but rather a line of transition, a mark either real or imagined that stands between where we are and where we would like to be.

Consider for a moment a physical threshold that people are anxious about crossing. It may be the door to a doctor's office when a biopsy is to be read. It may be the door to a principal's office for a high school student in trouble. It can be the door to an interview for a job that you desperately want, or the door to the CEO's office when you've been called in after making a significant mistake. It may simply be the door to your house, that you look at with tension as you return from a day of work because you have argued with your spouse or a child, and you are not sure what awaits you on the other side. Will you be welcomed and embraced or will the problems escalate beyond what they currently are?

The poet Adrienne Rich helps create this moment for us in one of her most well-known compositions, "Prospective Immigrants Please Note."

Either you will go through this door
or you will not go through.
If you go through
there is always the risk
of remembering your name.
Things look at you doubly
and you must look back
and let them happen.
If you do not go through
it is possible to live worthily
to maintain your attitudes
to hold your position
to die bravely
but much will blind you,
much will evade you,
at what cost who knows?
The door itself makes no promises.
It is only a door.

Every door, in Rich's construct, is a choice. Every choice has consequences. Not choosing is also a choice and may be an understandable choice, but it will also leave the questioner with the niggling doubt of "what if" moments. Knowing this, will you go through or not?

Yet, there is another aspect to this passage, another choice. How will you go through the door if you indeed decide to go through it? Will you hold your head up in pride or down in shame? Will there be dignity to the crossing or just humiliation?

When we turn to Jewish texts, we find the appearance of the word "*petaḥ*," door or threshold, as early as Genesis 4 as part of a narrative that is deeply familiar. God rejected Cain's sacrifice but accepted his brother's. God warned Cain to be attentive to his anger. The image of crossing over a threshold is fraught with anxiety:

The Lord looked with favor on Abel and his offering, but on Cain and his offering He did not look with favor. So Cain was very angry, and his face was downcast. Then the Lord said to Cain, "Why are you angry? Why is your face downcast? If you do what is right, will you not be accepted?

*But if you do not do what is right, sin is crouching at your **door**; it desires to have you, but you must master it."* Now Cain said to his brother Abel, "Let's go out to the field." And while they were in the field, Cain attacked his brother Abel and killed him. (Gen. 4:4–8)

God used questions to confront Cain with his own raw emotions. Cain had to understand the difficult passions swirling inside him: anger, rejection, fear, torment, jealousy. In the midst of this personal anguish, God taught Cain the most basic premise of free will, using a visual image to help Cain quell his impulse to kill. Sin appears in the form of a monster, an animal, or a demon – if you will – crouching at the door and ready to pounce. The door or threshold is the in-between place of decision. Cross this particular threshold, and it will have fatal consequences. God empowered Cain to shut the door on the constant presence of sin, telling him that even when sin is close by, you can overcome its seductions. Cain was not born in sin or born to sin. Sin exists but he could be its master, he was told. You will always have a choice to do right and when you do right, you will be uplifted.

Centuries later, a sage of the Talmud would take a similar approach in creating a framework for the everyday struggle against wrongdoing:

R. Shimon b. Lakish said: "A person's evil inclination overcomes him each day and seeks to kill him, as it is stated, 'The wicked watches the righteous and seeks to kill him' [Ps. 37:32]. And if not for the Holy One, Blessed be He, who assists him with the good inclination, he would not overcome it." (Sukka 52b)

To combat the persistent, nagging seduction of sin and to see it as the door – or choice – that it is, the Torah demanded that we place something on the door to warn us that we are about to step into a domain that may be morally unsafe, emotionally risky, or fraught with danger. Now, when we turn to this familiar trope in Deuteronomy in its context of everyday life, we may read the mitzva of mezuza a little bit differently:

Hear, O Israel: The Lord our God, the Lord is One. Love the Lord your God with all your heart and with all your soul and with all your strength. These commandments that I give you today are to be upon your hearts. Impress them on your children. Talk about them when you sit at home and when you walk along the road, when you lie down and when you get up. Tie them as symbols on your hands and bind them on your foreheads. Write them on the *doorframes* of your houses and on your *gates*. (Deut. 6:4–9)

In-between spaces, liminal territory, need to be noted and guarded precisely because we encounter their challenges and their ambiguities all the time. Most doors we go through on a daily basis are only wide enough for one person to cross at a time. On a metaphoric level, this enhances our anxiety about crossing thresholds. We generally have to traverse them alone. Even when we try to join with others to face risk collectively, on some level we understand that we are always existentially on our own. We may have company for part of the journey, but for the large inner battles, we fight on our own terms and with our own resources.

But look at a Jewish door for a moment. We place a *"shin"* on the outside of the mezuza, the Hebrew letter that stands for a particular name of God: *"Sh-adai,"* Protector. When we see that *shin* as we go through a door alone, we know that we are not ever really alone. If we are about to do wrong, God's presence is a gentle reminder to make a better choice. God is with us. Look inside the mezuza, and we find the first paragraph of *Shema*, the mission statement of the Jewish people. Not only are we with God when we undergo difficult transitions and passages, we are also armed with an ancient set of core beliefs observed by a community of believers who have made these words a living and ever-vibrant code of values. We have a mission statement and a people who go with us through these narrow places.

Exodus 12 takes place at twilight and demands that the Israelites place blood on a lintel. Liminal time. Liminal space. It was time to transition into a new life. To do that one must force oneself to go through that narrow, undefined time and space. On the other side of it waits another life. Go through.

BRINGING BACK THE PASCHAL LAMB

At the Seder, Rabban Gamliel reminds us that our evening of storytelling is incomplete without Pesaḥ, matza, and maror, but whereas the last two we ingest separately and together, the first we are not even allowed to lift up at the table lest it seem that we were trying to offer our own sacrifice, a post-Temple prohibition. Perhaps this is why we have traditionally spent less time delving into the Paschal lamb's significance and what it has to say about readying oneself for change.

Yet the very notion is foundational to storytelling on Passover, coupling transmission with transition:

> The blood *will be a sign for you* on the houses where you are; and when I see the blood, I will pass over you. No destructive plague will touch you when I strike Egypt…and when your children ask you, "What is this service to you?" you shall say, "It is a Pesaḥ offering for the Lord, *for He passed over the houses* of the Children of Israel in Egypt while He struck the Egyptians, but saved those in our homes" – and the people bowed down and prostrated themselves. (Ex. 12:13, 26–27)

At first, the text indicates that when God passes over the land of Egypt, *God* would see the blood and spare Israelite homes but later, the verse states explicitly that the blood "will be a sign *for you.*" We put blood on the doorposts that first Passover to signify that we were ready to leave. Whereas up until that point we were passive recipients of God's great kindnesses and miracles, now we had a moment to show our own commitment to the cause. God asked us to mark our homes so that *we* would self-select our redemption and become God's covenantal partner in intention and action.

The plagues were a remarkable display of power for the Egyptians to marvel at God and quake, but they would not teach the Israelites to grab destiny and change their fates. For that, they needed to do something proactive that would change every member of their household. Small, group-by-group influence began to spread until one after another in a family began to see that change was possible. Each day of the four, from the purchase of the Paschal lamb until its sacrifice, introduced new and exciting possibilities and helped shift every person from distance to dream. Little could be more shocking or jarring than being thrown into an impossible situation that required a paradigmatic shift in approach. No longer slaves but not freemen either, the Israelites left Egypt with an in-between identity that was reflected in time and place: by twilight and a doorpost. They woke up to the alarming reality that their ephemeral dream of freedom was held together not only by God but through their own personal visible commitment.

Emily Dickenson wrote, "I dwell in Possibility – a fairer House than Prose – More numerous of Windows – Superior – for Doors." Dwelling in possibility seemed improbable as slaves. Your sense of possibility narrows to the point of virtual non-existence. Your dreams are cut short until you stop dreaming altogether. But finally liberated of shackles, former slaves leapt into their own freedom and made all impossibilities possible, reminding those who came after them that we, too, must dwell in possibility.

LIFE HOMEWORK

- What is the most difficult door you have to push open in your life right now? Are you pushing it open or are you waiting for someone else to open it?
- Name three significant transitions in your life right now and the risks involved in each.
- What can you do right now – this Passover – to actualize a personal dream?

Day Eight

Men are children of this world
yet God has set eternity in my heart.

All my life I have been in the desert
but the world is a fresh stream.

I drink from it. How potent this water is!
How deeply I crave it!

An ocean rushes into my throat
But my thirst remains unquenched.

"Meditation," Moses ibn Ezra
(Translated by Carl Rakosi)

Day Eight

Pour Out Your Wrath, Pour Out Your Love

'Tis said that wrath is the last thing in a man to grow old.
Alcaeus of Mytilene

Pour out Your wrath" – the Haggada passage that follows Grace After Meals – is a collection of biblical quotes about a fiery divine anger to be directed at our enemies. We pour the last glass of wine, open the door for Elijah, and then a rush of indignation sweeps through the room. We create, in this moment, an odd and paradoxical sense of security and insecurity. Many have the custom of leaving the door unlocked the entire evening, creating easy access for Elijah should he arrive, because the night is called *"leil shimurim,"* a night of God's watchfulness.[1] God will protect us from harm, so much so that we do not lock our doors. And yet, at virtually the same moment that we open our doors wide, we also plead with God to eliminate any threats against us because we feel so insecure.

"Pour out Your wrath upon the nations that do not know You, and on the regimes that have not called upon Your name. For Jacob is devoured; they have laid his places waste" (Ps. 79:6–7). "Pour out Your great anger

---

1. See Exodus 12:42.

upon them, and let Your blazing fury overtake them" (Ps. 69:25). "Pursue them in Your fury and destroy them from under the heavens of the Lord" (Lam. 3:66).

These few verses sting with their violence, leaving no room for compassion or emotional ambivalence. The tone is unapologetic and confident. We know that certain nations deserve destruction, and we wish it upon them. The fact that these are biblical quotes without the usual rabbinic glue between them leaves us less room to minimize their significance or attribute them to a particularly grim phase of ancient Jewish oppression.

This text made its first appearances as a medieval addition in the shadow of the Crusades and, as Rabbi Jonathan Sacks points out in his Haggada, the text is intertwined with the glass of wine that is poured, in an intellectual and sensual intake of pain:

> One of the recurring events that made Pesaḥ in particular a time of fear was the blood libel. This originated in Norwich in 1144 and eventually spread throughout Europe. It is one of the few cases where persecution has left its mark on Jewish law. Several authorities ruled that though, preferably, the wine drunk on Pesaḥ should be red, in communities where there is risk of a blood libel, white wine may be used instead.[2]

The use of white wine at a Seder could only mean one thing: red wine spells the danger which the text speaks about in the abstract. We ask for God's help because, in reality, we could not survive without it. The threats of persecution are too great and ominous to ignore, even on this holy night of God's protection.

There are those who question how central *Shfokh Ḥamatkha* is to the ethos of the Hagadda, given its relatively late addition to the traditional text, as David Silber and Rachel Furst contend in their commentary on the Hagadda, *Go Forth and Learn*: "The recitation of these verses from Psalms and Lamentations is a custom that seems to derive from the medieval period, as it is not mentioned in either the Talmud or the geonic literature, nor is it cited by most medieval scholars. Subsequently, this recitation was accepted almost universally, with slight variations." Even if inspired by the punishing nature of the Crusades, the passage nevertheless found a home quickly as an enduring sentiment that needed articulation and affirmation for centuries beyond its origins.

---

2. Jonathan Sacks, *The Jonathan Sacks Haggada* (Jerusalem: Maggid, 2013), 121.

OUR EXISTENTIAL ANGST

"*Shfokh Ḥamatkha*" has been read for centuries with a sense of universal resignation. In the *Haggada Shleima*, Rabbi Menachem Kasher cites various customs
through the ages that speak of how geographically widespread this passage has
been for the centuries of its use. While it makes no appearance in the Haggada
of Rabbi Saadia Gaon (882–942) or Maimonides (1135–1204) and the *Maḥzor*
of Rome mentions only the first verse, Psalms 79:6, many communities added
to our current three verses – anywhere from two to an additional fifteen verses
on the same theme.[3] If you were not sure if God has the capacity to punish those
who punish us, the amalgamation of verses pushes home the message. We are
not alone. We do not have to fight alone.

Our people will have enemies in every generation. Because of this constant
and successive onslaught, we are compelled to repeat our Exodus narrative and
relive it in every generation, forcing us, through this Passover reading, to digest
the reality that is imposed upon us. There will always be someone who hates us.
Consequently, we ask for more than divine protection. We ask for divine retribution. We do not believe in vigilante justice, taking matters into our own hands.
We ask that God act justly because one of the great aspects of human suffering
is believing that this world is inherently unjust. The thought of this as a baseline
of the human condition is paralyzing and goes against the core of Jewish belief
and practice. And yet we are familiar with its seductions: the belief that nothing
we do will ever make a difference, that people do not get their just desserts, that
good people suffer and bad people are rewarded. It lulls us into passivity and
inertia. The promise of a world where the wicked get their recompense as do the
righteous is deeply satisfying and forms an understanding of a theological world
at its greatest ideal, a view of messianic-like proportions. We encounter this proposition at the very end of the last of the Prophetic books of the Bible, Malachi:

"Surely the day is coming; it will burn like a furnace. All the arrogant and
every evildoer will be stubble, and that day that is coming will set them on
fire," says the Lord Almighty. "Not a root or a branch will be left to them.
But for you who revere My name, the sun of righteousness will rise with
healing in its wings. And you will go out and leap like calves released from
the stall." (Mal. 3:19–20)

---

3. See Menachem Kasher, *Haggada Shleima* (Jerusalem: Makhon Tora Shleima, 1967), 177–178,
   for the practices of communities from Ashkenaz to Northern and Southern France, England,
   and Romania, among others.

This apocalyptic promise does not presage a day of disaster, as many have assumed. It is the day of divine retribution: "The sun of righteousness will rise with healing in its wings." The most regular of activities, the sun rising to signal a new day, will tell of righteousness and healing. Farmers who heard the prophet intone his message – the image of a calf released from its stall – could appreciate the joy of youth and the joy of movement. Justice brings joy.

MODERN SENSIBILITIES

Today, again, even in the shadow of a not-too-distant past of anguish, modern readers find that "Pour out Your wrath" does not fit in well with a worldview of acceptance and tolerance. Some have even changed the wording entirely to "Pour out Your love," in a grab for psychic relief from hatred, racism, and oppression of any kind, directed specifically to righteous gentiles who put their own safety at risk to save us. We celebrate those who made different, better, more loving choices. In *A Different Night*, a Haggada composed by Noam Zion, we find this passage attributed to descendants of Rashi, found in a manuscript from Worms (1521). Its authenticity, however, is under debate, even while its language touches us with its poignancy.

> Pour out Your love on the nations who have known you and on the kingdoms who call upon Your name. For they show loving-kindness to the seed of Jacob, and they defend the people Israel from those who would devour them alive. May they live to see the sukka of peace spread over Your chosen ones and to participate in the joy of Your nations.

Here, in place of biblical verses, we find snatches of familiar lines woven together to create a prayer quilt of intimacy and gratitude. We wish those who helped us peace and abiding joy. This text pushes us to another polarity: a world where the Jews are blessed and loved by all, the grateful beneficiaries of loving-kindness. When this text replaces the other, it is suggesting that our ultimate reality be a world not of divine justice and retribution but one of love and kindness alone.

Sometimes, there is no replacement text at all. To commemorate the twenty-fifth anniversary of their wedding day in 1891, Benjamin and Rebecca Cohen created their own Haggada which they affectionately dedicated to their children.[4] The actual Haggada has very few Hebrew words; in addition to the English translation of Haggada highlights, the Cohens added a synopsis of the

---

4. With gratitude to my friend Joy Katzenberg who shared her family Haggada with me.

story and a running commentary replete with history and politics. As they fill the wine glass toward the end of the Seder, they comment on the state of Jews in America. In place of "Pour out Your wrath," they offer an assessment of the Jewish people in exile. They note the destruction of the Temple in days of old but also the "inhuman treatment" Jews still received in their day in "Russia, Roumania [sic] and other benighted countries." In 1916 when this Haggada was created, they knew that Zionists fervently wanted their own state to relieve the Jews of these burdens, but felt that life on their side of the Atlantic was a lot more cheery for the Jews and wrote:

> While this movement through colonization and agitation may succeed in ameliorating the condition of our less-favored brethren, we do not consider the restoration of Palestine as a Jewish state either practical or necessary. The mission of Israel is spiritual, not political, and we who live in these United States, a land of liberty and equality, where we are accorded all the rights of citizenship, are proud of this, our native land.

As patriotic Americans, the Cohens at their Seder service then transitioned into the national song "My Country, 'Tis of Thee."

The Cohens felt uncomfortable with "Pour out Your wrath," so instead they created their modern version and applied it to, what was for them, contemporary situations of human injustice. In 1916, they thought that a state for the Jewish people to express their national identity and to relieve the peril of anti-Semitism was an unnecessary political and ideological move. They were, no doubt, voicing an opinion broadly shared by American Jews and those the world over who felt comfortable and settled in the Diaspora. A few decades later, the sheer loss of Jewish life across Europe dislodged the naiveté of those like the Cohens, unsettling the blissful ignorance embraced by many Jews of how unsafe their assumptions about Jewish security were.

Their naiveté is also ours. Many modern readers change or eliminate "Pour out Your wrath" even as Jews in Israel, France, and the Ukraine – to name but a few locations – live amidst ethnic hatred and with very regular threats and discomfort. We seem altogether confused about anti-Semitism, as if it is shocking and unacceptable to the open underpinnings of our education and world understanding. Modern additions to the Haggada that upend the desire for retribution help us formulate and collectively express appreciation, but if they are used as replacement texts to *Shfokh Ḥamatkha*, they miss the point entirely. We are *supposed* to read these verses from Psalms and Lamentations. It is part of the emotional script of the evening, and it begs understanding, especially given the biblical prohibition against revenge, because the world around us does not quickly let us relinquish these primal fears and subjugate them to the bin of history. "We have to combat evil, but evil sometimes does not let itself be defeated," concludes Rabbi Joseph Soloveitchik.[5] The stubborn persistence of evil is sobering. The liberal mindset struggles to grasp the extremist, the wicked, the fundamentalist, the person who is so driven by hatred that he can neither experience nor give love. On this night, we pause to take note of this crude and primitive hatred, its appearance and reappearance across the historical timeline of the Jewish people, and the way it has warped minds and hearts for centuries.

HUMAN REVENGE AND DIVINE RETRIBUTION

The scars of deep-seated persecution on victims of sustained violence and hatred are nearly impossible to remove. The scar tissue may harden and the scar's appearance may fade a little with time, but like a long-suffered wound, certain situations can reactivate the pain. The anger can be so overwhelming that a victim believes that the only way to be rid of the anguish is to seek revenge. The anger then has an effective emotional release and the revenge ensures that a situation does not repeat itself because the enemy becomes incapacitated. But those who study revenge know that it is a cycle that is rarely broken. It is at the heart of family and national conflicts.

The cyclical nature of human revenge is supposed to be stopped in its tracks by a biblical prohibition: "Don't take vengeance and don't bear a grudge against the members of your nation; love your neighbor as yourself" (Lev. 19:18). Many forget that the command to love one's neighbor is preceded by the prohibition to seek revenge or bear a grudge. The desire for revenge and the lodging of an old offense are obstructions to love. You will not love a neighbor you cannot forgive. The verse also contains a limitation to the law; you should not take vengeance or bear a grudge "against members of your nation." There seems to be an understanding that the verse may not extend to those outside of your family, your community, your nation. In these ever-widening, but still familiar clusters, revenge can become a devastating cancer that creates deep fissures in relationships, strained under the weight of too much closeness. But outside of these intimate bonds, revenge seems to be permitted and understandable.

---

5. Joseph Soloveitchik, *An Exalted Evening: A Passover Haggada*, ed. Menachem Genack (New York: OU Press, 2009), 138 (originally from *Festival of Freedom*).

This approach may offer the framework for understanding Genesis 34, the rape of Dinah. When Dinah is raped, her brothers are outraged and want to kill the perpetrator and his family and decimate his entire tribal enclave. The clash of cultures, the very otherness of them, allows for the revenge to take root. Dinah's brothers suggest circumcision for Shekhem's whole village, planning to kill all the village's men at the point of greatest vulnerability:

> All the men who went out of the city gate agreed with Hamor and his son Shekhem, and every male in the city was circumcised. Three days later, while all of them were still in pain, two of Jacob's sons, Simeon and Levi, Dinah's brothers, took their swords and attacked the unsuspecting city, killing every male. They put Hamor and his son Shekhem to the sword and took Dinah from Shekhem's house and left. The sons of Jacob came upon the dead bodies and looted the city where their sister had been defiled. They seized their flocks and herds and donkeys and everything else of theirs in the city and out in the fields. They carried off all their wealth and all their women and children, taking as plunder everything in the houses. Then Jacob said to Simeon and Levi, "You have brought trouble on me by making me a stench to the people living in this land, the Canaanites and Perizzites, and I being few in number, they shall gather together and slay me, and I shall be destroyed, I and my house." But they replied, "Should he have treated our sister like a prostitute?" (Gen. 34:24–31)

The brothers were overcome with righteous indignation; their sister was not to be treated like a harlot, allowing the man who did this to her to be free of punishment. Their behavior seems in keeping with the prohibition that is dispensed later: they seek revenge only on those outside themselves to enforce the laws, taboos, and culture of their own community. Yet Jacob does not allow them the luxury of violence. "You have brought trouble on me by making me a stench to the Canaanites and Perizzites, the people living in this land" (Gen. 34:30), he admonishes. A bad smell is not something corporeal. You can't touch it, but it pervades a space. Jacob challenged his sons' assumptions about community. Revenge will unravel security and community in the fragile ecosystem of Jacob's life in the ancient Near East.

Later, we encounter a more difficult text of revenge, a revenge that is immersed in a complex family dynamic around loyalty and betrayal. David invited his son Solomon to his deathbed and spoke his truth about his mortality and his legacy:

When the time drew near for David to die, he gave a charge to Solomon his son. "I am about to go the way of all the earth," he said. "So be strong, show yourself a man, and observe what the Lord your God requires: walk in His ways, and keep His decrees and commands, His laws and require-ments, as written in the Law of Moses, so that you may prosper in all you do and wherever you go, and that the Lord may keep His promise to me: 'If your descendants watch how they live, and if they walk faithfully before Me with all their heart and soul, you will never fail to have a man on the throne of Israel.'"

Up to this point, we are touched by David's faith and his desire to pass it on to the next generation. And then we stop suddenly, bothered by David's next words as he takes Solomon into his confidence:

"Now you yourself know what Joab son of Zeruiah did to me – what he did to the two commanders of Israel's armies, Abner son of Ner and Amasa son of Yeter. He killed them, shedding their blood in peacetime as if in battle, and with that blood stained the belt around his waist and the sandals on his feet. Deal with him according to your wisdom, but do not let his gray head go down to the grave in peace. But show kindness to the sons of Barzillai of Gilead and let them be among those who eat at your table. They stood by me when I fled from your brother Absalom. And remember, you have with you Shimei son of Gera, the Benjamite from Bahurim, who called down bitter curses on me the day I went to Mahanaim. When he came down to meet me at the Jordan, I swore to him by the Lord: 'I will not put you to death by the sword.' But now, do not consider him innocent. You are a man of wisdom; you will know what to do to him. Bring his gray head down to the grave in blood." Then David rested with his fathers and was buried in the City of David. He had reigned forty years over Israel – seven years in Hebron and thirty-three in Jerusalem. So Solomon sat on the throne of his father David, and his rule was firmly established. (1 Kings 2:1–12)

Solomon's rule had to be firmly established. David's enemies needed to know that they could not escape his withering judgment. He sought revenge through his son, bringing another generation into a circle of hatred and mistrust by ask-ing Solomon to take care of unfinished business. But he did not act directly. He merely stated the crimes and told Solomon that as a man of wisdom, he would know what to do.

These cases are ones in the "family" and involve serious crimes and misde-meanors. And yet the Talmud, when illustrating an example of revenge, chooses something relatively harmless with little consequence, a behavioral pettiness rather than a large-scale harm like rape or murder: "Taking revenge is when you ask someone, 'Lend me your sickle,' and he says no. The next day he comes to you and says to you, 'Lend me your hatchet.' You respond, 'I am not lending to you, just like you did not lend to me.' This is an example of revenge" (Yoma 23b). In this case, the lender has the item but will not lend it because previously – a day before – the borrower did not lend. The lender does it for no other reason than to irritate; he is perturbed by the lack of reciprocity.

The Talmud continues its discussion of revenge with an understanding that not acting in reprisal requires a great degree of personal maturity. "Those who are insulted but do not insult back, hear themselves slandered but do not respond, act with love and rejoice in tribulations, of these Scripture states that 'Those who love Him are like the sun rising with all its might.'"[6] Maimonides also describes the person who acts above the fray – rising like the sun – as someone who is not dragged down by trivial and trifling matters. "Taking revenge is an extremely bad trait. A person should be accustomed to rise above his feelings about all worldly matters; for those who understand [the deeper purpose of the world] consider all these matters as vanity and emptiness, which are not worth seeking revenge for."[7] The desire for these acts of revenge, however inconsider-able, is understandable but beneath a person's dignity.

Maimonides also mines the inner life of the revenge seeker, the secret chambers of the heart where no one else can go but an individual and God: "If someone who has wronged you comes to ask a favor, you should respond with a complete heart. As King David says in Psalms, 'Have I repaid those who have done evil to me? Behold, I have rescued those who hated me without cause.'"[8] A complete heart signals not only that acts of revenge are avoided but that the feel-ings of smallness that generally accompany them are not present either. Someone occupied with matters of greater consequence will not have time to be buried in insults, offenses, rejections, denials, or squabbles that drag down the spirit. King David is revisited in this passage by Maimonides not as a figure of dissension, bogged down by past wounds, but as a man who could save even those who hated him because he cared for the larger good. When he asked Solomon to use his

---

6. Yoma 23a. The verse is from Judges 5:31.
7. Maimonides, *Mishneh Torah*, Laws of Character Traits 7:7.
8. Ibid.

wisdom to take care of unfinished business, he was merely asking Solomon to act on behalf of his father's honor to restore integrity to the institution of leadership that was tarnished by David's enemies.

GOD'S JUSTICE

This conversation around revenge is limited to the machinations of human minds riddled with human limitations, the constant buzz and static of enmity and envy, judgment and negligible wrongdoings. Some elevate the entire discussion to a more Godly place. The medieval Spanish author of the *Sefer HaḤinukh*, a compilation of mitzvot according to Torah portions, identifies the goodness of those who avoid revenge as originating not in personal maturity but sourced in a deep and abiding faith.

> One of the roots of this commandment is that a person should know in his heart that all that happens to him, whether good or bad, is because it is God's will that it happens to him…. It was God who wished this to happen, and one should not consider taking revenge on the other person, because the other person is not the reason for what happened. (*Sefer HaḤinukh*, Mitzva #241)

God, who watches over us with divine providence and commanded us to live by laws that demand our personal best, has a larger plan. It behooves us, as a consequence of this larger narrative that we cannot see, to act in accordance with God's demands to achieve greater moral clarity and spiritual meaning. This wider landscape of concern also helps us return to *Shfokh Ḥamatkha* with renewed understanding. Humans can never act with objective justice. Only God can. Perhaps the only way we can understand the difference between human revenge and divine retribution is from a short verse in Deuteronomy: "Vengeance belongs to Me" (Deut. 32:35). We are flawed and failed, limited by our arrogance, fueled by anger and petty jealousies. How can we ever make the case for human revenge? We cannot. Because we cannot but suffer injustice, we ask God to intervene with a larger plan. We need the psychic assurance that all will be righted, even if we will not be witness to it.

DO NOT BEAR A GRUDGE

With the frequency of the insult comes its consequential partner: the grudge. Not every victim of insult is made of Teflon; many snubs hit us in the heart and then lodge in the gut. For decades. Some people take those grudges to the grave with them as permanent emotional scars. Since we are a nation that suffers insults and offenses, we have also become a nation that begrudges. We nurse our internal wounds. Perpetrators beware. The victims of a painful snub may hate you forever after. The recall of your name can bring up the bulbous bruise of the initial hurt as if it happened yesterday.

The same verse in Leviticus that prohibits taking revenge also warns against grudges: "Do not take vengeance and do not bear a grudge against the members of your nation; love your neighbor as yourself. I am God" (Lev. 19:18). This odd patchwork of commands ends on a strange theological high note. When read carefully, there is an emotional chronology that makes sense. As mentioned above, our immediate impulse when offended is to seek revenge, to plot a way to get back. If we do not act on that impulse for various reasons – ranging from a fear of confrontation to a fear of the consequences – revenge often morphs into a grudge. And there it stays as an immense barrier in a relationship. We may never get beyond one painful incident, reducing the totality of a complex relationship into the walnut of an insult.

God invites us to overcome negative emotions. The grudge will, after all, hurt us more than it can ever hurt someone else. It diminishes us, eats us alive, ruins happy occasions, and devours opportunities for growth and repair. If we can overcome it for no other reason than obligation to God, so be it. Alternatively, God may be summoned in this verse because any revenge demanding equivalence – like an eye for an eye – can never be satisfied literally.[9] Human beings are too biased, too small-minded, limited, and subjective to ever be truly fair about revenge. We leave ultimate judgments to higher powers.

Steve Maraboli in *Life, the Truth, and Being Free*, suggests that instead of our classic understanding of revenge, we "get even with people…but not with those who have hurt us, forget them, instead get even with those who have helped us."[10] We may just find that the more we "get even" for kindness, the less need we have to get even for wounds. If we work hard enough at it, we may even be able to find lost friends and recover family relationships that have been torn asunder by grudges.

---

9. To see this reasoning played out in legal texts, see Bava Kamma, the eighth chapter on how we measure damages to humans monetarily, based on the eye-for-an-eye verses that sound literal rather than metaphoric.

10. Steve Maraboli, *Life, the Truth, and Being Free* (Port Washington, New York: A Better Today Publishing, 2009).

OUR SPIRITUAL RESTRAINT

When we think about divine retribution, revenge, and the burden of bearing national grudges in light of the Exodus experience, we discover the phenomenal restraint that the Haggada actually asks of us. If we were a different people, informed by different texts, the Haggada from the very first page could have been a call for revenge, a way to fester and escalate our historic desire for retribution. But it isn't. Instead, we offer a thin chronology of our history and the Exodus in the context of it. We sing the Hallel. We eat an entire meal and enjoy three cups of wine first. We envelope ourselves in the joys of freedom. Only after we are packed with all this goodness and abundance, do we turn to the small relief valve offered by "Pour out Your wrath," and open up a miniscule but important hole to release the pressures of anger and indignation that may be developing along with our storytelling. Rabbi Sacks describes it thus:

> What is notable about this addition to the Haggada is its restraint. For centuries, Jews suffered a series of devastating blows – massacres, pogroms, forced conversions, inquisitions, confinement to ghettos, punitive taxation, and expulsions, culminating, in the very heart of "enlightened" Europe, in the Holocaust. Yet these verses…are almost the only trace left by this experience on the Haggada, the night we recall our past.[11]

When we open that relief valve to dispel the pressure built up within us as a people, we do so from a positive and safe place, a place where we no longer suffer the indignities that this night or so many others in our history could have fomented. The relief valve allows us to validate the tangled and complicated emotions of revenge and turn them into a healthy plea for God to craft a path of justice from our pain as we move on to the rest of Hallel, the last cup, the longing to return to Jerusalem, and the happiness of songs that carry us closer on this late night of redemption to the sleep of the righteous.

No different than the verse from Leviticus that prohibits revenge and the bearing of grudges, the Haggada asks us to float above petty worlds where victory is a function of getting back, getting even, or blaming, and go to a space of redemption where the world is redeemed because we have been redeemed.

ONE LAST PICTURE

A woodcut from the Prague Hagadda of 1574 depicts the passage "Pour out Your wrath" with a curious border. Above the central text is an illustration of the plagues.

---

11. Sacks, *Haggada*, 121.

God extended an arm of revenge on the Egyptians for persecuting the slave people in their midst. If divine retribution is what is called for, let it be, says the depiction. Part of that arm of retribution that gets extended happens through human instruments. Thus, on the left-hand column running vertically down the page, we find an image of Samson, an eccentric leader from the Book of Judges who lived among Philistines, butchering them, sleeping with their women, and dying with them. In this strange record, the text has Samson fulfill the divine promise that came with his birth when the angel announced to Samson's mother that she – a woman barren – would give birth to a child of wonder: "The boy is to be a Nazirite to God from the womb on. He shall be the first to deliver Israel from the Philistines" (Judges 13:5). His birth is bookended by his death, where in his humiliation he called upon God for retribution: "Let me die with the Philistines" (Judges 16:30), Samson cried out as he struggled in chains between two pillars of a Philistine temple. And then God, through the agent of Samson, returned Samson's passion as he pulled the pillars with all of the last strength he had: "Those who were slain by him as he died outnumbered those who were slain by him while he lived" (Judges 16:30).

The woodcut's subtle power continues. The left-hand column of the woodcut offers us a black-and-white image of Judith holding the head of the enemy

The Prague Haggada

army captain Holofernes with a sword in her other hand. The widow Judith, whose story is told in her eponymous book in the Apocrypha, beheaded this Assyrian general who was sent to wreak havoc on her home and her town, Betulia. She, like Samson, was an unusual and unexpected victor, a heroine who anticipated no glory. But victory came to her nonetheless.

Perhaps the artist of our woodcut included examples of human revenge with God's retribution to give strength to the underdogs of the world, the readers of the Haggada who, more often than not, suffered in humiliating silence. A small people can indeed overcome powerful enemies with brash displays of courage and heroism. These isolated incidents of revenge converge in the depiction across the bottom of the page. A man riding on a small donkey hints to us that revenge will unfold with the coming of the Messiah, when justice will finally reign and the possibility of redemption will finally become a reality.

Professor Yosef Yerushalmi, in *Haggada and History*, believes that this woodcut offered both solace and hope to its viewers, who were only too familiar with the volatility of ruling powers and capricious authorities. The sense that we have sought revenge and succeeded generates faith in our capacity for strength when needed. We ask for a tempered victory, one that is part of God's larger plan for a world where justice may take longer than we wish, but when it arrives, it will be heralded and celebrated. We ask not to be burdened by human revenge because we can never be truly objective. We ask that Passover be a time when our freedom is pure and clear of gloating over our enemies or rejoicing in their destruction.

Our freedom is enough.

Dayeinu.

LIFE HOMEWORK

- Have you ever personally experienced anti-Semitism? Describe it. Can you articulate the feelings that anti-Semitism creates in you and what you have done to manage it?
- If revenge is its own poison, what is your antidote? Think of a situation where you wanted to exhibit revenge but held back. Explain your restraint.
- Think of the longest grudge you have ever held or are still holding. Why are you still holding on? Think of three steps you can take right now to move you beyond the hurt and into a place of greater freedom this Passover.

Epilogue

Redemption Awaits

*We can be redeemed only to the extent to which we see
ourselves.*

Martin Buber

On the last day of Passover as the holiday was nearing its close,
the Baal Shem Tov had a meal in the late afternoon called a *"Seudat Mashiaḥ,"*
the festive meal of the Messiah. He believed that there was something special, something anticipatory, about this time that created the possibility of
redemption. Some have connected this auspicious time to the number eight;
it is the eighth day of the holiday, a number signifying that it is above the natural order of completion, embodied in Jewish tradition by the number seven.
In addition, the *haftara* read on the last day of Passover from the last chapter
of Malachi, which is the last book of the prophets, contains a prophecy with
messianic overtones:

> See, I will send you the prophet Elijah before that great and dreadful day
> of the Lord comes. He will turn the hearts of the fathers to their children,
> and the hearts of the children to their fathers; or else I will come and strike
> the land with a curse. (Mal. 3:23–24)

Elijah will come, and as a sign that he is bringing the Messiah, love and attention between parents and children will be rekindled. Great injustices and small family infractions will be swept away in cleansing fires.

These heady promises help us understand why a festive meal marking the end of Passover would be observed, to hasten this time of justice and intimacy. Early in the twentieth century, it became a custom in Lubavitch yeshivas to enact the same custom. The rebbe joined his students and insisted that everyone there partake of four cups of wine. By reenacting a ritual of redemption from the first day of Passover on the last day, Passover became an opportunity to express gratitude and a platform for dreams of future redemption, asking that Malachi's prophecy wax into reality. Rather than allowing the holiday to peter out with the sunset, this meal closes Passover with both a summation and an exclamation mark.

Those of us who do not observe this custom have a harder task. We have to reflect on the nature of redemption and how we will carry the hope and emotion forward without any tangible rituals. We must define and analyze what redemption means. When we redeem something, we buy it back. We pay it off. We exchange, recover, or convert something, transforming it into something we control from something we once lost. God redeemed us. With an outstretched arm, God brought us back under divine loving care from abject servitude. We were once God's small tribe in Canaan; we emerged from a family and became a nation, but in the process, lost our anchor and our autonomy. God redeemed us, recovering us from a culture that had engulfed us and isolated us. In the process – to achieve a truer freedom – God brought us to Sinai so that we could become redeemed yet again. In the wilderness, after Sinai, God commanded us to build a *Mishkan*, a portable prayer space where we could engage in divine worship and access transcendence. And this, too, was another act of redemption. Bringing sacrifices was a way we could atone for wrongdoing and say thank you, redeem ourselves, and start again. The three major sections of Exodus – slavery to freedom (1–15), Sinai (19–21), and the instructions and building of the Tabernacle (25–40) revolve around redemption, both national and personal. Together with God, we wrote this story. On so many levels, we were active participants and partners in the process of our freedom. As we end Passover, we realize that intimacy with God, our drive for social justice, and our need for spiritual depth have deep historical roots that must be lived and relived through our making of the future. Alexandre Dumas ends his book *The Count of Monte Cristo* with the following message: "Until the day God will deign to reveal the future to man, all human wisdom is contained in these two words, 'Wait and Hope.'" Wait. Hope. These are the two words that, in combination, help us best understand the process of redemption.

As we read Exodus, detailing the stories that created our long-sought-after freedom, we realize that the thread running through all of Exodus is the power of this redemptive possibility that brings joy, a force so strong that we cannot simply let it dissolve as the holiday ebbs. We appreciate that the hasidic custom of this last redemptive meal is a way of asking the holiday to spill over into our lives, a way to exchange mental frameworks that are limited and narrow for those which are expansive and full of future opportunities.

Redemption is not only about possibility. It is also about patience, the emotional fortitude required to wait for the small, interconnecting pieces of a story to come together organically. Patience demands the capacity to tolerate delay, to accept trouble, and often suffering, without anger or retaliation. But waiting is hard work. It can exhaust our patience and fill us with doubts and uncertainties. People get tired of waiting. We often find ourselves waiting for "real" life to begin, waiting to become something, someone, waiting for the next chapter or stage of life, finding ourselves on the edge of becoming, wondering when the timing will be right. We are continually on the verge, one step closer, waiting for the life we think we deserve and have worked hard to achieve.

Redemption always reflects these dialectic tensions of pushing and patience, knowing when to forestall and knowing when to force the end. Consequently, there have always been two schools regarding the Messiah's arrival. There are those who choose to wait patiently and check for signs, and there are those who wait proactively and try to create the kind of reality that they believe will bring the Messiah. This division, while somewhat superficial, is a dividing line among many Hasidim and religious Zionists who may look at the reality of a Jewish State through very different and conflicting lenses. But the story of waiting is not always one of anticipation alone – it is also one of enduring power. To wait is to exhibit a blend of strength and realism wrapped in a veil of optimism that has served the Jewish people admirably throughout history.

Our Exodus story offers us the elements of redemption within a political, rather than supernal, context. Stories of redemption – divine and human – need several staple ingredients, ones that are delivered in the Exodus master narrative. We need a hero, and we get a reluctant one who needs to be convinced. We need a villain who obstructs our redemption, so we get a hard-hearted one who time and again stands in our way. We need a community in need of salvation, and we get it in the form of a hesitant people who initially reject their hero for fear of the great unknown. We need a reason to be redeemed, and we get it in the form of a mountain where our future is foretold as a set of laws that will help us create an enduring society based on justice and goodness. We need an ultimate

Redeemer, and we get it in the God who provides eagle's wings to transport us to a higher freedom.

Each verse and chapter in Exodus helps this narrative unfold. We get to meet our cast of characters intimately and see them each at a place of vulnerability. We understand that in all stories of redemption, the individual components that will construct a change will take a long time to evolve separately, but when all the parts come together, they do so with an almost explosive intensity. Deliverance, at such times of confluence, cannot come fast enough. This explains another legendary aspect of messianic tales and speculations. There is a rabbinic expression about God's redemption. It will come upon us "keheref ayin," in the blink or twinkling of an eye, as we learn in Shabbat 34b. It is easy to miss someone blink or to bypass the momentary sparkle in someone's eye that expresses surprise or delight. It is not only that redemption happens quickly; it happens so quickly that unless we are particularly attuned and waiting for it, we can miss it altogether. The same expression is used in contemporary Hebrew to describe what happens when the bell rings and the children disappear from class "keheref ayin," in the blink of an eye. One quick look and they are gone. When you don't want to be somewhere and are awaiting that moment of freedom to break loose and it is suddenly offered, you expend no time in creating an escape route.

The Talmud records this very fast and dynamic process through an intriguing conversation that R. Yehoshua b. Levi allegedly had with Elijah, the prophet who is assigned to introduce, welcome, or be the harbinger of the Messiah. If Elijah will arrive before the Messiah, he should know when the Messiah is coming, information that R. Yehoshua b. Levi would have liked to have:

> R. Yehoshua b. Levi: "When will the Messiah come?"
> Elijah: "Go and ask him yourself."
> R. Yehoshua b. Levi: "Where is he sitting?"
> Elijah: "At the gates of Rome."
> R. Yehoshua b. Levi: "What will identify him?"
> Elijah: "He is sitting among the poor lepers. They are all untying their bandages, and he is rebandaging them one by one, saying, 'I may be needed, so I must not be delayed.'" (Sanhedrin 98a)

This is a striking interaction on a number of accounts. Elijah tells the rabbi that if he wants to know when the Messiah is coming, he can very well inquire himself. He does not need an intermediary. But he does need to find the Messiah, and Elijah knows where he will be. The Messiah is not sitting in the holy city of

Jerusalem, nor is he sitting with the religiously elite or learned. He is not engaged in lofty or ethereal work in preparation for his larger job. Instead, he is sitting in the capital city of an empire that controlled the Jews, an enemy, taking care of the most needy outcasts in society, who cannot even take care of themselves. The lepers are removing their bandages while the Messiah is seeing to each one of them personally and binding and healing them. He must do his work efficiently because he could get called at any moment to a larger task of redemption. But he knows that the way to prepare himself to save the world is through engaging in small acts of kindness and compassion for those who need it the most. He does not wait passively to redeem others. He brings about redemption quickly and with love and, in so doing, creates a world more ripe for redemption. We wait for the Messiah, and the Messiah waits for us.

As we say goodbye to Passover, we take the heartache of suffering, the joy of freedom, and the moral call to redeem others with us through the year and meld them together to experience authentic joy. It is why we must remember the Exodus from Egypt every day of our lives. It is our inspiration for better living and better loving. It guides us through the ethical imperative to move forward and advance instead of shrinking back into a trapped, flat, thin existence where we cannot exert our freedoms. It tells us that we cannot stop hoping for an improved world and acting to bring about change. It reminds us that redemption is about waiting patiently and then moving quickly when the moment arrives. Possibility exists but it may not last long. Harness it now and be forever changed.

Pesach 2016 / 5776

Dear Feders-

We wish you & your family
a joyous & meaningful Chag.

Warmly always,

Selya & Glynis

הגדה של פסח
Seder Talk
The Conversational Haggada

Erica Brown

הגדה של פסח
SEDER TALK
The Conversational Haggada

Maggid Books and OU Press

CONTENTS

For eight essays for the eight days of Pesaḥ turn to the other end of this volume.

Start with a Blessing

The Trees of Nisan

*Look! The winter is past; the rains are over and gone.
Flowers appear on the earth; the season of singing has come,
the cooing of doves is heard in our land. The fig tree forms
its early fruit; the blossoming vines spread their fragrance.*

Song of Songs 2:11–13

Passover is called the holiday of spring. Let's open our Haggada with a blessing of spring, a blessing that is only recited once a year in the month of Nisan, upon the earth's renewal. We mark the transition from winter to spring, noting that the change of seasons brings with it the power of possibility. With the budding of trees and flowers, we pause to thank God for the reawakening of the world and with it, the reawakening of a joyous self after a harsh winter. Rabbi Samson Raphael Hirsch, in his collected writings on Nisan, says, "How poor we would be, if we had not learned to celebrate our spring." The season of spring reminds us that just as nature renews itself, so does humanity. "When spring comes and nature bestirs itself outside our doors, there is a stirring in us too, a stirring among us, a stirring around us. Then the springtime comes to us, then our homes and dwellings come to life."

בָּרוּךְ אַתָּה יהוה אֱלֹהֵינוּ מֶלֶךְ הָעוֹלָם
שֶׁלֹּא חִסַּר בְּעוֹלָמוֹ כְּלוּם
וּבָרָא בוֹ בְּרִיּוֹת טוֹבוֹת וְאִילָנוֹת טוֹבִים לְהַנּוֹת בָּהֶם בְּנֵי אָדָם.

Blessed are You, LORD our God, King of the Universe,
who has withheld nothing from His world,
but has created in it beautiful creatures and trees for human beings to enjoy.

A different wind is blowing. Skies grow tall,
Bright distances unfold in limpid space.
Spring treads the hills, and in the village square,
The earth at dawn exhales a misty warmth,
And budding shoots appear upon wet trees.
A different wind is blowing through the world.

"Footsteps of Spring," Chaim Nachman Bialik
(Translated by Ruth Nevo)

Introduction

The Art of Order and Chaos

I shall not die but live to tell the story
of the LORD's deeds.

Psalm 118:17

On Passover, we create order to lose order. On this night, we balance between order and chaos, between organizing the Seder with a set chronology and in concrete stages and then telling a messy story that gets interrupted and upended with all of our commentary. It is a story of injustice and triumph, of human strain and divine salvation, of hesitation and progress. Of course, it must be told in fits and starts.

To begin telling the story, order is critical. We make sure that everything is in place. We clean our homes, scrub away any signs of leaven, and check every corner with the focused light of a candle. We organize the props that aid us in our storytelling: the symbolic food is prepared, the Seder plate is arranged, the cup of Elijah is poured, the Haggada – our script for the evening – is laid individually before each place setting for all to recount the Exodus. We make sure that the matzot we use for the night are whole, without cracks or the fissures of natural breakage. The table is beautifully set with our finest china. The children all shine in their new clothes and shoes. The cooking is finally done. There is a moment of pristine newness and perfection in all the order before us that has taken weeks to achieve. And we celebrate that order with a simple beginning that reflects this need for organization and method; we begin the Seder with a to-do

◀ list, a taxonomy

list, a taxonomy of rituals: *Kadesh, URehatz, Karpas, Yahatz* …. We recite fifteen tasks that must be completed by the evening's end. Some have the custom to return again and again to this list, musically checking off what has already been done by reciting only what is left to do, stage by stage. It is our laundry list, our planned statement of accomplishment that affirms our commitment to systems and goals, the rules that will signify the logic of the evening ahead. And in a way, this order takes us back to the very first days of Creation, making something out of the void, as Rebecca Goldstein notes:

> The celebration of Passover emphasizes the imposition of an ordered structure over the formlessness of time. From the beginning to the end of the Seder there is a multiplicity of stages, with procedural instructions overlaid along the way. First you must do this, we are told, and then you must do that. Differentiation creates order, creates the sense of significance that makes duration endurable.[1]

Human beings have a supreme need for order. It is the commitment to discipline that allows the randomness of events to have meaning. Things must be shaped and named, placed and organized. If "Seder" means order, then we begin as we intend to continue, emphasizing the imposition of order as our very first order of business.

But then all begins to unravel. We tell a story, and stories are never linear. We start with questions rather than definitive statements. Questions are always messier. We acknowledge that there are different types of children at our table who must all hear the story but who all need a different telling. Our story begins with baseless hatred, originating long before the Exodus, an illogical and unjust sentiment that drives the narrative. Even in a world so neatly crafted, we find that not all is under our control. We sing a slave song, "We were slaves." Slaves have no control over their fate or destiny. They are objects in the possession of a master.

Had God not redeemed us, we would still have been in Egypt, our Haggada reports. We would have become an absorbed people in a collapse of empires whose distinct identity had merged with the surrounding neighbors. We would have compromised our uniqueness. The small window of opportunity would have closed. As we read, this question of what would have happened makes the Haggada feel like a work of fiction where the reader can choose the next stage in the plot and flip the pages accordingly. Deep in the Haggada, we are momentarily arrested

1 Rebecca Newberger Goldstein, "Library," in *New American Haggada,* ed. Jonathan Safran Foer (New York: Little, Brown and Company, 2012), 13.

◂ by the possibility

by the possibility that in life there are so many possibilities: stymied beginnings, unexpected turns, alternate endings that often turn into different beginnings.

As we turn more and more pages, we begin to realize that the Haggada is far from an ordered telling of the story. It is the oddest mish-mash of passages. We sing a song of praise and then *talk* about the way our sages *talked* about the Exodus. A linear narration would require us to open up the Book of Exodus and read its first fifteen chapters, much the way Karaites and Samaritans mark the fifteenth of Nisan. But instead, in the Haggada, we read about the way that others read and told the story. A group of scholars in Benei Berak were so absorbed in the narration that they had no idea daybreak had come and that it was time to recite the *Shema*. R. Elazar b. Azaria did not know how to interpret a verse until the scholar Ben Zoma shed light on it. We skip around, beginning with "My father was a wandering Aramean" and jumping not long thereafter into a talmudic math lesson. Ten miracles soon become fifty and then 250. This is not storytelling. It is meta-storytelling. It is retelling how the Exodus has been told before. And with this realization, we feel that we have lost control over the story itself.

In fact, we are obligated to lose control. We are told to drink four cups of wine; after the first two, the world begins to get blurry. We recline, losing the stability of our physical positioning. With a few cups of wine, we find ourselves reclining naturally. Wine spills on the beautifully ironed tablecloth. The matza crumbles. How could it not? And soon, we discover, the order we imposed on the evening is forsaken. Even our to-do list of fifteen tasks is not really fifteen because we add song after song. Salt water drips onto the table. Then *ḥaroset* falls on the beautiful tablecloth, adding splotches of apples and nuts to the dark red wine stains. We hide the *afikoman,* and when we do not know where it is, we have lost control of that too. We pour more wine and talk about how our enemies still want to kill us. We are lost in random hatred. We push it aside and begin to sing, because to be a Jew means to sing in the face of adversity. We sing the Hallel and then, against all rational belief for most eras of our history, we sing "Next Year in Jerusalem." We turn to the Haggada's last pages and sing strange songs, like *Ḥad Gadya,* the Jewish version of "There Was an Old Lady Who Swallowed a Fly." Some conclude even later in the night with Song of Songs. By the end of the evening, the tablecloth has become a testament to entropy. Order has been replaced by story. Stories are always a muddle of fact and fiction; they involve digressions and details and defy logic. Then story is replaced by song. Singing reaches us in a different place; singing unites us with others on this night. We all sing so that we can feel true joy and release and togetherness with those around us at the table and with those in the past, people we have never met but who

◂ told the

told the same story once upon a time. We don't care if you have a good voice or not. Anyone can sing.

The pristine order that began the evening is long gone. The universe as we know it seems hazy. We are beyond tired. The children have dropped off to sleep. The songs buzz in our heads. We are free, blessedly free.

COMPONENTS OF MEMORY

One of the most chaotic mitzvot is the command to remember because memory is always messy, an inchoate jumble of lasting impressions combined with lapses and questions. Yet, this night to remember is based in large part on our capacity to remember. Because it is a night of order and chaos, we explore two competing components of memory: repetition and expectation, and surprise:

- We remember that which is repeated within a structured and logical framework.
- We remember that which is surprising and unexpected, a disturbance from the expected that is distinct. Something in the experience stands out.

Passover memory often comes in the form of a familiar pattern on the china that is unwrapped once a year or a family heirloom that graces the table annually. It comes in the expected and predictable presence of certain family members or friends who join us, and it is also formed by experiences that stick out in our memories because they were so different. It may be the first Seder you ever made yourself, or the Seder you had in a foreign country one year far from home. An elderly gentleman, a veteran, who was in one of my classes and barely spoke suddenly drew the class's attention when he told us in detail of a Seder in Japan with hundreds of American servicemen and servicewomen, all longing for the traditions of home. I remember the man who approached me after class to share with me the time he had Seder at his aunt's and a man missed the turnoff on their road and drove straight into his aunt's living room during the Seder. He'll never forget that night. It *was* different from every other night.

Memory is a strange mix of two conflicting experiences: order and disorder. We remember things that happen to us repeatedly, but those experiences tend to blend into one blur. And then we have the chaos – the disruption that stays with us as a powerful jolt out of the ordinary. We have no other meal in the Jewish calendar that relies on this balance of repetition and interruption for its drama. Ask family and friends around the Seder table to share what they look forward to every year, the traditions that they cannot be without, and then ask

◄ people to

people to recall their most distinctive Seder experiences and why they stand out. It is incumbent upon us this night to use both of these places, the place of order and the place of disorder, to trigger the Passover memory point.

THE MEMORY POINT

The *Sefat Emet*, Rabbi Yehuda Aryeh Leib Alter (1847–1905), was an important rebbe of the Gerer Hasidim in Poland and a highly regarded Bible commentator. He compared Passover to Shabbat because we count the days from Passover to Shavuot "from the day after the Sabbath" (Lev. 23:15), meaning that Passover is a Sabbath, a day when we cease all work. On Shabbat, we have a dual commitment both to remember and to keep the Sabbath, underscored in the Ten Commandments and elsewhere. Passover, too, is regarded as a day of remembrance, filled with triggers and props to aid memory. This command to remember Passover is repeated numerous times in the Bible (Ex. 12:14; Deut. 12:17, 16:1, 16:3). On this, the *Sefat Emet* writes: "For memory is a point within, one where there is no forgetfulness."[2] It is hard to force someone to remember something. You cannot demand something that people may not be able to deliver. But the *Sefat Emet* believes that there is a place where forgetfulness cannot reach: the memory point. He believes that this memory point was revealed on Shabbat in the single utterance that joined *zakhor* and *shamor*, remembering and keeping. On Shabbat there is an extra attempt to keep or preserve memory from "flowing into that place where forgetfulness occurs," like a drain that sluices away all the important imprints we put on our minds. By remembering the significance of Shabbat, we are motivated to keep it. By keeping or observing Shabbat we keep our memories alive in practice. Memory and observance were uttered together because they rely profoundly on each other, creating the spirit that is Shabbat.

For the *Sefat Emet*, this memory point is also drawn out on Passover in a unique way, helping us achieve an existential place of rebirth:

> On every Pesaḥ a Jew becomes like a new person, like the newborn child each of us was as we came forth from Egypt. The point within our hearts is renewed…every Jew has this inner point, to draw all our deeds to follow it. This is our job throughout the year, for better or worse. But the holiday of matzot is the time when the point itself is renewed, purified from any defilement.[3]

2 Judah Alter, *The Language of Truth: The Torah Commentary of the Sefat Emet*, trans. Arthur Green (Philadelphia: Jewish Publication Society, 1998), 389.
3 Ibid., 390.

◄ There is

There is a small spiritual trigger that is located in the heart and activated each Passover. It is the point of inspiration that translates into action. It is a point of motivation that provides the reason we do what we do as Jews. It is the point of peoplehood that links us deeply with those beside us and those before us and those who will come after us. We need to revisit this point every year, nurture it, and be nurtured by it.

Defilement of this point occurs throughout the year, when our inspiration flags or our motivation is low. Symbolically, this is the rising of the matzot into bread, for, like matza, that point is thin and must be preserved as such. On Passover, we want to return to that simpler, smaller place where we originally felt unified and whole. We must go back to our roots, our oppression and sudden freedom, and renew the feeling that the Passover memory brings with it: the newness of our relationship with God, the newness of justice, the newness of liberation. Just as in life, when people become successful they risk forgetting their roots, so too do we risk losing our capacity to marvel at miracles and freedom if we cannot renew this memory point. Passover is designed to help us identify that point anew and strengthen it, without bloating it into something large or narcissistic, symbolized by ḥametz.

This renewal is also critical in shaping a nation in that it forces us to renew our commitment to fighting injustice. When we become too comfortable, we can forget that we were once vulnerable to forces that enslaved us to ruinous effect, that we were beaten and downtrodden and in desperate need of salvation. But it is not merely events we risk forgetting; we can always read about our history to jog our recall. Passover demands that we do more than commit facts to memory. It demands that we relive all of the experiences that came with the facts of our history: the anxiety, the exclusion, the fear, the anticipation, the newness of a relationship, the first taste of freedom, the wonder of becoming. And so we understand the Haggada's requirement: "And even were we all wise, all intelligent, all aged, and all knowledgeable in the Torah, still the command would be upon us to tell of the coming out of Egypt; and the more one tells of the coming out of Egypt, the more admirable it is." Native intelligence may make it easier to access the facts of history but it cannot guarantee the imprint of that history on an enduring Jewish identity. This emotional aspect of memory ensures that the Jewish commitment to justice and freedom is renewed and strengthened with each retelling.

TELLING THE STORY OF OUR SUSTAINED HAPPINESS

Memory is often linked to tragedy. But memory can and should trigger deep joy as well. In addition to the pain of the experiences mentioned above, our

Passover memory point can recall miracles that create in us responses of gratitude, abundance, and happiness. If it does not do this, then perhaps we are denying ourselves a door into greater contentment and serenity. Passover can invite us to a happy memory point, but we must take God and our history up on the invitation, replacing the gloom-and-doom side of our story with joy and optimism instead.

The stories we tell always hold an opportunity for us to shape ourselves, depending on the narrative we choose. "All of us tell stories about ourselves. Stories define us," write Herminia Ibarra and Kent Lineback in their *Harvard Business Review* article "What's Your Story?"[4] When we know someone well, the authors remind us, it is because we know key aspects of his or her story: the experiences, trials, and turning points that have made them who they are. "When we want someone to know us, we share stories of our childhoods, our families, our school years, our first loves, the development of our political views, and so on,"[5] the authors tell us. They emphasize that people need a good story most at times of transition, for those who are doing the telling and for those who are doing the listening. A story about transitions explains why we are leaving or moving or joining or participating. In-between times beg for explanation, a compelling narrative that we tell ourselves and others. What we find most compelling about stories is how the world changes as a result of them, be it the narrow world we occupy or the world at large. It's the "change, conflict, tension, discontinuity" of stories that makes them dynamic and engaging. "If those elements are missing, the story will be flat. It will lack what novelist John Gardner called the profluence of development – the sense of moving forward, of going somewhere. Transition stories don't have this problem,"[6] point out Ibarra and Lineback.

Many people, however, do not want to share conflict or tension when they tell their stories because they are afraid it will look like personal failure or will communicate to others that they were lost or made poor decisions. But listeners are waiting for the conflict because it is the drama of the story that holds us. All good stories that inspire have heroes and villains, moments of trauma or critical decision-making, or poor beginnings that may turn into good endings. The Passover story has held our attention for so many centuries because of its drama, its quest for justice, and its resonance with so many other stories of people who were

---

4   Herminia Ibarra and Kent Lineback, "What's Your Story?" in *Harvard Business Review on Managing Yourself* (Boston: Harvard Business School Press, 2005), 45.
5   Ibid.
6   Ibid., 47.

◄ displaced

displaced or exploited but were nonetheless able to find a voice and a cause. As a result, we understand why Deuteronomy commands that this memory point be triggered daily: "so that you remember the day of your Exodus from Egypt all the days of your life" (Deut. 16:3). The Exodus was more than an event. It represented the most cherished values we have, and as such it must inform every other day from the day of the Exodus forward.

That same chapter of Deuteronomy mentions all of the major pilgrimage festivals and the joy that is attendant upon them, closing with the Hebrew expression "*vehayita akh same'aḥ*." Rabbi Samson Raphael Hirsch, the neo-Orthodox head of the Jewish community of Frankfurt am Main in Germany in the 1850s, translates this expression as, "you shall remain only joyful." He contrasts this command with the imperative "*vesamaḥta*," "you should be happy." Rabbi Hirsch believes that remaining joyful is a higher degree of happiness than merely being happy, a temporal state generated by a temporal action. He also believes there is a difference between the happiness of an individual in the context of a family and the joy of a person in the context of a community. National unity and a sense of living for a larger purpose has the power to sustain our happiness even when individual sources of joy dry up or wane.

It is on this last point that we turn to Rabbi Abraham Isaac Kook, first chief rabbi of Palestine, who never lived to see the State of Israel, the impossible possibility:

> The Exodus from Egypt only appears to be a past event. But, in truth, the Exodus never ceases. The arm of God that was revealed in Egypt to redeem the Jews is constantly outstretched, constantly active. The revelation of the hand of God is the breaking through of the light of God, shining great lights for all generations. (*Mo'adei HaRaya*, 292)

When we are surprised by positive developments and events, we become renewed by the energy and force of redemption, and we can indeed make impossible things possible. The positive spiral upward fuels more redemption, more possibility. The Exodus, as Rav Kook writes, is no longer a past event but one that occurs again and again, a breaking forth of a small light that becomes larger and increasingly radiant, sweeping us up with optimism and joy. Between the order and the chaos, the beauty of the familiar and the surprise of the unexpected, every Passover we find ourselves facing a choice of how each of us will contribute to our larger, national redemption. Redemption is a choice. Sustaining happiness is also a choice. Choose joy.

THIS HAGGADA

Stephen King wrote, "When you find a book that has both a good story and good words, treasure that book." We have that book in front of us – our Haggada. Reading and re-reading it, talking about it and interpreting it, is the way we show that we treasure the Haggada. In our family, one way we show how much we treasure the Haggada is that we purchase and use new Haggadot each year, as is the custom in many families. We own facsimile copies of medieval Haggadot, the standard scholarly Haggadot, and the quirkier contemporary ones – a Haggada of the Kibbutz Movement, several feminist versions, a vegetarian Haggada called "The Haggada for the Liberated Lamb," one telling the story through cartoons, and another with drawings from the Holocaust. Because we retell this story annually, we must search for new ways to engage ourselves.

With shelves of so many Haggadot, it is not hard to ask why another is necessary. My conclusion: it is not. Appropriately, I asked myself, "*Mi anokhi?*" – Who am I to write my own commentary to this enduring and majestic work? Very little in this life is necessary. Very little of what is written is original or enlightening or needed. We write and transmit our Passover truths not to be original but because it is how we satisfy the demand to relive the Exodus story in each generation through ourselves. We should all write our own commentary as a fulfillment of the commandment to make this story truly our own.

In the essays that follow, along with the journey into biblical and rabbinic texts and the work of modern scholarship, you will find art and poetry to engage you in the sensory emotions of the night. And just so the taste of the Seder stays with us until the end of Passover, there are eight essays on central Passover themes and texts, one for each day of the holiday, with life homework at the conclusion of each essay so that Passover becomes a time when we work on ourselves to achieve greater mindfulness, intention, and inner freedom.

Each year, I am drawn to the Haggada, the eclectic amalgamation of rabbinic passages, biblical prayers, symbolic foods, and strange closing songs. And I find myself singing back to it, expanding upon its ellipses and celebrating its language and intent. Consequently, writing a commentary on the Haggada induced feelings of euphoria and, at times, of panic in the face of such a task.

In my late teens I would create an annual collection of *divrei Torah*, short comments, on multiple aspects of the Seder. When I was in the midst of my seminary years in Jerusalem and for years after, I would search out a thick and dense Haggada in Hebrew and make notes in pencil before the Seder, preparing myself assiduously to have something of substance to contribute. I interrupted the flow when everyone was ready to move on, asking people to delve deeper and

engage the text with me. I was not unlike others my age who felt that Passover was a solemn occasion meant to be marked by serious thoughts and explications. I believed that the goal of the evening was to be smart or to impress with pilpulistic-like attention to detail. But my mind was narrow and shackled. My mouth was singing, but my heart was not. It was an evening of the intellect alone. And I was so very wrong. I embraced it analytically instead of mindfully. I was still in my grape juice years. I had not yet had the challenge of drinking a few cups of wine and trying to read the small print of a Haggada with Rashi script.

What was I thinking?

The moment wine was introduced into my ritual life, I understood the role of the Seder very differently. Locked in the nuances and minutiae of legal observance and commentary, I was hardly mentally free. I became conscious of moments when the text almost stood in the way of larger emotional objectives because understanding it had become the end goal instead of the portal to a higher freedom.

When I shifted the whole paradigm of the evening and made achieving a different emotional state my goal, the text was no longer the only, or even the central, conduit to achieving joy. The night was no longer about the text exclusively but the way the text in conjunction with the wine and the food and the song carried me to a different place, one of exaltation and redemption. My job for the night was to embody the sadness and darkness of the slave and then to be happy, deliriously overtaken with a joy that can only come when we can recall our history and are profoundly grateful that we are alive, that we have put our difficulties behind us, that we are able to celebrate together.

When we approach the text with imagination rather than mere intellection, we realize that the story and its subsequent retellings are designed to pull our emotions in contradictory directions. Matza is both the bread of affliction and the bread of freedom. The egg that represents the circle of life is dipped into salt water, which represents our tears. The horseradish and ḥaroset sandwich tells us to put bitter and sweet together and eat them because adult life demands that we swallow emotions that sometimes rip us in different directions, a bittersweet duality that most accurately reflects our daily, complex lives.

What you will find in the pages ahead is merely a small staging area, if you will, for you to experience the emotions of the evening with me. You will not find complex exegesis. You will find, instead, sections of commentary and sections of conversation. These are marginalia to share ideas and thoughts from past exegetes and interpreters and to encourage us all to do a slower, closer reading of the Haggada. The conversation section is an invitation to use the text to jump into your

◂ life and

life and into the lives of those around you at the Seder. Our scintillating dinner conversation these nights should revolve around the great questions of purpose and meaning and how the Haggada is relevant to those larger questions. This conversation starts with our Haggada text, but it doesn't end there; it is merely the starting point where we begin our night to remember. If we have done our job properly at the Seder, the messages of the story will lodge deep within us. Be selective about picking the questions for your conversations. Feel free to use the questions as a catalyst for your own areas of inquiry. On this night, there are so many more than four questions.

When we ask questions, we must also pay careful attention to answers – to listen with the totality of ourselves to what others say. This can be challenging when the Seder becomes the place of too many sidebar conversations, noisy interruptions, and relentless distractions. Very often, little authentic conversation takes place at the Seder table. This makes transmission very difficult, if not impossible. Professor of linguistics Deborah Tannen has researched the way Jews speak and observes that our enthusiastic conversational style – which she terms "high-involvement cooperative overlapping" – can come across as disinterest in what others say, narcissism, or rudeness to those who have a different conversational style.[7] If our job is to convey a remarkable story to the next generation, let us be sure to speak *and* listen well so we can faithfully bring the conversation of the ages into our lives and the lives of those who will carry it forward with hope and joy.

DAYEINU

To publish a Haggada of this complexity requires a great deal of editorial love. I am most grateful – in this season of gratitude – to Matthew Miller, Gila Fine, Tomi Mager, and the outstanding editorial team at Maggid Books for their commitment and hard work to see this project through to fruition and to all of my friends at the Orthodox Union for years of support. I would like to thank my good friend Aliza Sperling for her sensitive and thoughtful comments and edits and both David Brooks and Deborah Lipstadt for their friendship and help with the Haggada's title.

Many people prepare for Passover by cleaning and cooking. We have had the great fortune as a family to prepare for Passover by packing – but not as our ancient ancestors did. For eighteen virtually continuous years, my family has been

---

7   See Deborah Tannen, "New York Jewish Conversational Style," *International Journal of the Sociology of Language*, no. 30 (1991), 133–149. Online at http://faculty.georgetown.edu/tannend/NY%20conversational%20style.pdf.

hosted by a number of delightful Passover programs, allowing me the mental freedom to spend time learning, teaching, and trying to create meaningful and engaging Seder evenings for others. The results of much of that teaching are here on these pages. I join my family in thanking each and every one of those programs for one fun and meaningful Passover after another.

And my last thank you goes to the One who has made so much possible.

Had You only given me my remarkable husband,
    it would have been enough.
Had You only given me my beautiful children,
    it would have been enough.
Had You only given me a blessed extended family and wonderful friends,
    it would have been enough.
Had You only given me this amazing life,
    it would have been enough.

Instead, it has been more, so much more, than enough.

ערב פסח

EREV PESAḤ

THE SEARCH FOR ḤAMETZ

On the night before Pesaḥ, a search for ḥametz, such as breadcrumbs, and products containing leaven and grain alcohol, is made in the house. The custom is to do so at night by the light of a candle, but a flashlight may also be used. If Pesaḥ falls on Motza'ei Shabbat, the search is made on Thursday night. Those who plan to be away on Pesaḥ should conduct the search the night before their departure, but without making a blessing. Before the search, make the following blessing:

בָּרוּךְ Blessed are You, LORD our God, King of the Universe, who has made us holy through His commandments, and has commanded us about the removal of leaven.

---

a person of unusual beauty, strangeness, or wisdom requires that we be within the presence of that individual. This unusual blessing over leaven, made only once a year, is said over that which is consciously *not* in front of us, that which we must search out and obliterate. In fact, we do not complete the demand of the blessing until the next day with the actual burning of the *ḥametz* and the verbal acknowledgment that, to the best of our ability, all leaven in our presence has been removed totally. There are two commandments that surround matza, positive and negative: fulfilling the command to eat it is a positive way we consume the symbolism, but we also must make sure to remove all leavened food items, and our blessings before Passover and on the night of the Seder acknowledge the fulfillment of both demands. It is unusual to make a blessing on something that we take away. It reminds us that we are not only the sum total of what we have. Our identity is also framed by that which we rid from ourselves.

What are you so attached to that you cannot let go?

When do your attachments to the physical stand in the way of spiritual accomplishments?

How would a verbal acknowledgment of removal help you master detachment?

בְּדִיקַת חָמֵץ

On the night before פֶּסַח, a search for חָמֵץ, such as breadcrumbs, and products containing leaven and grain alcohol, is made in the house. The custom is to do so at night by the light of a candle, but a flashlight may also be used. If פֶּסַח falls on מוֹצָאֵי שַׁבָּת, the search is made on Thursday night. Those who plan to be away on פֶּסַח should conduct the search the night before their departure, but without making a blessing. Before the search, make the following blessing:

בָּרוּךְ אַתָּה יהוה אֱלֹהֵינוּ מֶלֶךְ הָעוֹלָם
אֲשֶׁר קִדְּשָׁנוּ בְּמִצְוֹתָיו
וְצִוָּנוּ עַל בִּעוּר חָמֵץ.

THE SEARCH FOR ḤAMETZ

On the fourteenth of Nisan, after nightfall, it is customary to search the house by candlelight for any leaven that may not have been located in the general cleaning and preparations for Passover. A blessing is uttered before this search. The blessing helps make us intentional about what we are doing and creates a distinction between cleaning and sacred searching. Sometimes we search for something we cannot name. We cannot bless that process because it does not necessarily have an outcome, but tonight we search for something specific and will perform an action upon finding it. Thus, the blessing is on the outcome rather than the process itself.

If you could make a blessing on a process rather than an outcome, what blessing would it be?

Is there anything specific in life you are searching for now? What blessing would you make upon finding it?

AND HAS COMMANDED US ABOUT THE REMOVAL OF LEAVEN

Usually we make blessings only upon things that we see in front of us or that we directly encounter through another one of our senses: food, lightening, thunder, notable smells. The blessing we make upon seeing

After the search, say:

כָּל חֲמִירָא May all *ḥametz* or leaven that is in my possession
which I have not seen or removed
be annulled and deemed
like the dust of the earth.

REMOVAL OF ḤAMETZ

The following morning, after burning the ḥametz, say:

כָּל חֲמִירָא May all *ḥametz* or leaven that is in my possession,
whether I have seen it or not,
whether I have removed it or not,
be annulled and deemed
like the dust of the earth.

---

we know about and that which we do not know about so that we can ready
ourselves for the Seder. Let go and let God in. Break with the daily pattern
of what you eat, and you may find yourself able to question other routines
and assumptions of daily life that you can then go on to repair.

Many Mizrahi Jews have a beautiful custom that reinforces this message.
After the burning, they recite a special *teḥina*, prayer:

May it be Your will, LORD our God and God of our fathers, to have mercy
on us and save us from the prohibition of leavened matter even in the
most minute amounts, us and our family, and all of Israel, in this year and
the coming years, all the days of our lives. Just as we did remove *ḥametz*
from our homes and burned it, so we pray that we should be able to
remove evil inclinations from within us always, all the days of our lives,
and we should merit always to cling to good intentions, to Your Torah,
to the fear and love of You: we, our children, and grandchildren. May
this be Your eternal pleasure. Amen Selah.

*Is there a personal bad habit you'd like to put on the fire and see go up in smoke
right now?*

*Is there something that took place from last Passover to this Passover that is
getting in the way of your experience of freedom and joy? Put it symbolically in
the fire and cleanse yourself.*

After the search, say:

כָּל חֲמִירָא וַחֲמִיעָא דְּאִכָּא בִרְשׁוּתִי
דְּלָא חֲמִתֵּהּ וּדְלָא בִעַרְתֵּהּ
לִבְטִיל וְלֶהֱוֵי הֶפְקֵר
כְּעַפְרָא דְאַרְעָא.

בִּיעוּר חָמֵץ

The following morning, after burning the חָמֵץ, say:

כָּל חֲמִירָא וַחֲמִיעָא דְּאִכָּא בִרְשׁוּתִי
דַּחֲמִתֵּהּ וּדְלָא חֲמִתֵּהּ, דְּבִעַרְתֵּהּ וּדְלָא בִעַרְתֵּהּ
לִבְטִיל וְלֶהֱוֵי הֶפְקֵר
כְּעַפְרָא דְאַרְעָא.

ALL ḤAMETZ OR LEAVEN

By making our *hametz* ownerless, *hefker*, we are consciously articulating the fact that we have no connection to it nor any desire to possess it. While this declaration is written in Aramaic, it can and should be said in any language so that the owner of the *hametz* says with certainty that he or she is devoid of it now. While this may seem easy to do with our unwanted crumbs, in actuality, it may have been very difficult in times of economic distress to part with perfectly edible food at a time of hunger. We hold on tightly to our anxiety around physical things: food, property, objects. We often define ourselves by what we own or the banal items that frame our daily rituals, activities, and concerns. What we have brings us comfort or status or satisfies basic needs. It is hard to watch our objects literally go up in smoke.

Many Haggadot do not contain the ritual of burning the *hametz* because it is not related to the Seder itself. Yet, it is integral to where the Seder should take us emotionally. By burning the *hametz*, we remove any chance of holding onto that which we should let go. Unlike Lot's wife, we cannot look back and try to keep the connection to that which we are leaving behind. Safeguarding the biblical commandment in Deuteronomy 16:3, "You shall not eat anything leavened for seven days," we relinquish that which

CANDLE LIGHTING

On Erev Pesah, say the following blessing and then light the candles from an existing flame. If also Shabbat, cover the eyes with the hands after lighting the candles and say the following blessing, adding the words in parentheses.

בָּרוּךְ Blessed are You, LORD our God, King of the Universe, who has made us holy through His commandments, and has commanded us to light (the Sabbath light and) the festival light.

בָּרוּךְ Blessed are You, LORD our God, King of the Universe, who has given us life, sustained us, and brought us to this time.

Prayer after candle lighting (add the words in parentheses as appropriate):

יְהִי May it be Your will, LORD my God and God of my forebears, that You give me grace – me (and my husband/and my father/and my mother/and my sons and my daughters) and all those close to me, and give us and all Israel good and long lives. And remember us with a memory that brings goodness and blessing; come to us with compassion and bless us with great blessings. Build our homes until they are complete, and allow Your presence to live among us. And may I merit to raise children and grandchildren, each one wise and understanding, loving the LORD and in awe of God, people of truth, holy children, who will cling to the LORD and light up the world with Torah and with good actions, and with all the kinds of work that serve the Creator. Please, hear my pleading at this time, by the merit of Sarah and Rebecca, Rachel and Leah, our mothers, and light our candle that it should never go out, and light up Your face, so that we shall be saved, Amen.

As you prepare to light the candles and bring more light and blessing into your home, think of the person who stood beside you when you learned to light candles. Think of those who are no longer with you when you light candles and think of those you will teach how to light candles, passing on the light to yet another sacred generation.

As we say the SHEHEḤEYANU prayer this Passover, let us say it a little louder than usual. Say it loudly for Toby, who gave her six-line Haggada to her friend before the death march that claimed her life. Her friend preserved it and passed it on so that we could preserve it and also proclaim that we survive and thrive and now have a homeland and a refuge. We, thank God, have made it to this day. We pray for our abundant blessings and also in memory of those who did not make it to this day.

הדלקת נרות

On ערב פסח, *say the following blessing and then light the candles from an existing flame.*
If also שבת, *cover the eyes with the hands after lighting the candles and*
say the following blessing, adding the words in parentheses.

בָּרוּךְ אַתָּה יהוה אֱלֹהֵינוּ מֶלֶךְ הָעוֹלָם
אֲשֶׁר קִדְּשָׁנוּ בְּמִצְוֹתָיו וְצִוָּנוּ לְהַדְלִיק נֵר שֶׁל (שַׁבָּת וְשֶׁל) יוֹם טוֹב.

בָּרוּךְ אַתָּה יהוה אֱלֹהֵינוּ מֶלֶךְ הָעוֹלָם
שֶׁהֶחֱיָנוּ וְקִיְּמָנוּ, וְהִגִּיעָנוּ לַזְּמַן הַזֶּה.

Prayer after candle lighting (add the words in parentheses as appropriate):

יְהִי רָצוֹן מִלְּפָנֶיךָ יהוה אֱלֹהַי וֵאלֹהֵי אֲבוֹתַי, שֶׁתְּחוֹנֵן אוֹתִי (וְאֶת אִישִׁי/ וְאֶת אָבִי/
וְאֶת אִמִּי/ וְאֶת בָּנַי וְאֶת בְּנוֹתַי) וְאֶת כָּל קְרוֹבַי, וְתִתֶּן לָנוּ וּלְכָל יִשְׂרָאֵל חַיִּים טוֹבִים
וַאֲרֻכִּים, וְתִזְכְּרֵנוּ בְּזִכְרוֹן טוֹבָה וּבְרָכָה, וְתִפְקְדֵנוּ בִּפְקֻדַּת יְשׁוּעָה וְרַחֲמִים, וּתְבָרְכֵנוּ
בְּרָכוֹת גְּדוֹלוֹת, וְתַשְׁלִים בָּתֵּינוּ וְתַשְׁכֵּן שְׁכִינָתְךָ בֵּינֵינוּ. וְזַכֵּנִי לְגַדֵּל בָּנִים וּבְנֵי בָנִים
חֲכָמִים וּנְבוֹנִים, אוֹהֲבֵי יהוה יִרְאֵי אֱלֹהִים, אַנְשֵׁי אֱמֶת זֶרַע קֹדֶשׁ, בַּיהוה דְּבֵקִים
וּמְאִירִים אֶת הָעוֹלָם בַּתּוֹרָה וּבְמַעֲשִׂים טוֹבִים וּבְכָל מְלֶאכֶת עֲבוֹדַת הַבּוֹרֵא. אָנָּא
שְׁמַע אֶת תְּחִנָּתִי בָּעֵת הַזֹּאת בִּזְכוּת שָׂרָה וְרִבְקָה וְרָחֵל וְלֵאָה אִמּוֹתֵינוּ, וְהָאֵר נֵרֵנוּ
שֶׁלֹּא יִכְבֶּה לְעוֹלָם וָעֶד, וְהָאֵר פָּנֶיךָ וְנִוָּשֵׁעָה. אָמֵן.

CANDLE LIGHTING

What follows is a meditation from the *Auschwitz Haggada of Freedom*,
by Toby Trackeltaub from Munkacs, Hungary, prepared in Auschwitz in
1945 on small scraps of toilet paper, bound by threads from her prisoner
uniform, with which she embroidered the word "Zion" on the cover. Cited
in Aliza Lavie's book, *A Jewish Woman's Prayer Book*:

> We wish to celebrate but we are unable to.
>
> We desire to believe and that is the only thing that we have that they
> are unable to take from us; in it is memory, that alone can give us hope
> for a better and more beautiful future that we wish to think about and
> not to lower our heads.
>
> And if God redeemed our forefathers from Egypt, He will also save us
> from our bitter enslavement,
>
> And restore us to the land of our forefathers.

הגדה של פסח

PESAH HAGGADA

matza located symbolically beneath the plate on shelves. The Rema has matza in the middle of his plate and then going clockwise, has the shankbone, the bitter herbs, the parsley (*karpas*), the salt water, the *ḥaroset*, and the egg. The Vilna Gaon has matza in the middle and then going clockwise, has the bitter herbs, shankbone, egg, and *ḥaroset*. The other items were deemed extraneous or merely subservient to the central food items. The Ari has bitter herbs in the center of his plate, with the shankbone, *ḥaroset*, other vegetable (*karpas*), and roasted egg in clockwise order. The plate is not only a container of the symbolic foods of the evening. It is also a platform for the experience. The placement of the foods on it signifies the way we are supposed to feel and takes us through the Exodus experience. Each sage who wrote about the placement of the foods on the Seder plate wanted to make sure that we achieve our evening's emotional goal and maximize this experience.

In creating the bittersweet theme of the evening, we move between foods with a positive association and those with a negative association, often combining them to achieve "food contradictions." Our egg can symbolize the circle of life and our fertility in Egypt and, at the same time, remind us of the pain and loss of life as slaves since eggs are eaten as part of a mourner's meal. Our shankbone from the ancient Paschal lamb is the most compelling symbol of our redemption on the plate, but it sits in a circle with bitter herbs, representing the weight of our persecution. The circular shape of the plate itself keeps these emotions spiraling through us, encircling us with their constant change of meaning. We take *karpas*, often associated with the verdant green of spring, and dip it in salt water, emblematic of our tears. Later we will put horseradish and *ḥaroset* together on matza to achieve the same emotional push and pull that the evening is designed to create. In so doing, we take a page from Walt Whitman's playbook: "Do I contradict myself? Very well, then I contradict myself. I am large. I contain multitudes." We, as a people, tell our story from a point of strength and can afford to experience its contradictions.

Think about the order of items you have placed in a specific way – on your desk or dresser or in your office – that you see often. What were you trying to achieve emotionally with that placement?

Do you get upset when physical things in your life are out of order? If so, why?

קערת הסדר
THE SEDER PLATE

ביצה
THE EGG

זרוע
THE SHANKBONE

מרור
THE BITTER HERB

כרפס
THE KARPAS

חרוסת
THE ḤAROSET

חזרת
**THE MAROR
FOR THE SANDWICH**

THE SEDER PLATE

There are many intricate legal discussions about the ordering of the Seder plate. Generally, we follow the arrangement of Rabbi Moses Isserles – the Rema, Rabbi Elijah of Vilna – the Vilna Gaon, or Rabbi Isaac Luria – the Ari – who, in addition to organizing the plate a specific way, also has the

THE ORDER

We are about to read the fifteen steps (Motzi Matza is considered two steps) we have to undertake in order to fulfill the basic legal requirements of the Seder. Many families read this list again and again, stopping at each step, revisiting and restating the order to demonstrate that they are moving along a trajectory of freedom encased in rituals. Some regard these fifteen rituals as corresponding to the fifteen psalms in the section of the Song of Ascents (120–134), a corpus of psalms that were read in the days of the Temple by the Levites as they stood on the fifteen semi-circular steps leading from one hall of the Temple into another. We have a vivid depiction of this ceremony during the intermediate days of the Temple described in the *mishnayot* of the Tractate Sukka. In addition to the singing, the Levites had "harps, lyres, cymbals, and trumpets." It was a time of such great joy that the Mishna claims that if you did not see the Temple at this time, it was as if you had never seen true happiness in your life. These Songs of Ascent were sung as a spiritual climb, taking us to a peak intimacy with God. These steps represented the ladder we ascend to reach God, rung by rung by rung, as we grow our joy incrementally until it engulfs and overwhelms us.

Think of an activity or self-improvement project you are currently working on and think of the next step you have to achieve. What will it take to get you there?

What does the top of that ladder look like and what strategy will you employ to make the total ascent?

The order for the evening is announced beforehand
in the following form:

קדש		KIDDUSH
ורחץ		WASHING
כרפס		KARPAS
יחץ		SPLITTING
מגיד		TELLING
רחצה		WASHING
מוציא מצה		MOTZI MATZA
מרור		BITTER HERBS
כורך		WRAPPING
שלחן עורך		TABLE SETTING
צפון		HIDDEN
ברך		BLESSING
הלל		PRAISING
נרצה		PARTING

KADESH / KIDDUSH

The first cup of wine is poured.
Lift the cup with the right hand and say the following:

On Shabbat add:

Quietly: And it was evening, and it was morning –   Gen. 1
יוֹם הַשִּׁשִּׁי the sixth day.
Then the heavens and the earth were completed,   Gen. 2
and all their array.
With the seventh day, God completed the work He had done.
He ceased on the seventh day from all the work He had done.
God blessed the seventh day and declared it holy,
because on it He ceased from all His work He had created to do.

On other evenings Kiddush starts here:

When saying Kiddush for others, add:

Please pay attention, my masters.

Blessed are You, LORD our God,
King of the Universe,
who creates the fruit of the vine.

BLESSED ARE YOU…WHO CREATES THE FRUIT OF THE VINE
As we make Kiddush and think of all of the cups of wine ahead on this
sacred night, we recall that the *gefen,* vine, is not an incidental image in the
Haggada. The prophet Hosea called us a vine: "Israel was a spreading vine;
he brought forth fruit for himself" (10:1). Jeremiah created a nurturing
image of God as the careful gardener who tended to us: "Let them glean
the remnant of Israel as thoroughly as a vine; pass your hand over the
branches again, like one gathering grapes" (6:9). For this wondrous night,
the image of Israel as a vine takes on even greater significance when we read
Psalm 80:

You brought a vine out of Egypt; You drove out the nations and planted
it. You cleared the ground for it; it took deep root and filled the land.
The mountains were covered with its shade, the mighty cedars with its

Continued on the next page.

קדש

The first cup of wine is poured.
Lift the cup with the right hand and say the following:

On שבת add:

בראשית א

Quietly וַיְהִי־עֶרֶב וַיְהִי־בֹקֶר

יוֹם הַשִּׁשִּׁי:

בראשית ב

וַיְכֻלּוּ הַשָּׁמַיִם וְהָאָרֶץ וְכָל־צְבָאָם:

וַיְכַל אֱלֹהִים בַּיּוֹם הַשְּׁבִיעִי מְלַאכְתּוֹ אֲשֶׁר עָשָׂה

וַיִּשְׁבֹּת בַּיּוֹם הַשְּׁבִיעִי מִכָּל־מְלַאכְתּוֹ אֲשֶׁר עָשָׂה:

וַיְבָרֶךְ אֱלֹהִים אֶת־יוֹם הַשְּׁבִיעִי, וַיְקַדֵּשׁ אֹתוֹ

כִּי בוֹ שָׁבַת מִכָּל־מְלַאכְתּוֹ, אֲשֶׁר־בָּרָא אֱלֹהִים, לַעֲשׂוֹת:

On other evenings קידוש starts here:

When saying קידוש for others, add:

סברי מרנן

בָּרוּךְ אַתָּה יהוה אֱלֹהֵינוּ מֶלֶךְ הָעוֹלָם

בּוֹרֵא פְּרִי הַגָּפֶן.

KADESH / KIDDUSH

Note how often in the Kiddush for Shabbat we mention how much God worked during Creation. In imitation of God, we not only rest when God declared rest. We work because God worked. We create. We build. We master. We learn. We do not stop until we stop. And then, like God, we make time holy by transcending the convention of work, rising above it. Rest takes on meaning because of work.

Name the last time you had a complete rest. How long ago was it, and what made it different?

What creative act makes you feel most alive, as if you have fulfilled the purpose of creation?

On Shabbat, add the words in parentheses.

בָּרוּךְ Blessed are You, Lord our God,
King of the Universe,
who has chosen us from among all peoples,
raised us above all tongues, and made us holy
through His commandments.
You have given us, Lord our God,
in love (Sabbaths for rest),
festivals for rejoicing,
holy days and seasons for joy,
(this Sabbath day and)
this day of the Festival of Matzot,
the time of our freedom
(with love), a holy assembly in memory
of the Exodus from Egypt.
For You have chosen us
and sanctified us above all peoples,
and given us as our heritage
(Your holy Sabbath in love and favor and)
Your holy festivals for joy and gladness.
Blessed are you, Lord,
who sanctifies (the Sabbath and) Israel and the festivals.

---

nurturing and careful gardener once again and take care of the vine He planted. As we bless the wine multiple times this night, we are – in essence – blessing the metaphor and asking that God bless us and continue to tend to us lovingly.

What is it about gardening that brings out a creative impulse?

Think of and name activities from the world of agriculture and horticulture that we use to describe other activities, particularly spiritual ones. Why is this language so rich in metaphors?

On שבת, add the words in parentheses.

בָּרוּךְ אַתָּה יהוה אֱלֹהֵינוּ מֶלֶךְ הָעוֹלָם, אֲשֶׁר בָּחַר
בָּנוּ מִכָּל עָם, וְרוֹמְמָנוּ מִכָּל לָשׁוֹן, וְקִדְּשָׁנוּ בְּמִצְוֹתָיו
וַתִּתֶּן לָנוּ יהוה אֱלֹהֵינוּ בְּאַהֲבָה (שַׁבָּתוֹת לִמְנוּחָה
וּ)מוֹעֲדִים לְשִׂמְחָה, חַגִּים וּזְמַנִּים לְשָׂשׂוֹן, אֶת
יוֹם (הַשַּׁבָּת הַזֶּה וְאֶת יוֹם) חַג הַמַּצּוֹת הַזֶּה
זְמַן חֵרוּתֵנוּ (בְּאַהֲבָה) מִקְרָא קֹדֶשׁ
זֵכֶר לִיצִיאַת מִצְרָיִם, כִּי בָנוּ
בָחַרְתָּ וְאוֹתָנוּ קִדַּשְׁתָּ
מִכָּל הָעַמִּים, (וְשַׁבָּת)
וּמוֹעֲדֵי קָדְשֶׁךָ
(בְּאַהֲבָה וּבְרָצוֹן)
בְּשִׂמְחָה וּבְשָׂשׂוֹן הִנְחַלְתָּנוּ.
בָּרוּךְ אַתָּה יהוה, מְקַדֵּשׁ (הַשַּׁבָּת וְ)יִשְׂרָאֵל וְהַזְּמַנִּים.

───────────────────────────

branches; it sent out its branches to the sea, and its shoots to the river. Why then have You broken down its walls, so that all who pass along the way pluck its fruit? The boar from the forest ravages it, and all that move in the field feed on it. Turn again, O God of hosts; look down from heaven, and see; have regard for this vine, the stock that Your right hand planted. (8–15)

God brought a small vine out of Egypt and planted it in the Holy Land, where it could develop deep and enduring roots. That vine was protected and sustained so it did what all well-cared-for vines do. It spread. As it spread, others tried to pluck its fruits and endanger it. In this psalm, the vine calls out to God to ask for further protection. We ask God to be a

On Motza'ei Shabbat, the following Havdala is added:

בָּרוּךְ Blessed are You, LORD our God,
King of the Universe,
who creates the lights of fire.

Blessed are You, LORD our God,
King of the Universe,
who distinguishes between sacred and secular,
between light and darkness,
between Israel and the nations,
between the seventh day and the six days of work.
You have made a distinction
between the holiness of the Sabbath
and the holiness of festivals,
and have sanctified the seventh day
above the six days of work.
You have distinguished and sanctified
Your people Israel with Your holiness.
Blessed are You, LORD,
who distinguishes between sacred and sacred.

בָּרוּךְ Blessed are You, LORD our God,
King of the Universe,
who has given us life, sustained us,
and brought us to this time.

Drink while reclining to the left.

Take a few moments to think of other SHEHEḤEYANU *opportunities in your life
from last Passover to this one.*

*Go around the room and invite everyone to share a new "arrival" moment in
one brief sentence that has carried them to this Seder.*

On מוצאי שבת, *the following* הבדלה *is added:*

בָּרוּךְ אַתָּה יהוה אֱלֹהֵינוּ מֶלֶךְ הָעוֹלָם
בּוֹרֵא מְאוֹרֵי הָאֵשׁ.

בָּרוּךְ אַתָּה יהוה אֱלֹהֵינוּ מֶלֶךְ הָעוֹלָם
הַמַּבְדִּיל בֵּין קֹדֶשׁ לְחֹל
בֵּין אוֹר לְחֹשֶׁךְ
בֵּין יִשְׂרָאֵל לָעַמִּים
בֵּין יוֹם הַשְּׁבִיעִי לְשֵׁשֶׁת יְמֵי הַמַּעֲשֶׂה
בֵּין קְדֻשַּׁת שַׁבָּת לִקְדֻשַּׁת יוֹם טוֹב הִבְדַּלְתָּ
וְאֶת יוֹם הַשְּׁבִיעִי מִשֵּׁשֶׁת יְמֵי הַמַּעֲשֶׂה קִדַּשְׁתָּ
הִבְדַּלְתָּ וְקִדַּשְׁתָּ אֶת עַמְּךָ יִשְׂרָאֵל בִּקְדֻשָּׁתֶךָ.
בָּרוּךְ אַתָּה יהוה הַמַּבְדִּיל בֵּין קֹדֶשׁ לְקֹדֶשׁ.

בָּרוּךְ אַתָּה יהוה אֱלֹהֵינוּ מֶלֶךְ הָעוֹלָם
שֶׁהֶחֱיָנוּ וְקִיְּמָנוּ וְהִגִּיעָנוּ
לַזְּמַן הַזֶּה.

Drink while reclining to the left.

WHO HAS GIVEN US LIFE

This blessing is one of the shortest and most potent of the Haggada. It is
a blessing we make on time. It offers us an opportunity at each holiday to
reflect on the newness of our lives at that point in time, on both the simple
accomplishment of just living to reach the day again and on allowing us
the privilege of marking it with those we love.

URḤATZ / WASHING

Water is brought to the leader.
The participants wash their hands but do not say a blessing.

KARPAS

A small quantity of radish, greens, roots of parsley, or potato is dipped in salt water.
Say the following over the karpas, with the intent to include the maror in the blessing:

בָּרוּךְ Blessed are You, LORD our God, King of the Universe, who creates the fruit of the ground.   *Eat without reclining.*

YAḤATZ / SPLITTING

The middle matza is broken in two.

The bigger portion is then hidden away to serve as the Afikoman with which the meal is later concluded.
The smaller portion is placed between the two whole matzot.

---

prop: a broken piece of matza. Matza is such a fragile food. It is so easily broken, it may be hard to find a whole piece upon which to make a blessing. The optimal way to make a blessing is over food that is whole and without blemish. Its perfection demands a more perfect blessing. But before we tell the story of our freedom, we note our brokenness. We hold it up and pay attention to it. We bless God with broken hearts because so much of life is painful, but we are still here. We survive. As the Kotzker Rebbe said, "There is nothing more whole than a broken heart." We look around the table and notice who might not be at the table this year, who has suffered loss, who seems broken. We don't close our eyes to it. We know that when we are vulnerable our hearts are softer and more open. Leonard Cohen famously sang in *Anthem*: "Forget your perfect offering. There is a crack, a crack in everything. That's how the light gets in." We will let the light in on this remarkable night not by ignoring what is broken but by drawing attention to it. That is how all redemption begins.

Spend a moment thinking about what seems broken in your life right now.

Spend a moment thinking about what seems broken in the world right now.

Don't try to fix anything. Not yet. Just hold it up for a little while. Sometimes we rush to solutions because we want to fix everything that is broken, but in our haste – because we failed to really look at the brokenness carefully – we never solved what was truly broken.

ורחץ

Water is brought to the leader.
The participants wash their hands but do not say a blessing.

כרפס

A small quantity of radish, greens, roots of parsley, or potato is dipped in salt water.
Say the following over the karpas, with the intent to include the maror in the blessing:

בָּרוּךְ אַתָּה יהוה אֱלֹהֵינוּ מֶלֶךְ הָעוֹלָם

Eat without reclining. בּוֹרֵא פְּרִי הָאֲדָמָה.

יחץ

The middle מצה is broken in two.
The bigger portion is then hidden away to serve as the אפיקומן
with which the meal is later concluded.
The smaller portion is placed between the two whole מצות.

KARPAS

So much of Jewish history might be told through the taste of a potato. Just think of Van Gogh's famous painting, "The Potato Eaters." Take a moment to contemplate the humble potato before making the blessing. Pretend that there is no large meal on the way. Imagine your life as a slave and the delight you feel at this small morsel of food. Think of the potatoes that sustained your ancestors who may not have had meat or fish to eat and sustained their feelings of fullness through this simple meal. It was Sholem Aleichem who said: "One cannot live on potatoes alone. It is said that one wants bread with potatoes. And when there's not bread, a Jew takes his stick, and goes through the village in search of business." The potato is a blessed food for us. It sustained us in our darkest moments.

Name a food that sustained you during a particularly vulnerable or challenging time in your life.

What have you done or what do you currently do to honor and acknowledge this food?

YAHATZ / SPLITTING

Hardly sated by our small potato, with our bellies asking for more food, we sit as slaves about to tell our story in a distant past. We prepare our central

MAGGID / TELLING

*During the recital of this paragraph, the Seder plate is held up
and the middle matza is displayed to the company.*

הָא לַחְמָא עַנְיָא

THIS IS THE BREAD OF OPPRESSION

our fathers ate in the land of Egypt.
Let all who are hungry come in and eat;
let all who are in need come and join us for the Pesaḥ.
Now we are here; next year in the Land of Israel.
Now – slaves; next year we shall be free.

---

literature is capable of bringing new horizons and new perspectives – philosophical, religious, esthetical, and even social. In the history of old Jewish literature there was never any basic difference between the poet and the prophet. Our ancient poetry often became law and a way of life.

What do we talk about when we talk about the Exodus? We are called upon this night to become master storytellers: to entertain, to preach, to be relevant, to engage, to empathize, to argue, to discuss, to dissuade, to encourage. We are asked to be prophets and poets, who use the words of prophets and poets as a script for engaging the world and perfecting it. We start with talking because all redemption begins with the word. Thoughts breed words. Words breed deeds. Deeds bring about salvation. We talk about what happened in the past so we can understand what we must do in the present.

What goes into a great story that compels you to read more?
Why and how is language the beginning of redemption?
How does talking set you free? When does it get in the way?

THIS IS THE BREAD OF OPPRESSION

What kind of hosts are we? We invite guests at the last minute and then when they join us, we give them the bread of affliction? No one wants to

Continued on the next page.

מגיד

During the recital of this paragraph, the קערה *(Seder plate) is held up*
and the middle מצה *is displayed to the company.*

הָא לַחְמָא עַנְיָא
דִּי אֲכָלוּ אֲבָהָתָנָא בְּאַרְעָא דְמִצְרָיִם
כָּל דִּכְפִין יֵיתֵי וְיֵיכֹל, כָּל דִּצְרִיךְ יֵיתֵי וְיִפְסַח
הָשַׁתָּא הָכָא   לְשָׁנָה הַבָּאָה בְּאַרְעָא דְיִשְׂרָאֵל
הָשַׁתָּא עַבְדֵי   לְשָׁנָה הַבָּאָה בְּנֵי חוֹרִין.

MAGGID / TELLING

What are we talking about when we talk about the Exodus? The Seder is
the perfect holiday for Jews because it asks us to talk and then talk some
more. The more we talk, the more praiseworthy we are. In December 1978,
Isaac Bashevis Singer said this in his Nobel Prize acceptance speech about
storytelling:

> The storyteller of our time, as in any other time, must be an entertainer
> of the spirit in the full sense of the word, not just a preacher of social and
> political ideals. There is no paradise for bored readers and no excuse for
> tedious literature that does not intrigue the reader, uplift his spirit, give
> him the joy and the escape that true art always grants.

> Nevertheless, it is also true that the serious writer of our time must
> be deeply concerned about the problems of his generation.... As the
> son of a people who received the worst blows that human madness can
> inflict, I must brood about the forthcoming dangers. I have many times
> resigned myself to never finding a true way out. But a new hope always
> emerges telling me that it is not yet too late for all of us to take stock and
> make a decision...

> I am not ashamed to admit that I belong to those who fantasize that

The Seder plate and the matzot are now covered and the second cup of wine is poured.
The youngest child asks the following questions:

מַה נִּשְׁתַּנָּה

WHAT MAKES
THIS NIGHT UNLIKE ALL OTHER NIGHTS,
so that every other night
>> we eat either bread or matza,
>> but tonight
>>>> there is only matza?

And that every other night
>> we eat many different greens,
>> but tonight
>>>> we will eat bitter herbs?

This year we are slaves. Next year we may be in Jerusalem. Those who can love and support us in failure, will love and support us in success and be there beside us in joy.

Name something that you shared that was hard for you to give up, but you wanted someone else to get pleasure from it more than you wanted to keep it.

What is the difference between an act of giving and an act of sacrifice?

WHAT MAKES THIS NIGHT UNLIKE ALL OTHER NIGHTS?
Questions are the platform by which great stories begin. They are there to answer a question. Why am I here? Why does the world exist? What is my purpose? When done correctly and well, a good question has transformative powers, lifting us and helping us transcend the banalities of everyday existence and touch on that which is ultimate and enduring. American artist and writer Erin Morgenstern helps us understand the power of a transformative story: "You may tell a tale that takes up residence in

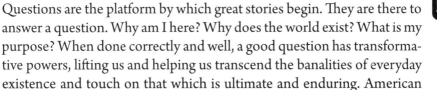

Continued on the next page.

The ‏קערה‏ *and the* ‏מצות‏ *are now covered and the second cup of wine is poured.*
The youngest child asks the following questions:

מַה נִּשְׁתַּנָּה
הַלַּיְלָה הַזֶּה מִכָּל הַלֵּילוֹת

שֶׁבְּכָל הַלֵּילוֹת
אָנוּ אוֹכְלִין חָמֵץ וּמַצָּה
הַלַּיְלָה הַזֶּה
כֻּלּוֹ מַצָּה

שֶׁבְּכָל הַלֵּילוֹת
אָנוּ אוֹכְלִין שְׁאָר יְרָקוֹת
הַלַּיְלָה הַזֶּה
מָרוֹר

join us for that. But wait. We are slaves. We could not invite guests because we didn't know that food was on its way. But then miraculously we found a bit of food. It wasn't much, but it was worth sharing. A Holocaust survivor wrote in her memoir: "Ilse, a childhood friend of mine, once found a raspberry in the camp and carried it in her pocket all day to present to me that night on a leaf. Imagine a world in which your entire possession is one raspberry and you gave it to your friend." This beautiful recollection is shared on a pillar of the New England Holocaust Memorial. When we have the capacity to give away even the most meager thing we have to give someone else pleasure, we have achieved light through darkness. And we tell those we invite for our modest meal that we know something else about true friendship. We never forget those who extend us kindness during hardship when we finally find ourselves in the position to enjoy success.

And that every other night
> we do not dip [our food] at all,
> but tonight
>> we will dip it twice?

And that every other night
> some sit to eat and some recline,
> but tonight
>> we are all reclining?

---

story to get us there. British novelist Phillip Pullman once wrote: "After nourishment, shelter, and companionship, stories are the things we need most in the world." When our basic needs are satisfied, we turn to higher-level needs, like the need for meaning. Storytellers make meaning. Storytellers are weavers. They understand that to capture interest, stories need not only information to be engaging. Content needs to be supported by drama, the theater of a narrative. Storytellers are strategic and intentional. They drop a nugget of suspense and conflict just as our attention span flags. They know how to raise interest and generate anticipation. One of the most important aspects of storytelling is how to begin a tale, how to draw in listeners from the very first words. Every story starts somewhere. Storytellers who are good at their job do not rely on chronology or purely linear accounts. They puncture time with an arresting aspect of the story and then work forward or backward. How do we ever know where to start a story? Our master narrative starts with one critical detail that demands us to shackle ourselves and imagine the limitations to our freedoms. We begin with a synopsis that tells all before we build and embellish, elaborate and analyze: "We were slaves." And then we were redeemed. "The LORD our God brought us out of there." If the Passover story could only be told in two sentences, it would be these.

Tell your family story in one great sentence.
Where did you start?
What was the most important moment in the story's trajectory?

שֶׁבְּכָל הַלֵּילוֹת
אֵין אָנוּ מַטְבִּילִין אֲפִלוּ פַּעַם אֶחָת
הַלַּיְלָה הַזֶּה
שְׁתֵּי פְּעָמִים

שֶׁבְּכָל הַלֵּילוֹת
אָנוּ אוֹכְלִין בֵּין יוֹשְׁבִין וּבֵין מְסֻבִּין
הַלַּיְלָה הַזֶּה
כֻּלָּנוּ מְסֻבִּין

---

someone's soul, becomes their blood and self and purpose. That tale will move them and drive them and who knows what they might do because of it, because of your words. That is your role, your gift." On this night, we are asked to be master storytellers. It is our role. It is our gift. It is the opportunity of a lifetime offered to us annually. We can embrace another person with words of justice and injustice, song and praise, spellbinding details and sweeping endings. We want the Exodus narrative to take residence in our souls. It is the story that speaks to a sense of Jewish purpose in the world: to hear the cries of another and do something about them, to celebrate small and unexpected victories as a sacred community, to join forces and tell the world that the few and the brave can still triumph. We refuse to let people languish in servitude of any kind. We do that under the rubric of God and not only out of our commitment to humanity. We believe that spiritual forces are at work that we may not always understand, but we partner with God to improve an already blessed world.

Name one personal reason you tell the Exodus story.

How does the mandate to tell the kind of story that takes residence in someone else's soul change the way you will tell the Exodus story tonight?

WHAT MAKES THIS NIGHT UNLIKE ALL OTHER NIGHTS?
On this night, we are different. Every day offers us an opportunity to be different. It is our choice. Tonight, we *must* be different. We use the

The Seder plate and the matzot are uncovered.

עֲבָדִים הָיִינוּ

WE WERE SLAVES to Pharaoh in Egypt,

and the LORD our God brought us out of there
with a strong hand and an outstretched arm.
And if the Holy One, Blessed Be He,
had not brought our fathers out of Egypt –
then we, and our children, and the children of our children,
would still be enslaved to Pharaoh in Egypt.
And even were we all wise, all intelligent,
all aged and all knowledgeable in the Torah,
still the command would be upon us
to tell of the coming out of Egypt;
and the more one tells of the coming out of Egypt,
the more admirable it is.

---

indicates the intensity of their storytelling. They were so absorbed that they lost all track of time.

But another reading is even more likely because it is hard not to notice the transition from night to the natural light of day unless you are hiding in a dark space, perhaps a cave or an attic, when you are discussing the Exodus. These sages were likely hiding from soldiers or representatives of the Roman administration, who may have persecuted them for external expressions of their religion. The magic of this passage is not only the length of the Exodus recollections or the passionate retelling on this Passover night long ago. It is also that despite outside dangers, they kept talking. A story worth telling is told again and again. Danger only makes the story more meaningful because it offers the reason that we endure.

Think of a story that is told and retold because it continues to inspire.

Name the last time you lost track of time because you were so absorbed in what you were doing.

Why would the Haggada make us read about the way other people read, rather than reading the story directly?

The קערה *and the* מצות *are uncovered.*

עֲבָדִים הָיִינוּ לְפַרְעֹה בְּמִצְרָיִם

וַיּוֹצִיאֵנוּ יהוה אֱלֹהֵינוּ מִשָּׁם

בְּיָד חֲזָקָה וּבִזְרוֹעַ נְטוּיָה.

וְאִלּוּ לֹא הוֹצִיא הַקָּדוֹשׁ בָּרוּךְ הוּא

אֶת אֲבוֹתֵינוּ מִמִּצְרַיִם

הֲרֵי אָנוּ וּבָנֵינוּ וּבְנֵי בָנֵינוּ מְשֻׁעְבָּדִים הָיִינוּ לְפַרְעֹה בְּמִצְרָיִם.

וַאֲפִלּוּ

כֻּלָּנוּ חֲכָמִים, כֻּלָּנוּ נְבוֹנִים, כֻּלָּנוּ זְקֵנִים

כֻּלָּנוּ יוֹדְעִים אֶת הַתּוֹרָה

מִצְוָה עָלֵינוּ לְסַפֵּר בִּיצִיאַת מִצְרָיִם

וְכָל הַמַּרְבֶּה לְסַפֵּר בִּיצִיאַת מִצְרַיִם

הֲרֵי זֶה מְשֻׁבָּח.

WE WERE SLAVES

We open our Haggada with a quick précis of what happened and with an invitation. Tell us more. Use this as a framework rather than a script. Speak and speak more because with every articulation of this ancient freedom, our appreciation deepens.

Since the close of this passage tells us that the more we speak, the more praiseworthy we are, we turn next to sages of the Talmud who could not stop speaking about the Exodus. If you set out to tell the story of our Exodus, chances are you would not have come up with a Haggada. It does not read at all like Exodus 1–15, with its mounting tensions and ultimate relief. Instead, we have a number of passages which tell us how others read this story. Rabbi Eliezer and his colleagues were telling this story all night. They, too, could not stop speaking about the Exodus. They didn't even realize that the time for the morning recitation of the *Shema* was upon them. Many commentators believe that this

מַעֲשֶׂה

ONCE,

Rabbi Eliezer and Rabbi Yehoshua and Rabbi Elazar ben Azaria
and Rabbi Akiva and Rabbi Tarfon
reclined [for the Seder] in Benei Berak.
And they told of the Exodus from Egypt all that night;
until their students came in and said,
"Teachers – the time for saying the *Shema* of the morning has come."

Rabbi Elazar ben Azaria said:
I am almost seventy years old,
and never have I merited to find the command
to speak of the Exodus from Egypt at night –
until Ben Zoma interpreted:

Berakhot
12b

He did not view learning separately from one's relationship to God, from character development, emotional intelligence, or financial responsibilities. Therefore, it seems unlikely that he would give self-praise.

Instead, this anecdote is a perfect illustration of the principle above that even those who are wise, intelligent, *aged*, and knowledgeable in Torah must retell the story of leaving Egypt. And the passage before it illustrates the next principle established in the Haggada, namely that the more one speaks about the Exodus, the more praiseworthy he or she is. A group of sages spoke about this story for so many hours that the sun was rising, and they were still talking.

Rabbi Elazar ben Azaria was regarded as a scholar of repute from a very young age. The Talmud records that hundreds of seats had to be brought into the study hall to accommodate the crowds that came to hear his Torah. When he died, the Talmud states that the "crown of the sages had been removed" (Sota 49b). It was as if true, authoritative learning could not take place without him. Yet when Ben Zoma shared his insight about the reference to the Exodus in the evening *Shema*, Rabbi Elazar brings us into a beautiful moment of intellectual discovery; that elated feeling of clarifying confusion, elucidating that which had remained elusive for years – maybe even what felt to him like seventy years of misunderstanding. In ancient

Continued on the next page.

מַעֲשֶׂה

בְּרַבִּי אֱלִיעֶזֶר וְרַבִּי יְהוֹשֻׁעַ וְרַבִּי אֶלְעָזָר בֶּן עֲזַרְיָה
וְרַבִּי עֲקִיבָא וְרַבִּי טַרְפוֹן
שֶׁהָיוּ מְסֻבִּין בִּבְנֵי בְרַק
וְהָיוּ מְסַפְּרִים בִּיצִיאַת מִצְרַיִם כָּל אוֹתוֹ הַלַּיְלָה
עַד שֶׁבָּאוּ תַלְמִידֵיהֶם וְאָמְרוּ לָהֶם
רַבּוֹתֵינוּ, הִגִּיעַ זְמַן קְרִיאַת שְׁמַע שֶׁל שַׁחֲרִית.

ברכות יב: אָמַר רַבִּי אֶלְעָזָר בֶּן עֲזַרְיָה
הֲרֵי אֲנִי כְּבֶן שִׁבְעִים שָׁנָה
וְלֹא זָכִיתִי שֶׁתֵּאָמֵר יְצִיאַת מִצְרַיִם בַּלֵּילוֹת
עַד שֶׁדְּרָשָׁהּ בֶּן זוֹמָא

 RABBI ELAZAR BEN AZARIA SAID

This is one of the most curious passages in the Haggada. Many have interpreted the statement, "I am almost seventy years old" as a reflection of
wisdom: Rabbi Elazar ben Azaria was so wise, he was like a person with
the intellectual maturity of a seventy-year-old. Yet this reading is problematic if we believe that humility is the better part of wisdom. Someone may
have said this of him, but it would make little sense if he said it of himself,
especially because he stated that one who has wisdom but no good deeds
is like a tree with many branches but no roots, easily able to be overturned
(*Avot DeRabbi Natan* 22:1). He is also the famous author of the statement
in *Ethics of the Fathers*:

> Without religion there is no true wisdom. Without wisdom, there is no
> religion. Where there is no wisdom, there is no fear of God. Where there
> is no fear of God, there is no wisdom. Where there is no understanding,
> there is no learning. Where there is no learning, there is no understand-
> ing. Where there is a lack of bread, Torah study cannot thrive. Without
> Torah study, there is no bread. (3:21)

It is written,

"So that you remember the day of your exodus from Egypt
all the days of your life."

Deut. 16

> "The days of your life" would mean in the days;
> "all the days of your life" includes the nights.

But the sages say,

> "The days of your life" would mean only in this world;
> "all the days of your life" brings in the time of the Messiah.

בָּרוּךְ הַמָּקוֹם

BLESSED IS THE OMNIPRESENT –

BLESSED IS HE.

BLESSED IS THE ONE

WHO GAVE HIS PEOPLE ISRAEL THE TORAH –

BLESSED IS HE.

---

interjecting a familiar tune but into a seemingly odd place. It seems inter-
ruptive but actually provides an excellent transition between the sages of
old and the four sons. In this song we celebrate and bless the God who gave
us Torah. It is the Torah that bridges the old and new, from generation to
generation. The sages were absorbed in the story of the Exodus and always
open to new interpretations that could layer their knowledge. Then they
passed it down to the next generation: the children, who would then carry
it forward and transmit it. We stop here to bless this moment of transition
and the God who required this legacy. We acknowledge the beauty of
spiritual succession which is captured majestically in the *UVa LeTziyon*
morning prayer: "'My spirit which is upon you, and My words which I
have put in your mouth shall not depart from your mouth, nor from the
mouth of your children, nor from the mouth of your children's children,'
said God, 'from now until eternity.'"

What is the beauty in succession?

*Name one value or pearl of wisdom about life that you received from someone
before you that you will transmit to someone after you.*

Reduce all your advice into one saying to be passed on. What is that saying?

שֶׁנֶּאֱמַר

לְמַעַן תִּזְכֹּר אֶת־יוֹם צֵאתְךָ מֵאֶרֶץ מִצְרַיִם

כֹּל יְמֵי חַיֶּיךָ:

יְמֵי חַיֶּיךָ   הַיָּמִים

כֹּל יְמֵי חַיֶּיךָ   הַלֵּילוֹת.

וַחֲכָמִים אוֹמְרִים

יְמֵי חַיֶּיךָ   הָעוֹלָם הַזֶּה

כֹּל יְמֵי חַיֶּיךָ   לְהָבִיא לִימוֹת הַמָּשִׁיחַ.

בָּרוּךְ הַמָּקוֹם

בָּרוּךְ הוּא

בָּרוּךְ שֶׁנָּתַן תּוֹרָה לְעַמּוֹ יִשְׂרָאֵל

בָּרוּךְ הוּא

───

Jewish tradition, it was believed that there were seventy nations and seventy languages. Seventy was the number of Israelites who went down to Egypt and emerged as a nation (Gen. 46:27; Ex. 1:5). Seventy elders were gathered to help Moses teach and adjudicate Jewish law (Num. 11:16). Seventy men made up the Great Court (Sanhedrin 2a). Using this number was not necessarily literal but the way that R. Elazar conveyed how long he had struggled to understand something that perplexed him. He shows us what it means to hold on to issues that are mentally perplexing for as long as it takes until wisdom builds around them and reveals a way forward.

Name a recent insight into a long-held problem and how it felt.

Share one conundrum that you still wonder about and for which you wish you had a better, more satisfying answer.

BLESSED IS THE OMNIPRESENT

This short song offers a welcome break from the story of storytelling,

כְּנֶגֶד אַרְבָּעָה בָנִים

The Torah relates
to four types of sons –
    one who is wise,
    one who is wicked,
    one with a simple nature,
    and one who does not know how to ask.

---

shall say to him, 'With a strong hand the LORD brought us out of Egypt, from the grip of slavery'" (Ex. 13:14).

The last verse is the meaning of ritual and action as a result of our history. It is our opportunity to explain, when prompted, why we do what we do as a result of what happened to us. "When in time your children ask you, 'What are the testimonies, the statutes, and laws that the LORD our God commanded you?' you shall say to your children, 'We were slaves to Pharaoh in Egypt and the LORD our God brought us out of there with a strong hand'" (Deut. 6:20–21).

The sages of the Talmud identified four sons who all needed to hear the same story but needed to hear it differently to understand it and to be inspired by it. But these verses can also tell us that curiosity works differently at different life stages or moments. We ask questions about what is happening to us when it is happening. We listen to those who witness events that did not happen to us and try to understand the meaning it has for them. Sometimes we seek wisdom to understand the repercussions of events in our own lives. We make choices and then the choices make us, shaping us and those around us.

We often like to assign these parts to different siblings or those with different personality traits. Why?

Parents are often stymied by just how different their children are, one from the other. For a few minutes, engage in the reverse of this exercise. Name four qualities that are similar in all of your children/siblings or those around the table. Too often we look for differences rather than highlighting similarities. Let tonight be really different and seek commonalities.

כְּנֶגֶד אַרְבָּעָה בָנִים דִּבְּרָה תוֹרָה
אֶחָד חָכָם
וְאֶחָד רָשָׁע
וְאֶחָד תָּם
וְאֶחָד שֶׁאֵינוֹ יוֹדֵעַ לִשְׁאֹל

THE TORAH RELATES TO FOUR TYPES OF SONS

The four children identified here are based on the four verses in the Haggada, three in Exodus and one in Deuteronomy. When examined carefully, they each reveal a different context in which you would address a child. They represent not only four types of children (as described in detail in "The Four Sons, the Right Question" in the essay section of this book), but four different types of telling. In the first verse, the ritual of the Paschal lamb is taking place in real time. It is an experiential question, a question asked at the very moment to explain an action. Why are you taking this lamb that is holy in Egypt and slaughtering it and sacrificing it and putting its blood on the doorpost? I have never seen this. It does not make sense. This is the telling of explanation, an origin story, the etiology of why we do what we do. "And when your children ask you, 'What is this service to you?' you shall say, 'It is a Pesaḥ offering for the LORD, for He passed over the houses of the Children of Israel in Egypt while He struck the Egyptians, but saved those in our homes'" (Ex. 12:26–27).

The second verse is an act of witnessing. It is not prompted by a question asked by a child but by the need and responsibility that the one who experiences something monumental must transmit it to one who has not seen it. "And you shall explain to your son on that day, 'Because of this the LORD acted for me when I came out of Egypt'" (Ex. 13:8). The child is part of the experience in the first verse. This second child is only told about it.

The third verse offers an explanation of meaning. We describe not what is happening or what happened once but the significance of it for our lives now. It is the story of what events mean to us personally and nationally: "And when, in time to come, your son asks you, saying, 'What is this?' you

The

WISE SON

what does he say?

"What are the testimonies, the statutes, and laws,

Deut. 6

that the LORD our God commanded you?"

And you must tell him the laws of Pesaḥ:

"After eating the Pesaḥ offering

one does not eat anything more."

The

WICKED SON

what does he say?

"What is this service to you?"

Ex. 12

"To you," he says, not to him.

When he sets himself apart from the community,

he denies the very core of our beliefs.

And you must set his teeth on edge and tell him,

"Because of this

Ex. 13

the LORD acted for me when I came out of Egypt."

"For *me*," and not for *him*;

had he been there he would not have been redeemed.

---

the nature of intelligence. Wisdom can express itself in asking about the detailed laws around a holiday – "what are the testimonies, the statutes, and laws" – or it can come in the broad philosophical sweep of history that comes with perspective – "with a strong hand the LORD brought us out of Egypt."

What do you think: is intelligence about the trees or the forest?

How do we measure intelligence in children? How should we?

חָכָם

מַה הוּא אוֹמֵר

דברים ו

מָה הָעֵדֹת וְהַחֻקִּים וְהַמִּשְׁפָּטִים
אֲשֶׁר צִוָּה יהוה אֱלֹהֵינוּ אֶתְכֶם:
וְאַף אַתָּה אֱמָר לוֹ כְּהִלְכוֹת הַפֶּסַח
אֵין מַפְטִירִין אַחַר הַפֶּסַח אֲפִיקוֹמָן.

רָשָׁע

מַה הוּא אוֹמֵר

שמות יב

מָה הָעֲבֹדָה הַזֹּאת לָכֶם:
לָכֶם וְלֹא לוֹ
וּלְפִי שֶׁהוֹצִיא אֶת עַצְמוֹ מִן הַכְּלָל
כָּפַר בָּעִקָּר
וְאַף אַתָּה הַקְהֵה אֶת שִׁנָּיו, וֶאֱמָר לוֹ

שמות יג

בַּעֲבוּר זֶה עָשָׂה יהוה לִי בְּצֵאתִי מִמִּצְרָיִם:
לִי וְלֹא לוֹ
אִלּוּ הָיָה שָׁם, לֹא הָיָה נִגְאָל.

THE WISE SON

In the Jerusalem Talmud, the answers given to the simple son and the wise
son are reversed. This touch of irony clues us into different perspectives on

The
SIMPLE-NATURED SON
what does he say?
"What is this?" Ex. 13
> And you must tell him,
> "With a strong hand Ibid.
> the LORD brought us out of Egypt,
> from the grip of slavery."

And the
ONE WHO DOES NOT KNOW HOW TO ASK
you must open [the story] for him,
as it is said:
> "And you shall tell your child Ex. 13
> on that day,
> 'Because of this the LORD acted for me
> when I came out of Egypt.'"

---

child not only of a family but of our entire community. This child has the obligation to know this story because he owns it the same way as any other Jewish child. The parent of this child has the obligation to find a way to make this story meaningful regardless. There is room at this table for all. Be the storyteller who finds the way inside every heart.

Share a life discovery you made because someone with a disability taught you something you could not learn on your own.

Do you think Jewish life has created enough room for those with special needs?

AND THE ONE WHO DOES NOT KNOW HOW TO ASK
"You must open for him" is the literal translation and a resplendent verb
choice. This night is not only about opening up the story, but about

Continued on the next page.

תָּם

מָה הוּא אוֹמֵר

שמות יג

מַה־זֹּאת

וְאָמַרְתָּ אֵלָיו

שם

בְּחֹזֶק יָד הוֹצִיאָנוּ יהוה מִמִּצְרַיִם

מִבֵּית עֲבָדִים:

וְשֶׁאֵינוֹ יוֹדֵעַ לִשְׁאֹל

אַתְּ פְּתַח לוֹ

שֶׁנֶּאֱמַר

וְהִגַּדְתָּ לְבִנְךָ

שמות יג

בַּיּוֹם הַהוּא לֵאמֹר

בַּעֲבוּר זֶה עָשָׂה יהוה לִי

בְּצֵאתִי מִמִּצְרָיִם:

THE SIMPLE-NATURED SON

In the Jerusalem Talmud, this child is called not a "*tam*," a simpleton, but a "*tipesh*," a stupid child. We often regard this son as simply too young to ask a sophisticated question about history and memory, but the Jerusalem Talmud, with its bald use of language, offers a different interpretation that is at once more harsh and more radical. The young child of our rendition will grow into knowledge even if he developmentally cannot understand this story with its narrative complexities. The child of the Jerusalem Talmud is the child with limited mental capacity. We do not give up on this child because this is the story of the community we have created. This child is a

וְהִגַּדְתָּ לְבִנְךָ

"AND YOU SHALL TELL YOUR CHILD" –
One might have thought
this meant from the beginning of the month.
And so it says,
> "on that day."

Had it said only
> "on that day,"

one might have thought [the obligation] applied during the day.
And so it also says, "Because of this" –
"because of *this*" can only be said
when matza and bitter herbs are there before you.

ONE MIGHT HAVE THOUGHT THIS MEANT
FROM THE BEGINNING OF THE MONTH

This passage references the verse that marks the beginning of Jewish time, so to speak. God approached Moses and Aaron in the land of Egypt and said, "This month shall mark for you the beginning of the months; it shall be the first of the months of the year for you" (Ex. 12:1). This chapter mentions time again and again; days take on special significance and they will become festive occasions of memory and delight later in history. It is as if the entire chapter conveys a sense that time only begins when you leave servitude, and time is your own for the first time to determine and shape. You have the autonomy to use your time as you see fit, an act of independence and freedom. But the days in this biblical chapter do not refer merely to the time that the sun is up, the Haggada tells us, but to the nights as well, specially the nights when the props of the Seder sit before us and invite us to tell their story. We transition immediately to the header "beginnings" because we now begin our story anew as *our* story, one that is self-determined.

Throw out the calendar for a moment and imagine a date/event when your life really started.

Is there a life-defining event or time that you find yourself often thinking about day and night? If so, why?

וְהִגַּדְתָּ לְבִנְךָ

יָכוֹל מֵראשׁ חֹדֶשׁ

תַּלְמוּד לוֹמַר:

בַּיּוֹם הַהוּא.

אִי בַּיּוֹם הַהוּא יָכוֹל מִבְּעוֹד יוֹם

תַּלְמוּד לוֹמַר:

בַּעֲבוּר זֶה.

בַּעֲבוּר זֶה לֹא אָמַרְתִּי

אֶלָּא

בְּשָׁעָה שֶׁיֵּשׁ מַצָּה וּמָרוֹר

מֻנָּחִים לְפָנֶיךָ.

identifying the nexus where an idea and an individual can meet and a story takes on relevance, personal meaning, and urgency. Find the opening, the portal. The sages were master educators, and like all great educators, they were interested in opening minds, in building capacity to learn. What gets in the way of that opening? It is the child or adult who is closed, who cannot open up emotionally or intellectually. It is the person who cannot change his or her mind or experience pain and joy fully because of layers of protection: defensiveness, criticism, sarcasm, a false coating of strength. Let it all go. Dissolve it in the beauty of the evening, in the majesty of the family, and the divinity of the story. We ask this night that all at the Seder stop needlessly protecting themselves. God watches this night. Make yourself as open as possible and possibilities will open up for you as they once opened up for our ancestors.

 Think of an opening that you once grabbed that changed your life. Share it. When is the last time you did something for the first time? How was it?

מִתְּחִלָּה

IN THE BEGINNING, our ancestors were idol worshippers.

BUT NOW the Omnipresent has drawn us close in His service;
as it is said: "Joshua said to all the people,   *Josh. 24*
'This is what the LORD God of Israel has said:
Beyond the river your ancestors always dwelled –
Terah the father of Abraham, the father of Nahor –
and they served other gods.
But I took your father Abraham from beyond the river,
and I led him all the way across the land of Canaan,
and I multiplied his offspring and gave him Isaac.
And to Isaac I gave Jacob and Esau,
and I gave Esau Mount Seir as an inheritance,
**WHILE JACOB AND HIS CHILDREN
WENT DOWN TO EGYPT.'"**

———————————————————————————————————

arm, were once idol worshippers? This will grab you, the storyteller thinks.
And then the tale continues…

Begin an intriguing sentence with something you once were that you are not
any more.
Now explain why. We want to understand the transformation.

IN THE BEGINNING, OUR ANCESTORS WERE IDOL WORSHIPPERS
We did not expect our beginning in the Book of Joshua, but in the beginning of Genesis. Instead, we get the perspective of a storyteller looking
back at those beginnings, helping us make intentional choices about the
beginnings of the story we will tell tonight. Joshua tells this to people who
have crossed into their own land, finally, and returned. In order to heighten
the momentous nature of this journey, Joshua returns to our humble, unexpected beginnings, which makes our arrival that much sweeter.

Now offer a sentence about yourself in an imagined future, but state it in the
present as if you were currently experiencing it.
Try the same exercise, but this time with an aspiration of someplace or someone
you would really like to be.

מִתְּחִלָּה עוֹבְדֵי עֲבוֹדָה זָרָה הָיוּ אֲבוֹתֵינוּ

וְעַכְשָׁו קֵרְבָנוּ הַמָּקוֹם לַעֲבוֹדָתוֹ

שֶׁנֶּאֱמַר

יהושע כד

וַיֹּאמֶר יְהוֹשֻׁעַ אֶל־כָּל־הָעָם, כֹּה־אָמַר יהוה אֱלֹהֵי יִשְׂרָאֵל

בְּעֵבֶר הַנָּהָר יָשְׁבוּ אֲבוֹתֵיכֶם מֵעוֹלָם

תֶּרַח אֲבִי אַבְרָהָם וַאֲבִי נָחוֹר

וַיַּעַבְדוּ אֱלֹהִים אֲחֵרִים:

וָאֶקַּח אֶת־אֲבִיכֶם אֶת־אַבְרָהָם מֵעֵבֶר הַנָּהָר

וָאוֹלֵךְ אוֹתוֹ בְּכָל־אֶרֶץ כְּנָעַן

וָאַרְבֶּה אֶת־זַרְעוֹ, וָאֶתֶּן־לוֹ אֶת־יִצְחָק:

וָאֶתֵּן לְיִצְחָק אֶת־יַעֲקֹב וְאֶת־עֵשָׂו

וָאֶתֵּן לְעֵשָׂו אֶת־הַר שֵׂעִיר לָרֶשֶׁת אוֹתוֹ

וְיַעֲקֹב וּבָנָיו יָרְדוּ מִצְרָיִם:

IN THE BEGINNING, OUR ANCESTORS WERE IDOL WORSHIPPERS

When does a story begin? It begins when the storyteller makes a choice. Open the page of any book and you will see a choice. Beginnings are intentional. Rashi writes that, "*kol hathalot kashot,*" all beginnings are difficult (Ex. 19:5). They are difficult primarily because they involve choices and limitations. If I start something at some time then I have excluded something else. If I start somewhere then I have not started somewhere else. The beginning signals to us that this is where a tale really starts, where a lesson derives its meaning, where enough context has been offered so that the inherent drama and conflict make sense and the plot is ready to take flight. The beginning must get your attention quickly. The Haggada's beginning is this: our ancestors were idol worshippers. This is a striking confession. We begin with a surprise – did you know that the founders of monotheism, who built their relationship with God on the premise of His outstretched

**BLESSED IS THE ONE
WHO HAS KEPT HIS PROMISE TO ISRAEL –**
blessed is He.
For the Holy One calculated the end
and fulfilled what He had spoken to our father Abraham
in the Covenant Between the Pieces.
As it is said: "He said to Abram, 'Know that your descendants   *Gen. 15*
will be strangers in a land not their own, and they will be enslaved
and oppressed for four hundred years;
but know that I shall judge the nation that enslaves them,
AND THEN THEY WILL LEAVE WITH GREAT WEALTH.'"

וְהִיא שֶׁעָמְדָה   *The matzot are covered and the wine cup is raised.*

AND THIS

[promise] is what has stood by our ancestors and us;
for it was not only one man who rose up to destroy us:
in every single generation people rise up to destroy us –

**BUT THE HOLY ONE, BLESSED BE HE,
SAVES US FROM THEIR HANDS.**

The wine cup is put down and the matzot are uncovered.

Abraham to understand that the suffering he faced as an individual who
was yet unable to have a child was a microcosm of the difficulties ahead as a
nation. Do not fall victim to the fate in front of you. It is still the beginning.

*Think of a time when you were thwarted by the way your life was unraveling.
How did you overcome it and get to a better ending/beginning?*

*This is a prayer about celebrating promises that were kept. Can you construct a
short prayer about a promise you kept or want to keep to someone or a promise
that someone else kept for you?*

AND THIS [PROMISE] IS WHAT HAS STOOD
Taking the long view demands that we see what stands in our way; in
fact, we recognize that someone or something always will. But we will be

Continued on the next page.

בָּרוּךְ שׁוֹמֵר הַבְטָחָתוֹ לְיִשְׂרָאֵל

בָּרוּךְ הוּא

שֶׁהַקָּדוֹשׁ בָּרוּךְ הוּא חִשַּׁב אֶת הַקֵּץ

לַעֲשׂוֹת כְּמָה שֶׁאָמַר לְאַבְרָהָם אָבִינוּ בִּבְרִית בֵּין הַבְּתָרִים

שֶׁנֶּאֱמַר, וַיֹּאמֶר לְאַבְרָם יָדֹעַ תֵּדַע כִּי־גֵר יִהְיֶה זַרְעֲךָ בְּאֶרֶץ לֹא לָהֶם

וַעֲבָדוּם וְעִנּוּ אֹתָם אַרְבַּע מֵאוֹת שָׁנָה:

וְגַם אֶת־הַגּוֹי אֲשֶׁר יַעֲבֹדוּ דָּן אָנֹכִי

וְאַחֲרֵי־כֵן יֵצְאוּ בִּרְכֻשׁ גָּדוֹל:

בראשית טו

The מצות are covered and the wine cup is raised.

וְהִיא

שֶׁעָמְדָה לַאֲבוֹתֵינוּ וְלָנוּ

שֶׁלֹּא אֶחָד בִּלְבַד עָמַד עָלֵינוּ לְכַלּוֹתֵנוּ

אֶלָּא שֶׁבְּכָל דּוֹר וָדוֹר עוֹמְדִים עָלֵינוּ לְכַלּוֹתֵנוּ

וְהַקָּדוֹשׁ בָּרוּךְ הוּא מַצִּילֵנוּ מִיָּדָם

The wine cup is put down and the מצות are uncovered.

BLESSED IS THE ONE WHO HAS KEPT HIS PROMISE

Now we turn to Genesis to look forward. Joshua asked us to look backwards. God asked Abraham to look forward. At a time when Abraham had not yet had one son, God promised that he would become a nation, so large that we would be countless in number. We would be a nation that formed itself in a strange land and suffered in that land, but also became great in number and great in wealth. This brief synopsis of our history tells Abraham to take the long-range view in a chapter when he perseverated on the fact that he did not have a child. If you believe that everything will be good in the end, and things are now decidedly bad, then it is not yet the end. God also wanted

צֵא וּלְמַד

GO [to the verse]
AND LEARN
what Laban the Aramean
sought to do to our father Jacob:
Pharaoh condemned only the boys to death,
but Laban sought to uproot everything,

This is the same advice we are given on this night. We cannot possibly cover the entire Exodus story. The Haggada offers us a helpful summation but then puts the responsibility back on us. Go forth and learn. Bring the text to the table and study together, and the Divine Presence will rest on your gathering.

When did you last "go and learn" simply for the sake of learning?
"Go and learn" is descriptive of a posture of ongoing curiosity. Who is the most curious person you know?

GO [TO THE VERSE] AND LEARN
The sages of the Talmud will now pastiche a group of texts together from the Book of Exodus and elsewhere to create a narrative quilt of scraps and fragments that they believe tells the Exodus story, highlighting what they felt were critical details. Three themes emerge in their understanding of what made us a nation and then what inspired the Exodus: our unexpected fertility, the change in the political landscape of Egypt, and our anguished enslavement. Each of these factors pushed on each other until we found ourselves unable to remain in Egypt. All three of these factors appear in the very first chapter of Exodus, setting the early groundwork for what would follow. We learn that Joseph dies, as do his brothers and "all that generation." This, however, does not signal the demise of the Jews. The very next verse – one that we will read a piece of momentarily – tells us just how prolific we became: "And the Children of Israel were fertile, and they swarmed, and grew more and more numerous and strong, and the land was filled with them." This verse contains every element of what would become the Exodus.

Continued on the next page.

צֵא וּלְמַד

מַה בִּקֵּשׁ לָבָן הָאֲרַמִּי
לַעֲשׂוֹת לְיַעֲקֹב אָבִינוּ
שֶׁפַּרְעֹה לֹא גָזַר
אֶלָּא עַל הַזְּכָרִים
וְלָבָן בִּקֵּשׁ לַעֲקֹר אֶת הַכֹּל

resilient and find ways to overcome it. Survival demands hope and it demands faith. When we look back at our impossible history, we find obstructions and obstructionists everywhere. We could not always overcome them. We just outlived them. Resilience involves grit, the capacity to make mistakes, live with pain, and multiply successes despite all of it.

Consider a persistent hurdle to your success and how you managed it time and again.

GO [TO THE VERSE] AND LEARN

The suggestion that we "go [to the verse] and learn" comes to us originally from Hillel the Elder's suggestion to a convert (Shabbat 31a). The convert came to Hillel after going to his famous debater Shammai and asking to be taught the Torah on one foot. That was the condition of his conversion. Shammai dismissed him outright. Hillel used a different approach. He offered an underlying Torah value, a fundamental principle of all relationships: "What is hateful to you, do not do to your neighbor" (an inversion of Lev. 19:18), which may be both a chastisement of Shammai – to dismiss a convert – and also a rebuke of the convert himself for asking a scholar to do that which is hateful – teach a Torah of superficiality. The rest is commentary, Hillel told him. Go and learn it. Hillel, like Shammai, was not prepared to teach the whole Torah through summation. He created a portal and then put the onus of education back on the convert. I cannot teach it all, but you must learn it all.

as it is written:

"MY FATHER WAS A WANDERING ARAMEAN,   *Deut. 26*
AND HE WENT DOWN TO EGYPT
AND RESIDED THERE,
JUST A HANDFUL OF SOULS;
AND THERE HE BECAME A NATION –
LARGE, MIGHTY, AND GREAT."

"AND HE WENT DOWN TO EGYPT" –
    Compelled by what had been spoken.

---

king "did not know Joseph." He had no institutional memory of Joseph's contributions to the Egyptian economy and the loyalty of his people that may have come with gratitude. Leadership transitions and successions are always risky and potentially perilous. We do not know what we do not know, but since the text tells us that one generation has passed and another has emerged that cares little about old allegiances, we know that tensions are on the horizon.

3. *Slavery* – Forced labor was the way that this new Pharaoh intended to control the population. No longer would the Jews enjoy the choice land of Egypt without paying a steep price. Curiously, the king spoke to his people rather than his ministers to develop a strategy to handle the population growth and possibility of a fifth column: "Look, the Israelite people are much too numerous for us. Let us deal cleverly with them." Instead of being an economic boon, the Jews were becoming an economic and security burden to Pharaoh. He searched for a strategy and in consulting with the people, was heightening their awareness of a growing problem in their midst. He made the Israelites economically useful by having them build his garrison cities, ironically becoming an instrument to secure Egyptian might. When this did not wear them down and stop the fertility march forward, the Egyptians became increasingly ruthless as taskmasters. This, too, failed. They could not find the clever strategy

Continued on the next page.

שֶׁנֶּאֱמַר

אֲרַמִּי אֹבֵד אָבִי

וַיֵּרֶד מִצְרַיְמָה

וַיָּגָר שָׁם בִּמְתֵי מְעָט

וַיְהִי־שָׁם לְגוֹי גָּדוֹל עָצוּם וָרָב

וַיֵּרֶד מִצְרַיְמָה

אָנוּס עַל פִּי הַדִּבּוּר

───────────────────────────────────

1. Sudden Population Explosion – Seventy people came down to Egypt – Joseph and his family – as we learn in Exodus. That is not "just a handful of souls" but it is a contrast to the large, mighty, and great nation we became there. Size is critical in creating a nation, but fertility problems lace all of Genesis. In the first chapter of Genesis, Adam and Eve were told to be fruitful and multiply. Yet we were unable to fulfill this mandate until the first chapter of Exodus; the text uses the very same language as Genesis. In addition to the words that we were finally fruitful, multiplied, and filled the earth, we have two more beguiling words: we were prolific, and we swarmed (the same word used in Genesis 1 to describe the proliferation of reptiles). The text is offering us two opposing views of fertility at the same time: where the Hebrews saw in their growth the realization of a divine vision, the Egyptians saw the population growth as a threat. And it seems that nothing could stop our sudden expansion and the Egyptian response to it: "But the more they were oppressed, the more they increased and spread out, so that the Egyptians came to dread the Israelites" (Ex 1:12).

2. Political Changes – In just three words, we learn that political change was on the horizon. "*Vayakam melekh ḥadash*" – a new king arose. This

"AND RESIDED THERE" –

From this,
learn that our father Jacob went down
not to be absorbed into Egypt,
but only to reside there for a time.
As it is said:
"They said to Pharaoh,   *Gen. 47*
'We have come to *reside* in this land,
for there is no pasture for your servants' flocks,
for the famine is heavy in the land of Canaan;
and now, if you please,
let your servants dwell in the land of Goshen.'"

"JUST A HANDFUL OF SOULS" –

As it is said:
"Your ancestors were but seventy souls   *Deut. 10*
when they went down to Egypt –
and now the LORD has made you
as many as the sky has stars."

Think beyond the Seder table tonight. What factors are contributing to Jewish growth and outreach?

What factors are diminishing our size and influence in the world today?

In Egypt, we needed numbers to become a nation. What do we need today to strengthen Jewish peoplehood?

AND NOW THE LORD HAS MADE YOU

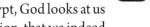

Stop right here. This verse in Deuteronomy should astound us. In evaluating who we became as a result of our immense growth in Egypt, God looks at us and concludes, in the words of Moses' farewell to the nation, that we indeed became as numerous as the stars. This promise of our future countlessness

Continued on the next page.

וַיָּגָר שָׁם

מְלַמֵּד שֶׁלֹּא יָרַד יַעֲקֹב אָבִינוּ
לְהִשְׁתַּקֵּעַ בְּמִצְרַיִם
אֶלָּא לָגוּר שָׁם
שֶׁנֶּאֱמַר

בראשית מז

וַיֹּאמְרוּ אֶל־פַּרְעֹה
לָגוּר בָּאָרֶץ בָּאנוּ
כִּי־אֵין מִרְעֶה לַצֹּאן אֲשֶׁר לַעֲבָדֶיךָ
כִּי־כָבֵד הָרָעָב בְּאֶרֶץ כְּנָעַן
וְעַתָּה יֵשְׁבוּ־נָא עֲבָדֶיךָ בְּאֶרֶץ גֹּשֶׁן:

בִּמְתֵי מְעָט

כְּמָה שֶׁנֶּאֱמַר

דברים י

בְּשִׁבְעִים נֶפֶשׁ יָרְדוּ אֲבֹתֶיךָ מִצְרָיְמָה
וְעַתָּה שָׂמְךָ יהוה אֱלֹהֶיךָ
כְּכוֹכְבֵי הַשָּׁמַיִם לָרֹב:

---

they sought. Next step: approach the midwives and force them to dispose of the males and have the females absorbed into the Egyptian people. But the midwives refused. Pharaoh then returned to the very body he had engaged at the beginning: his people. "Then Pharaoh charged all his people, saying, 'Throw every boy who is born into the river, and the girls let live.'" As we know too well in history, it is impossible to get rid of a population unless all of society is induced to participate in it and have something to gain by it.

"AND THERE HE BECAME A NATION" –

From this,
learn that Israel was distinct there.

"LARGE, MIGHTY" –

As it is said:
"And the Children of Israel were fertile,   *Ex. 1*
and they swarmed,
and grew *more and more numerous*
and strong,
and the land was filled with them."

FROM THIS, LEARN THAT ISRAEL WAS DISTINCT THERE

Jewish distinction according to one midrash (*Mekhilta* 12:28) lay in the
fact that we retained our Jewish names and our language. We also refrained
from gossip and did not engage in the immoral acts of the Egyptians
around us. These are foundational to nationhood. By keeping Jewish names
and our own distinctive language, we protected ourselves from the two
most obvious and public ways that people acculturate in a society. These
are internal decisions with external signs that tell others something about
our identity. Not gossiping or engaging in immorality are harder and require deeper inner work but are no less important because they shape the
reputation that we have when we live among others. There is always a risk
in distinction. Social differences and moral differences make any minority
stand out, hopefully for the good.

What, if anything, makes you distinctly Jewish among non-Jews in an external
way?

What, if anything, makes you distinctly Jewish among non-Jews in an internal
way?

וַיְהִי־שָׁם לְגוֹי
מְלַמֵּד שֶׁהָיוּ יִשְׂרָאֵל מְצֻיָּנִים שָׁם

גָּדוֹל עָצוּם
כְּמָה שֶׁנֶּאֱמַר
שמות א

וּבְנֵי יִשְׂרָאֵל פָּרוּ וַיִּשְׁרְצוּ וַיִּרְבּוּ
וַיַּעַצְמוּ בִּמְאֹד מְאֹד
וַתִּמָּלֵא הָאָרֶץ אֹתָם:

---

was given to Abraham multiple times – Genesis 12:2, 13:16, 15:5 – specifically at times when a fertility option for Abraham failed. Don't lose hope, Abraham. One day far into the future, you will not struggle with the identity of one heir but your people will spread out far beyond any imaginable number. Rabbi Samson Raphael Hirsch notes the connection between our verse, Deuteronomy 10:22, and the next one, which begins "And you shall love God." He writes, "This growth of the family into a nation occurring under God's miraculous power makes that nation regard itself as the sign of God's special care and by its very existence already feel in duty bound to God in love." God loved us so He made sure that that love grew with our own growth, nurturing us from a relatively small family to a vibrant, bustling nation. If you love something, you want more of it, not less of it. But there is more in our verse. We are not only numerous as the stars, because being a number has never been as important as the quality of each and every member. We *are* stars: elevated, sparkling, transcendent, luminous.

Take a moment at the Seder to reflect on the star power of our nation and feel group pride. Note some "Jewish" accomplishments of significance this past year or ones that have special significance for you.

How did you and those around you right now sparkle this past year?

"AND GREAT" –
As it is said:
"I let you *grow wild* like meadow plants,
and you grew and matured and came forth in all your glory,
your breasts full and your hair grown,
and you were naked and exposed."

Ezek. 16

Some add:
"And I passed by you
and saw you wallowing in your own blood –
and I said to you, 'In your blood, live!'
and I said, 'In your blood, live!'"

Ibid.

---

her, covering her with a mantle to signify their new boundedness to each other, their covenantal relationship. These verses are used here to reflect the romance of a budding nation taken from harsh beginnings to a magical ending. The verse specifically points to a time of rapid growth in the life of an adolescent woman, and the references in the Haggada to fertility and growth are naturally associated with women. Suddenly, a young girl discovers adulthood in her changing body, a metaphor here for the unexpected changes that the Israelites underwent almost overnight, as they go from a family of seventy to a slave nation beyond count. God is the "first-person" of the verse, so to speak, letting the Israelites grow wild in this setting of oppression so that when maturation takes place, the people will come "forth in all their glory." But the verse also notes another development that is not so positive. Just as you begin to notice the changes in yourself, so do others, creating a sense of uncomfortable exposure. Few adolescents emerge from this time in their lives without feeling vulnerable and awkward as changes take place. Many want to hide because not every change can be easily concealed. As the Israelites grew in number, the Egyptians noticed them and could not stop noticing them and the impact of their population explosion. It made them take action against us. It made God take action for us.

What is or was the hardest part of adolescence for you?
When you were at your most miserable at this stage of life, who mentored you and helped you emerge into adulthood?

וָרָב

יחזקאל טז

כְּמָה שֶׁנֶּאֱמַר

רְבָבָה כְּצֶמַח הַשָּׂדֶה נְתַתִּיךְ

וַתִּרְבִּי וַתִּגְדְּלִי, וַתָּבֹאִי בַּעֲדִי עֲדָיִים

שָׁדַיִם נָכֹנוּ וּשְׂעָרֵךְ צִמֵּחַ, וְאַתְּ עֵרֹם וְעֶרְיָה:

Some add:

שם

וָאֶעֱבֹר עָלַיִךְ וָאֶרְאֵךְ מִתְבּוֹסֶסֶת בְּדָמָיִךְ

וָאֹמַר לָךְ בְּדָמַיִךְ חֲיִי   וָאֹמַר לָךְ בְּדָמַיִךְ חֲיִי:

I LET YOU GROW WILD LIKE MEADOW PLANTS

These verses are among the hardest to understand in the Haggada, in part because they require translation into their metaphoric context and in part because in the biblical book from which they are excerpted, they appear in the reverse order. Only with a careful read of the passage do we begin to understand the way the rabbis of old wove together Ezekiel with the Exodus story:

> On the day you were born your cord was not cut, nor were you washed with water to make you clean, nor were you rubbed with salt or wrapped in cloths. No one looked on you with pity or had compassion enough to do any of these things for you. Rather, you were thrown out into the open field, for on the day you were born you were despised. And I passed by you and saw you wallowing in your own blood – and I said to you, "In your blood, live!" and I said, "In your blood, live!" I let you grow wild like meadow plants, and you grew and matured and came forth in all your glory, your breasts full and your hair grown, and you were naked and exposed. Later I passed by, and when I looked at you and saw that you were old enough for love, I spread the corner of my garment over you and covered your nakedness. I gave you my solemn oath and entered into a covenant with you, declares the Sovereign LORD, and you became Mine. (Ezek. 16:4–8)

A poor infant was left to die in an open field. The child was despised and neglected, wallowing in her blood. The one who passed by her willed her to live and nurtured her through a blooming adolescence and then married

"AND THE EGYPTIANS DEALT CRUELLY WITH US

AND OPPRESSED US,

AND IMPOSED HARD LABOR ON US."

Deut. 26

"THE EGYPTIANS DEALT CRUELLY WITH US" –
    As it is said:
    "We must act wisely against [this people],
    in case it grows great,
    and when we are called to war
    they may join our enemies,
    fight against us,
    and rise up to leave the land."

Ex. 1

"AND OPPRESSED US" –
    As it is said:
    "They placed taskmasters over [the people]
    to *oppress* them under their burdens;
    they built store cities for Pharaoh:
    Pithom and Raamses."

Ex. 1

And yet, from Pharaoh's perspective, population control must be handled with care. Saadia Gaon suggests that Pharaoh wanted to confuse us. Rashi says that the term *"hava"* is an invitation for readiness and preparation. In other words, let us be strategic. Any empire builder must take pains to ensure that the provinces and nations that comprise his empire are not decimated willy-nilly, creating grounds for confusion and rebellion. Nahmanides suggests as much when he says that Pharaoh and his counselors never suggested outright death by the sword because it would throw his country into panic. In the animal world, populations are kept down in size through hunting. Pharaoh tried a more magnanimous approach that he thought was strategic. If you make life hard enough for a

Continued on the next page.

דברים כו

וַיָּרֵעוּ אֹתָנוּ הַמִּצְרִים
וַיְעַנּוּנוּ
וַיִּתְּנוּ עָלֵינוּ עֲבֹדָה קָשָׁה:

וַיָּרֵעוּ אֹתָנוּ הַמִּצְרִים

שמות א

כְּמָה שֶׁנֶּאֱמַר
הָבָה נִתְחַכְּמָה לוֹ פֶּן־יִרְבֶּה
וְהָיָה כִּי־תִקְרֶאנָה מִלְחָמָה
וְנוֹסַף גַּם־הוּא עַל־שֹׂנְאֵינוּ
וְנִלְחַם־בָּנוּ
וְעָלָה מִן־הָאָרֶץ:

וַיְעַנּוּנוּ

שמות א

כְּמָה שֶׁנֶּאֱמַר
וַיָּשִׂימוּ עָלָיו שָׂרֵי מִסִּים
לְמַעַן עַנֹּתוֹ בְּסִבְלֹתָם
וַיִּבֶן עָרֵי מִסְכְּנוֹת לְפַרְעֹה
אֶת־פִּתֹם וְאֶת־רַעַמְסֵס:

AND THE EGYPTIANS DEALT CRUELLY WITH US AND OPPRESSED US
Pharaoh said he wanted to act wisely, but we understand it as acting
shrewdly, with a piercing and callous sort of strategy. We don't view his
strategy as particularly wise because we were victimized on its account.

"AND IMPOSED HARD LABOR ON US" –

> As it is said:
> "The Egyptians enslaved the Children of Israel
> with *heavy labor.*"

Ex. 1

> may not be ruined by the famine. The plan seemed good to Pharaoh and
> to all his officials. (Gen. 41:34–37)

The plan worked so spectacularly that Egypt dominated the global market
as a result:

> When all Egypt began to feel the famine, the people cried to Pharaoh for
> food. Then Pharaoh told all the Egyptians, "Go to Joseph and do what he
> tells you." When the famine had spread over the whole country, Joseph
> opened the storehouses and sold grain to the Egyptians, for the famine
> was severe throughout Egypt. And all the countries came to Egypt to
> buy grain from Joseph, because the famine was severe in all the world.
> (Gen. 41:55–57)

The Pharaoh of old understood nothing about economics and sent all
who inquired to Joseph to "do what he tells you." The new Pharaoh of
our slave labor perhaps learned too well from Joseph to tackle large-scale
problems – like famine and population control – with a strategic eye to
the future. Storing food in times of abundance for leaner years became
the norm. It became such a conventional solution that Jews were forced
to build additional storehouses in Pithom and Raamses to implement
the plan that Joseph originally put in place. The hard labor referenced
in the verse we read here may be more than simple manual drudgery. Attached to the physical burden was the psychic burden of knowing that this
plan of storing grain in large amounts was traced back to their very own
ancestor.

*Life takes ironic turns. When in history did we pay a negative price for an earlier
positive development?*

*When in your life did you pay a negative price for an earlier positive develop-
ment?*

וַיִּתְּנוּ עָלֵינוּ עֲבֹדָה קָשָׁה
כְּמָה שֶׁנֶּאֱמַר
וַיַּעֲבִדוּ מִצְרַיִם אֶת־בְּנֵי יִשְׂרָאֵל בְּפָרֶךְ:

שמות א

---

minority, they will not flood your borders nor will they grow internally, because people do not want to create new life when the old life is hard and unyielding. Intensive labor seemed like a reasonable solution. Over the course of chapter 1, Pharaoh's methods increase in cruelty and scope because his strategy kept failing. His incremental approach was wise in the sense that had he started off by throwing male children into the river, the Israelites may have seen sharper warning signals and done more to either leave or change. The slow developments in Pharaoh's plan may have thrown off the Israelites from understanding the true evil behind Pharaoh's plot.

Think of a time when you dealt wisely with something. What do you mean by this?

Consider instances where your intelligence failed or frustrated you and simple-mindedness would have served you better.

AND IMPOSED HARD LABOR ON US

Ironically, we may have created the conditions for our own downfall. When Joseph interpreted Pharaoh's dreams of economic success followed by economic downfall, Joseph dealt wisely and created a strategy of savings that augmented Pharaoh's largesse and kept the people fed through famine. Joseph interpreted Pharaoh's dream into two distinct phases of the Egyptian economy:

> Let Pharaoh appoint commissioners over the land to take a fifth of the harvest of Egypt during the seven years of abundance. They should collect all the food of these good years that are coming and store up the grain under the authority of Pharaoh, to be kept in the cities for food. This food should be held in reserve for the country, to be used during the seven years of famine that will come upon Egypt, so that the country

"AND WE CRIED OUT TO THE LORD,
GOD OF OUR ANCESTORS,
AND THE LORD HEARD OUR VOICE,
AND HE SAW OUR OPPRESSION
AND OUR LABOR AND SLAVERY."

"AND WE CRIED OUT TO THE LORD,
GOD OF OUR ANCESTORS" –

> As it is said:
> "It came to be,
> as a long time passed,
> that the king of Egypt died,
> and the Children of Israel
> groaned under the burden of work,
> and they *cried out,*
> and their plea rose to God from amid the work."

Ex. 2

---

only now because only now has a leader been identified. If there is no one to hear our cries, then we withhold them and become numb to our own pain. Once a human partner in our salvation is introduced, we can begin to cry. Silence turns into groaning. Anguish turns into prayer. Prayer turns into advocacy. Advocacy turns into song. In only fifteen chapters, we moved from silence to song because a leader was introduced who shepherded that miraculous trajectory. Never believe that one person cannot change history. Great leaders have always been able to muster singular commitment to change.

Describe a time in your life when you moved all the way from silence to song, either literally or metaphorically.

When was the last time you gave voice for someone who could not speak up?

וַנִּצְעַק אֶל־יהוה אֱלֹהֵי אֲבֹתֵינוּ
וַיִּשְׁמַע יהוה אֶת־קֹלֵנוּ
וַיַּרְא אֶת־עָנְיֵנוּ
וְאֶת־עֲמָלֵנוּ
וְאֶת־לַחֲצֵנוּ:

וַנִּצְעַק אֶל־יהוה אֱלֹהֵי אֲבֹתֵינוּ

כְּמָה שֶׁנֶּאֱמַר

וַיְהִי בַיָּמִים הָרַבִּים הָהֵם
וַיָּמָת מֶלֶךְ מִצְרַיִם
וַיֵּאָנְחוּ בְנֵי־יִשְׂרָאֵל מִן־הָעֲבֹדָה
וַיִּזְעָקוּ
וַתַּעַל שַׁוְעָתָם אֶל־הָאֱלֹהִים מִן־הָעֲבֹדָה:

AND WE CRIED OUT TO THE LORD

Why didn't the Jews cry out in the first chapter of Exodus, when they first experienced the Egyptian change of heart, their new harsh and cruel treatment? Rabbi Joseph Soloveitchik answers this by posing what is, on the surface, a literary question. The first twenty-two verses of Exodus chapter 2 tell the early biography of Moses as a leader: his birth and early upbringing, his killing of a taskmaster and his flight of refuge in Midian that ended with marriage and childbirth. The last three verses of the chapter offer a different view. At this time, the Israelites cried to God and God remembered the covenant as we read here in the Haggada. They cry

"AND THE LORD HEARD OUR VOICE" –

As it is said:
"And God *heard* their groans,
and God remembered His covenant
with Abraham, Isaac, and Jacob."

Ex. 2

"AND HE SAW OUR OPPRESSION" –

The separation of husband from wife,
as it is said:
"And God saw the Children of Israel,
and God knew."

Ex. 2

---

the burden of our work as if it weighed us down and covered us. He heard our cry and rather than see our broken faith, God returned us to the faith of our ancestors and saved us because of those relationships, trying to help us reconnect to them the way God did. We were not broken links in a chain but bent links, our belief bent and misshapen because we no longer knew what to believe. Oppressive labor bends people out of shape physically and spiritually. It makes our backs and our beliefs crooked.

Oppression takes many forms. One aspect of persecution is that the existential pain of existence is so great that couples decide not to have children. No one wants to bring children into a world of pain and suffering, particularly when relief is unimaginable. One way to control a population growth is to make the world so miserable that people begin to shrink themselves. Children are all about hope in a future unseen. That is why so much is made of the midwives and the birth of Moses. Our growth in spite of oppression is a sign that we never lost hope in redemption, that we sought our revenge by multiplying our hope in a future unseen.

Can you recall a time when your faith felt bent by difficult circumstances?

Can you recall a time when your faith was strengthened by difficult circumstances?

וַיִּשְׁמַע יהוה אֶת־קֹלֵנוּ

כְּמָה שֶׁנֶּאֱמַר

שמות ב

וַיִּשְׁמַע אֱלֹהִים אֶת־נַאֲקָתָם

וַיִּזְכֹּר אֱלֹהִים אֶת־בְּרִיתוֹ

אֶת־אַבְרָהָם

אֶת־יִצְחָק

וְאֶת־יַעֲקֹב:

וַיַּרְא אֶת־עָנְיֵנוּ

זוֹ פְּרִישׁוּת דֶּרֶךְ אֶרֶץ

כְּמָה שֶׁנֶּאֱמַר

שמות ב

וַיַּרְא אֱלֹהִים אֶת־בְּנֵי יִשְׂרָאֵל, וַיֵּדַע אֱלֹהִים:

AND HE SAW OUR OPPRESSION

When we tell our story this night, we must speak of our emotional state. We were oppressed. We cried out. Because we cried out, God heard us and remembered our covenant. When we say this, we are struck with a terrible thought. Could it be that God forgot our covenant and, therefore, let us suffer willingly under Egyptian cruelty? This lapse in protection made us feel abandoned and neglected. Alternatively, we can read this not as God's break with us but our break with God. As our difficulties thickened, we did not plead with God for salvation but blamed God for our fate and harsh treatment, as is often the case with man-made calamities that we shoulder onto God. We removed ourselves from Him and distanced ourselves from any intimacy with and dependency on the Divine Presence. In fact, we turned Divine Presence into Divine Absence, which itself became another form of oppression: apartness from God. God heard us groan from under

"AND OUR LABOR" –
> [The killing of] the sons,
> as it is said:
> "Throw every boy who is born into the river,
> > and the girls let live."

Ex. 1

"AND SLAVERY" –
> The forced labor that was pressed down on them,
> as it is said:
> "I have seen the *slavery*
> that Egypt forced upon you."

Ex. 3

"AND THE LORD BROUGHT US OUT OF EGYPT
WITH A STRONG HAND AND AN OUTSTRETCHED ARM,
IN AN AWESOME HAPPENING,
WITH SIGNS AND WITH WONDERS."

Deut. 26

"AND THE LORD BROUGHT US OUT OF EGYPT" –
> Not through an angel,
> not through a seraph,
> not through any emissary.
> No, it was the Holy One, His glory,
> His own presence.

AND THE LORD BROUGHT US OUT OF EGYPT WITH A STRONG HAND

Although we do not believe in anthropomorphism, we do enlist an image of God's outstretched arm again and again, such that the Haggada will later pick up on the image of a hand and its fingers with numerical word-plays. Hand imagery abounds in this section. Hands can be instruments of violence or loving affection. When we think of the relationship between God and man through this imagery, we are often drawn to Michelangelo's

Continued on the next page.

וְאֶת־עֲמָלֵנוּ

אֵלוּ הַבָּנִים

כְּמָה שֶׁנֶּאֱמַר

שמות א

כָּל־הַבֵּן הַיִּלּוֹד, הַיְאֹרָה תַּשְׁלִיכֻהוּ
וְכָל־הַבַּת תְּחַיּוּן:

וְאֶת־לַחֲצֵנוּ

זֶה הַדְּחַק

כְּמָה שֶׁנֶּאֱמַר

שמות ג

וְגַם־רָאִיתִי אֶת־הַלַּחַץ
אֲשֶׁר מִצְרַיִם לֹחֲצִים אֹתָם:

דברים כו

וַיּוֹצִאֵנוּ יהוה מִמִּצְרַיִם

בְּיָד חֲזָקָה וּבִזְרֹעַ נְטוּיָה
וּבְמֹרָא גָּדֹל
וּבְאֹתוֹת וּבְמֹפְתִים:

וַיּוֹצִאֵנוּ יהוה מִמִּצְרַיִם
לֹא עַל יְדֵי מַלְאָךְ
וְלֹא עַל יְדֵי שָׂרָף
וְלֹא עַל יְדֵי שָׁלִיחַ
אֶלָּא הַקָּדוֹשׁ בָּרוּךְ הוּא בִּכְבוֹדוֹ וּבְעַצְמוֹ

As it is said:

 "I shall pass through the land of Egypt on that night;   *Ex. 12*
 I shall kill every firstborn son in the land of Egypt,
 man and beast,
 and I shall pass judgment on all the gods of Egypt:
 I am the LORD."

 "I shall pass through
 the land of Egypt on that night" –
      I and no angel.
 "I shall kill every firstborn son in
     the land of Egypt" –
     I and no seraph.
 "And I shall pass judgment on all
     the gods of Egypt" –
     I and no emissary.
 "I am the LORD" –
     It is I and no other.

I SHALL PASS THROUGH THE LAND OF EGYPT ON THAT NIGHT
If you look carefully at the verses above, they all have a stirring and startling
"I" in them, usually at the beginning of the verse. This "I" emphasizes the
intimacy of salvation. God wanted to be at the very heart of this transformation, speaking and acting the redemption, personally vested in the success
of the mission. These verses also stress the divine nature of the cause. While
Moses was the human conduit, this was not merely what we would call lob-
bying for social justice. It needed to be encased in a sense of transcendence,
that which goes beyond and above humanity since humans, sadly, cannot
always be counted on for both passion and compassion in proper balance.

*Name a time when you knew that a job well done had to be done by you
alone.*

*When has it happened that responsibility called and you could not delegate it
to someone else?*

שֶׁנֶּאֱמַר

שמות יב

וְעָבַרְתִּי בְאֶרֶץ־מִצְרַיִם בַּלַּיְלָה הַזֶּה

וְהִכֵּיתִי כָל־בְּכוֹר בְּאֶרֶץ מִצְרַיִם, מֵאָדָם וְעַד־בְּהֵמָה

וּבְכָל־אֱלֹהֵי מִצְרַיִם אֶעֱשֶׂה שְׁפָטִים

אֲנִי יהוה:

וְעָבַרְתִּי בְאֶרֶץ־מִצְרַיִם

אֲנִי וְלֹא מַלְאָךְ

וְהִכֵּיתִי כָל־בְּכוֹר

אֲנִי וְלֹא שָׂרָף

וּבְכָל־אֱלֹהֵי מִצְרַיִם אֶעֱשֶׂה שְׁפָטִים

אֲנִי וְלֹא הַשָּׁלִיחַ

אֲנִי יהוה

אֲנִי הוּא וְלֹא אַחֵר

---

iconic finger of God touching Adam's finger, bringing him to life. When
we think of injustice, we think of the righteous indignation of a clenched
fist raised high in the air. We think of the outstretched arm picking up the
vulnerable and injured. We imagine the handshake in a peace negotiation
and the arms used to embrace those who were once enemies. Moses' signs
and wonders came from holding out his staff, almost acting as an extension
of his arm. Moses, like God, offered an outstretched arm. The biblical texts
and the mandate to act in *imitatio Dei* – in God's image – ask us to think
about how we should outstretch our own arms to lend a hand to others,
and about all the kindnesses we could extend.

Name a mitzva you do with your hands.

*Think of a time when someone stretched out an arm to help you in your time
of need.*

When did you last outstretch your arm in protest or charity?

"WITH A STRONG HAND" –

This refers to the pestilence,
as it is said:
"You shall see the *hand* of the LORD   *Ex. 9*
among your cattle in the field,
among your horses and donkeys and camels,
in the herd and in the flock,
bringing harsh, heavy pestilence."

"AND AN OUTSTRETCHED ARM" –

This refers to the sword,
as it is said:
"And His sword was drawn in His hand,   *1 Chron.*
stretched out over Jerusalem."   *21*

---

tion and not merely convenience for human beings. God intended it that
way. We learned this straight from the Book of Job: "He teaches us from the
animals of the land, and from the birds of the heavens, He makes us wise"
(35:11). The Talmud says that "Had the Torah not been given, we would
have learned modesty from a cat, not to steal from an ant, fidelity from the
dove, and good manners in sexual relationships from the rooster" (Eiruvin
100b). Rashi there specifically comments that God put wisdom in each of
the animals to teach us lessons in character as human beings.

Think of your pets or animals that you have observed. Name one character trait
that you have witnessed in an animal that you would like to work on in your
own personal growth.

The Talmud also implies that humans should behave more like animals, who act
in obedience to their master, rather than humans, who so often rebel or question
their purpose (Kiddushin 82b). Do you think this is true?

THIS REFERS TO THE SWORD
In these passages, we move from the sword to the staff, two objects of
authority that communicate opposing messages. One is the language of

Continued on the next page.

בְּיָד חֲזָקָה

זוֹ הַדֶּבֶר

כְּמָה שֶׁנֶּאֱמַר

שמות ט

הִנֵּה יַד־יהוה, הוֹיָה בְּמִקְנְךָ אֲשֶׁר בַּשָּׂדֶה
בַּסּוּסִים בַּחֲמֹרִים בַּגְּמַלִּים, בַּבָּקָר וּבַצֹּאן
דֶּבֶר כָּבֵד מְאֹד:

וּבִזְרֹעַ נְטוּיָה

זוֹ הַחֶרֶב

כְּמָה שֶׁנֶּאֱמַר

דברי הימים
א׳ כא

וְחַרְבּוֹ שְׁלוּפָה בְּיָדוֹ
נְטוּיָה עַל־יְרוּשָׁלָ͏ִם:

THIS REFERS TO THE PESTILENCE

Many regard this plague as the death of a domestic workforce and source
of food. With the demise of horses and cattle, transportation, farming,
and food consumption would be severely compromised. All true. But
perhaps there is something deeper occurring in this plague. Often the
death of animals ironically moves us to compassion more than the death
of human beings. Perhaps we see humans as more capable of their own
defense or as riddled with a deviousness and intention to harm that we
do not attribute to animals. In his commentary on the Book of Jonah, the
eighteenth-century German commentator Rabbi David Altschuler (the
Metzudat David VeTziyon) observes that the animals of Nineveh wore
sackcloth not because they were repenting or had any understanding of
personal transformation but because the citizens of Nineveh, when witnessing their animals fasting and in sackcloth, would feel more motivated
to change themselves. From the cattle of Nineveh to the great fish to the
small worm in the story of Jonah, we find that animals are vehicles of salva-

"IN AN AWESOME HAPPENING" –

    This refers to the revelation of His presence,
    as it is said:
    "Has any god ever tried to come   *Deut. 4*
    and take a nation out of the midst of another,
    with trials
    and with signs
    and wonders, in war
    and with a strong hand,
    with an outstretched arm,
    inspiring *great awe,*
    as the Lord your God has done all this
    for you in Egypt,
    before your eyes?"

---

was unsure about himself even with Aaron's partnership, God's support, and his new, magical staff. "What if they do not believe me and do not listen to me?" he asked God in Exodus 4. God asked him to look at his staff – "What is that in your hand?" After all, Moses had been out shepherding when he encountered the burning bush. This is such an obvious question – asking a shepherd what he is holding. But it is only obvious if you believe that it is merely a stick and does not represent your own sense of authority, direction, and conviction. God told Moses to cast it on the ground. It became a snake and then turned back into a staff. But more importantly, God was teaching Moses a lesson about self-belief. "What is that in your hand?" – what is it that you already possess that will be a source of strength for you? You already hold it. Recognize your strength for what it is.

When did you discover a hidden source of your own strength at a time of in-security?

What challenge did you think was beyond you that you eventually overcame?

וּבְמֹרָא גָדֹל

זֶה גִּלּוּי שְׁכִינָה
כְּמָה שֶׁנֶּאֱמַר
אוֹ הֲנִסָּה אֱלֹהִים
לָבוֹא לָקַחַת לוֹ גוֹי מִקֶּרֶב גּוֹי
בְּמַסֹּת בְּאֹתֹת
וּבְמוֹפְתִים וּבְמִלְחָמָה
וּבְיָד חֲזָקָה, וּבִזְרוֹעַ נְטוּיָה
וּבְמוֹרָאִים גְּדֹלִים
כְּכֹל אֲשֶׁר־עָשָׂה לָכֶם יהוה אֱלֹהֵיכֶם בְּמִצְרַיִם
לְעֵינֶיךָ:

דברים ד

---

obedience through violence and coercion; the other inanimate object speaks the language of obedience through influence. One is the tool of the soldier, the other the tool of the shepherd. The staff was a remarkable gift to Moses, given after he confessed the inadequacies of his speech. Typically this speech "defect" is rendered as a stutter or stammer. But it may simply mean that Moses understood that the power of words was what would ultimately force Pharaoh's hand and inspire his own people, and he felt inadequate to the urgent task of advocacy. One contemporary scholar regards Moses' difficulty as a content issue. When the Bible says that Moses is heavy of speech, it means that he spoke about topics of weight and intensity but understood the role of leader as making small talk, the chatter of politics, niceties, and community organizing. God sought to allay his anxieties by giving him a staff, an object that would work in place of his mouth, an object that would deflect visual attention away from him and toward the task at hand, an object that would signal actions because actions are the ultimate measure of leadership. Moses

"WITH SIGNS" –
> This refers to the staff,
> as it is said:
> "Take this staff in your hand,
> and with it
> you shall perform the *signs*."

Ex. 4

"AND WITH WONDERS" –
> This refers to the blood,
> as it is said:
> "I shall make *wonders* in the sky
> and on the earth –

Joel 3

A drop of wine is spilled from the cup
as each wonder is mentioned:

BLOOD,
AND FIRE,
AND PILLARS OF SMOKE."

דָּבָר אַחֵר

Another interpretation:

"With a strong hand" –	Two.
"And an outstretched arm" –	Two.
"In an awesome happening" –	Two.
"With signs" –	Two.
"And with wonders" –	Two.

וּבְאֹתוֹת

זֶה הַמַּטֶּה

כְּמָה שֶׁנֶּאֱמַר

שמות ד

וְאֶת־הַמַּטֶּה הַזֶּה תִּקַּח בְּיָדֶךָ

אֲשֶׁר תַּעֲשֶׂה־בּוֹ אֶת־הָאֹתֹת:

וּבְמֹפְתִים

זֶה הַדָּם

כְּמָה שֶׁנֶּאֱמַר

יואל ג

וְנָתַתִּי מוֹפְתִים בַּשָּׁמַיִם וּבָאָרֶץ

A drop of wine is spilled from the cup
as each wonder is mentioned:

דָּם וָאֵשׁ וְתִימְרוֹת עָשָׁן:

דָּבָר אַחֵר

שְׁתַּיִם	בְּיָד חֲזָקָה
שְׁתַּיִם	וּבִזְרֹעַ נְטוּיָה
שְׁתַּיִם	וּבְמֹרָא גָּדֹל
שְׁתַּיִם	וּבְאֹתוֹת
שְׁתַּיִם	וּבְמֹפְתִים

THESE WERE
THE TEN PLAGUES
that the Holy One
brought upon Egypt,
and these are they –

A drop of wine is spilled from the cup as each plague, and each of the acronyms,
Detzakh, Adash, and Be'aḥav, is mentioned:

BLOOD	FROGS	LICE
WILD ANIMALS	PESTILENCE	BOILS
HAIL	LOCUSTS	DARKNESS

THE STRIKING DOWN OF THE FIRSTBORN.

Now this is what the LORD Almighty says: "Give careful thought to your ways. You have planted much but have harvested little. You eat, but never have enough. You drink, but never have your fill. You put on clothes, but are not warm. You earn wages, only to put them in a purse with holes in it." This is what the LORD Almighty says: "Give careful thought to your ways." (Haggai 1:5–7)

Wrapped in day-to-day problems of a significant nature, we sometimes forget to step back and identify larger patterns of failure or consequences. In the list form in the Haggada, the plagues offer us the litany of devastation that one can only truly consider when standing at the distance offered by time. The Egyptians were hammered again and again. Blood, frogs, lice … a verse-by-verse reading may soften out the punishments meted to the Egyptians. A list of one after another creates an image of a breathless onslaught that did not let up.

We mark each vocalization with a symbolic action, the release of a drop of wine on the plate. By the time we read all ten, our plates are a mess. We are taken visually to the plague that started them all: blood. We recall the loss of life created by the plagues for the Egyptians but also mark that

Continued on the next page.

אֵלּוּ עֶשֶׂר מַכּוֹת

שֶׁהֵבִיא הַקָּדוֹשׁ בָּרוּךְ הוּא
עַל הַמִּצְרִים בְּמִצְרָיִם
וְאֵלּוּ הֵן

A drop of wine is spilled from the cup as each plague, and each of the acronyms,
בְּאַחַ״ב, עֵד״שׁ, דְּצַ״ךְ, and is mentioned:

כִּנִּים	צְפַרְדֵּעַ	דָּם
שְׁחִין	דֶּבֶר	עָרוֹב
חֹשֶׁךְ	אַרְבֶּה	בָּרָד

מַכַּת בְּכוֹרוֹת.

THESE WERE THE TEN PLAGUES

In the Torah, the five chapters of Exodus that describe the plagues (chapters 7–12) are reduced here to a list, exchanging the narrative buildup, rejection, and drama of each plague for creative numerological manipulation. When we read the chapters, it is easy to get lost in the details of the plagues or the tiresome arrogance of Pharaoh and his ministers as they dismiss one sign and wonder after another. We also have no idea from the biblical text how long the plagues took to unfold. Was it days, months, or years? The likelihood is that it was years from Aaron turning his rod into a snake until the plague of the firstborn; disasters and their aftermath, advocacy, and the political entanglements they involve are long and bureaucratic processes. Yet if much time elapsed, it may have been easy for the Egyptians to ignore a pattern or the totality of the decimation and attribute each plague to an unfortunate natural disaster rather than the hand of God. This parallels the way the prophet Haggai told the Israelites that if they ignore God's warnings in the form of agricultural problems, they will not reform:

Rabbi Yehuda
grouped these under acronyms –

DETZAKH, ADASH, BEʾAḤAV.

non-words to remember ten easy words? Maybe this is not a mnemonic at all but Rabbi Yehuda's way of suggesting that the plagues must be viewed in clusters. Some cluster them in tropes of three because of who performed them or the warnings that accompanied them. But perhaps Rabbi Yehuda was saying something deeper about their location that signaled an intensification of the difficulty that finally broke the Egyptians. Blood, frogs, and lice are all plagues that happened close to or below the earth. They seem more manageable because human beings look down upon the ground. Maybe these plagues could be ignored altogether. Pharaoh was not fazed by the plague of blood at all. One midrash records Pharaoh's dismissal as banal. "In Egypt, all schoolchildren can do this. Even my wife can do this!" Wild animals, pestilence, and boils, however, affect human beings at eye level and upon the body. It is harder to ignore the presence and impact of this cluster of plagues. Finally, the first three of the last group – hail, locusts, and darkness – come from the sky, moving the Egyptians from below the earth to the earth to the heavens. It is no coincidence that Pharaoh's first real breakdown in the competition he wages between his power and God's is in his response to hail:

> Throughout Egypt hail struck everything in the fields – both men and animals; it beat down everything growing in the fields and stripped every tree. The only place it did not hail was the land of Goshen, where the Israelites were. Then Pharaoh summoned Moses and Aaron. "This time I have sinned," he said to them. "The LORD is in the right, and I and my people are in the wrong. Pray to the LORD, for we have had enough thunder and hail. I will let you go; you don't have to stay any longer." (Ex. 9:25–28)

What patterns have become prisons in our lives?

We fail to notice most problems we have until they require urgent and immediate attention. Is there any "plague" in your life that is increasing in intensity and must be handled now?

רַבִּי יְהוּדָה
הָיָה נוֹתֵן בָּהֶם סִימָנִים
דְּצַ"ךְ עַדַ"שׁ בְּאַחַ"ב

with each plague, we separated ourselves a bit more from the familiar surroundings in which we were entrenched for centuries. Isak Dinesen, the author of *Out of Africa*, did not believe in evil, only in horror: "In nature there is no evil, only an abundance of horror: the plagues and the blights and the ants and maggots." The plagues of Egypt tell us otherwise. There is a horror of nature here used to combat the evil of human nature. Where many traditional commentaries root this ritual of dripping wine in the verse, "Rejoice not when your enemy falls" (Prov. 24:17), perhaps we might offer an alternative understanding more in keeping with the historic realities of all resistance movements: each drop of wine symbolically commemorates Israelite blood that was shed as the cruelty of slavery intensified with each plague. Rebellions are not clean victories; they cost precious lives. They eat their children, as the expression goes. Those most courageous often sacrifice most. We have to acknowledge that the horror of nature mingled with and escalated by the evil of human nature resulted in great loss of life for the Israelite slaves. And with each drop, we recall not only our slave lives of old but those who fought back and lost during the Crusades and the Inquisition, pogroms, partisans at the time of the Holocaust, and Israeli soldiers on the front lines who gave up their lives so that we can be free in our own country. We laud their courage. We mourn their loss.

 Consider a time when you did not see a long-term pattern of behavior because you were too busy dealing with day-to-day problems.

You may want to use this time to read a brief biography of a WWII Jewish partisan or a fallen Israeli soldier or add a moment of silence to consider the loss of life.

 RABBI YEHUDA GROUPED THESE UNDER ACRONYMS

The abbreviations sound harder to remember than the plagues themselves. Why did Rabbi Yehuda need to create a mnemonic of three difficult

רַבִּי יוֹסֵי הַגְּלִילִי

RABBI Yossei HaGelili says:

How can you know
that the Egyptians were struck with ten plagues in Egypt
and another fifty at the sea?

For in Egypt it is said,
"The astrologers said to Pharaoh, 'This is the *finger* of God,'"   *Ex. 8*

while at the sea it is said,
"When Israel saw the great *hand*   *Ex. 14*
the LORD raised against the Egyptians,
the people feared the LORD,
and they believed in the LORD and in His servant Moses."

If a finger struck
them with ten plagues,
conclude from this that
THEY WERE STRUCK WITH TEN PLAGUES IN EGYPT
AND WITH FIFTY PLAGUES AT THE SEA.

The way this math works is that we focus on different parts of God's "arm" and through them, identify the plethora of goodness and abundance of each aspect. We start with one. We begin with God's finger, which is one, then move to God's hand, which is five. The outstretched arm uses all of these to leverage God's power. Turning to Isaiah 42, we begin to understand that the rabbis' playful math used the imagery of the hand intentionally: "I the LORD, in My grace, have summoned you. *And I have grasped you by the hand.* I created you and appointed you a covenant people, a light to the nations" (6–7). You can point a finger to the future but for people to actualize opportunity they sometimes need a firm grasp and sometimes a shove. God holds our hand through the anxiety of transition, the way we might hold the hand of a small child made nervous by the large and strange world he sees all around him.

Name some aspect of your life where numbers really matter.
What numbers do you hold onto as treasures, numbers you will not forget?

רַבִּי יוֹסֵי הַגְּלִילִי אוֹמֵר

מִנַּיִן אַתָּה אוֹמֵר

שֶׁלָּקוּ הַמִּצְרִים בְּמִצְרַיִם עֶשֶׂר מַכּוֹת

וְעַל הַיָּם לָקוּ חֲמִשִּׁים מַכּוֹת

בְּמִצְרַיִם מַה הוּא אוֹמֵר

שמות ח

וַיֹּאמְרוּ הַחַרְטֻמִּם אֶל־פַּרְעֹה, אֶצְבַּע אֱלֹהִים הוּא:

וְעַל הַיָּם מַה הוּא אוֹמֵר

שמות יד

וַיַּרְא יִשְׂרָאֵל אֶת־הַיָּד הַגְּדֹלָה

אֲשֶׁר עָשָׂה יְהוָה בְּמִצְרַיִם

וַיִּירְאוּ הָעָם אֶת־יְהוָה

וַיַּאֲמִינוּ בַּיהוָה וּבְמֹשֶׁה עַבְדּוֹ:

כַּמָּה לָקוּ בָאֶצְבַּע

עֶשֶׂר מַכּוֹת.

אֱמֹר מֵעַתָּה

בְּמִצְרַיִם לָקוּ עֶשֶׂר מַכּוֹת

וְעַל הַיָּם לָקוּ חֲמִשִּׁים מַכּוֹת.

RABBI YOSSEI HAGELILI SAYS

This is one of the most challenging passages in the Haggada, sort of like new math. It's actually miracle math. We know that when people contemplate tragedy and joy, they often take it apart looking at the tragedy within the tragedy and the joy within the joy. Miracles induce the same kind of multiplication. Just as with *Dayeinu*, the more we delve into what befell us in history, the more our gratitude grows in exponential ways, so too with the miracles that God created that pushed us out of Egypt and through the Reed Sea.

Rabbi Eliezer says: How can you know
    that each and every plague
    the Holy One brought upon the Egyptians in Egypt
    was in fact made up of four plagues?
    For it is said,
    "His fury was sent down upon them,   *Ps. 78*
    great anger, rage, and distress,
    a company of messengers of destruction."
    "Great anger" –   one,
    "rage" –   two,
    "distress" –   three,
    "a company of messengers of destruction" –   four.
    Conclude from this that
    THEY WERE STRUCK WITH FORTY PLAGUES IN EGYPT
    AND WITH TWO HUNDRED PLAGUES AT THE SEA.

Rabbi Akiva says: How can you know
    that each and every plague
    the Holy One brought upon the Egyptians in Egypt
    was in fact made up of five plagues?
    For it is said,
    "His fury was sent down upon them,   *Ps. 78*
    great anger, rage, and distress,
    a company of messengers of destruction."
    "His fury" –   one,
    "great anger" –   two,
    "rage" –   three,
    "distress" –   four,
    "a company of messengers of destruction" –   five.
    Conclude from this that
    THEY WERE STRUCK WITH FIFTY PLAGUES IN EGYPT
    AND WITH TWO HUNDRED AND FIFTY PLAGUES
    AT THE SEA.

תהלים עח

רַבִּי אֱלִיעֶזֶר אוֹמֵר מִנַּיִן שֶׁכָּל מַכָּה וּמַכָּה
שֶׁהֵבִיא הַקָּדוֹשׁ בָּרוּךְ הוּא עַל הַמִּצְרִים בְּמִצְרַיִם
הָיְתָה שֶׁל אַרְבַּע מַכּוֹת, שֶׁנֶּאֱמַר: יְשַׁלַּח־בָּם חֲרוֹן אַפּוֹ
עֶבְרָה וָזַעַם וְצָרָה, מִשְׁלַחַת מַלְאֲכֵי רָעִים:

אַחַת	עֶבְרָה
שְׁתַּיִם	וָזַעַם
שָׁלוֹשׁ	וְצָרָה
אַרְבַּע	מִשְׁלַחַת מַלְאֲכֵי רָעִים

אֱמֹר מֵעַתָּה

בְּמִצְרַיִם לָקוּ אַרְבָּעִים מַכּוֹת
וְעַל הַיָּם לָקוּ מָאתַיִם מַכּוֹת.

תהלים עח

רַבִּי עֲקִיבָא אוֹמֵר מִנַּיִן שֶׁכָּל מַכָּה וּמַכָּה
שֶׁהֵבִיא הַקָּדוֹשׁ בָּרוּךְ הוּא עַל הַמִּצְרִים בְּמִצְרַיִם
הָיְתָה שֶׁל חָמֵשׁ מַכּוֹת, שֶׁנֶּאֱמַר: יְשַׁלַּח־בָּם
חֲרוֹן אַפּוֹ, עֶבְרָה וָזַעַם וְצָרָה, מִשְׁלַחַת מַלְאֲכֵי רָעִים:

אַחַת	חֲרוֹן אַפּוֹ
שְׁתַּיִם	עֶבְרָה
שָׁלוֹשׁ	וָזַעַם
אַרְבַּע	וְצָרָה
חָמֵשׁ	מִשְׁלַחַת מַלְאֲכֵי רָעִים

אֱמֹר מֵעַתָּה

בְּמִצְרַיִם לָקוּ חֲמִשִּׁים מַכּוֹת
וְעַל הַיָּם לָקוּ חֲמִשִּׁים וּמָאתַיִם מַכּוֹת.

כַּמָּה מַעֲלוֹת טוֹבוֹת

HOW MUCH GOOD, LAYER UPON LAYER,
THE OMNIPRESENT HAS DONE FOR US:

Had He brought us out of Egypt
without bringing judgment upon [our oppressors],
that would have been enough for us.

Had He brought judgment upon them
but not upon their gods,
that would have been enough for us.

Had He brought judgment upon their gods
without killing their firstborn sons,
that would have been enough for us.

Had He killed their firstborn sons
without giving us their wealth,
that would have been enough for us.

Had He given us their wealth
without splitting the sea for us,
that would have been enough for us.

God taken us out of Egypt but not taken us to Sinai or not brought us to Israel? Probably not. This song is directed to God but from the perspective of human experience. As we moved through each stage of our deliverance, we felt immensely grateful and could not imagine as we were looking forward what we experienced looking backwards.

Dayeinu not only helps us understand God's love as we experienced it, it is in a format that gives us lessons in appreciation. Scholar Sol Schimmel in the book *The Psychology of Gratitude* observes that the format is intentional: "One interpretation of the structure of this poem is that when we reflect on a benefit that God [or by extension, another person] has done for us, we should break it into its multiple components, meditating on each element." For gratitude to be truly felt on both sides, it must be enumerated in specifics. A general thank-you gets lost.

Continued on the next page.

כַּמָּה מַעֲלוֹת טוֹבוֹת לַמָּקוֹם עָלֵינוּ

אִלּוּ הוֹצִיאָנוּ מִמִּצְרַיִם

דַּיֵּנוּ   וְלֹא עָשָׂה בָהֶם שְׁפָטִים

אִלּוּ עָשָׂה בָהֶם שְׁפָטִים

דַּיֵּנוּ   וְלֹא עָשָׂה בֵאלֹהֵיהֶם

אִלּוּ עָשָׂה בֵאלֹהֵיהֶם

דַּיֵּנוּ   וְלֹא הָרַג אֶת בְּכוֹרֵיהֶם

אִלּוּ הָרַג אֶת בְּכוֹרֵיהֶם

דַּיֵּנוּ   וְלֹא נָתַן לָנוּ אֶת מָמוֹנָם

אִלּוּ נָתַן לָנוּ אֶת מָמוֹנָם

דַּיֵּנוּ   וְלֹא קָרַע לָנוּ אֶת הַיָּם

THAT WOULD HAVE BEEN ENOUGH

Right after we enumerate God's miracles, we pause to say "thank you" with the Seder's most famous song: *Dayeinu*. Just saying the name induces the tune, which is itself joyous and expansive.

Doctor and theologian Albert Schweitzer (1875–1965) helps us understand this sudden transition from lots of numbers to lots of thank-yous: "Train yourself never to put off the word or action for the expression of gratitude." Sometimes in the rush to move forward, we forget to say "thank you." The Haggada makes us stop and express our gratitude with joy and at length. Schweitzer reminds us that even an unintentional omission is not excusable because we are not entitled to any of the gifts we are given: "Nothing that is done for you is a matter of course." Just think of regulation #5 at USP Alcatraz, "You are entitled to food, clothing, shelter, and medical attention. Anything else you get is a privilege."

Dayeinu has an unforgettable structure that is regularly subjected to the same question by commentators. Would it really have been enough had

Had He split the sea for us
  but not brought us through it dry,
    that would have been enough for us.

Had He brought us through [the sea] dry
  without drowning our enemies in it,
    that would have been enough for us.

Had He drowned our enemies in it
  without providing for our needs
  for forty years in the desert,
    that would have been enough for us.

Had He provided for our needs for forty years in the desert,
  without feeding us with manna,
    that would have been enough for us.

Had He fed us with manna
  without giving us Shabbat,
    that would have been enough for us.

Had He given us Shabbat
  without drawing us close around Mount Sinai,
    that would have been enough for us.

Had He drawn us close around Mount Sinai
  without giving us the Torah,
    that would have been enough for us.

Had He given us the Torah
  without bringing us to the Land of Israel,
    that would have been enough for us.

Had He brought us to the Land of Israel
  without building for us the House He chose
    that would have been enough for us.

---

now grateful because you wouldn't be who you are without those trials. As the writer Melodie Beattie says, "Gratitude unlocks the fullness of life. It turns what we have into enough, and more."

אִלּוּ קָרַע לָנוּ אֶת הַיָּם
וְלֹא הֶעֱבִירָנוּ בְּתוֹכוֹ בֶּחָרָבָה   דַּיֵּנוּ

אִלּוּ הֶעֱבִירָנוּ בְּתוֹכוֹ בֶּחָרָבָה
וְלֹא שִׁקַּע צָרֵינוּ בְּתוֹכוֹ   דַּיֵּנוּ

אִלּוּ שִׁקַּע צָרֵינוּ בְּתוֹכוֹ
וְלֹא סִפֵּק צָרְכֵּנוּ בַּמִּדְבָּר
אַרְבָּעִים שָׁנָה   דַּיֵּנוּ

אִלּוּ סִפֵּק צָרְכֵּנוּ בַּמִּדְבָּר אַרְבָּעִים שָׁנָה
וְלֹא הֶאֱכִילָנוּ אֶת הַמָּן   דַּיֵּנוּ

אִלּוּ הֶאֱכִילָנוּ אֶת הַמָּן
וְלֹא נָתַן לָנוּ אֶת הַשַּׁבָּת   דַּיֵּנוּ

אִלּוּ נָתַן לָנוּ אֶת הַשַּׁבָּת
וְלֹא קֵרְבָנוּ לִפְנֵי הַר סִינַי   דַּיֵּנוּ

אִלּוּ קֵרְבָנוּ לִפְנֵי הַר סִינַי
וְלֹא נָתַן לָנוּ אֶת הַתּוֹרָה   דַּיֵּנוּ

אִלּוּ נָתַן לָנוּ אֶת הַתּוֹרָה
וְלֹא הִכְנִיסָנוּ לְאֶרֶץ יִשְׂרָאֵל   דַּיֵּנוּ

אִלּוּ הִכְנִיסָנוּ לְאֶרֶץ יִשְׂרָאֵל
וְלֹא בָנָה לָנוּ אֶת בֵּית הַבְּחִירָה   דַּיֵּנוּ

After DAYEINU, *pause and have every member of the Seder express thanks for three positive aspects of his or her life in the structure of the song, "Had I only… it would have been enough." Alternatively, every person at the Seder can thank the person to his or her right within this format. If you want to be truly consistent with form and content, you can identify difficult challenges for which you are*

עַל אַחַת כַּמָּה וְכַמָּה

HOW MANY AND MANIFOLD THEN,
THE OMNIPRESENT'S KINDNESSES ARE TO US –

for He brought us out of Egypt
   and brought judgment upon [our oppressors]
   and upon their gods,
   and He killed their firstborn sons
   and gave us their wealth,
   and He split the sea for us
   and brought us through it on dry land
   and drowned our enemies there,
   and He provided for our needs for forty years in the desert
   and fed us manna,
   and He gave us Shabbat,
   and He drew us close around Mount Sinai
   and gave us the Torah,
   and He brought us to the Land of Israel
   and built for us the House He chose,

SO WE COULD FIND ATONEMENT [THERE]
FOR ALL OUR SINS.

---

all our sins." We might think we are ending this frenzy of appreciation on a down note but perhaps the praise in excess ends with a plea for a place of atonement for not saying "thank you" when we needed to, for withholding praise of God and others, for being stingy with a compliment or a pat on the back for a job well done.

Think of a time when you should have praised someone but missed the moment. How would you apologize or make up for it now? Don't miss this moment. Add your own note of humility and love at the end of this section of the Haggada by asking each person at the Seder to turn to the person to their right and offer a thoughtful compliment. Let's not hold back on the capacity we each have to make someone else feel praised and valued.

עַל אַחַת כַּמָה וְכַמָה
טוֹבָה כְּפוּלָה וּמְכֻפֶּלֶת לַמָּקוֹם עָלֵינוּ

שֶׁהוֹצִיאָנוּ מִמִּצְרַיִם

וְעָשָׂה בָהֶם שְׁפָטִים

וְעָשָׂה בֵאלֹהֵיהֶם

וְהָרַג בְּכוֹרֵיהֶם

וְנָתַן לָנוּ אֶת מָמוֹנָם

וְקָרַע לָנוּ אֶת הַיָּם

וְהֶעֱבִירָנוּ בְתוֹכוֹ בֶּחָרָבָה

וְשִׁקַּע צָרֵינוּ בְּתוֹכוֹ

וְסִפֵּק צָרְכֵּנוּ בַּמִּדְבָּר אַרְבָּעִים שָׁנָה

וְהֶאֱכִילָנוּ אֶת הַמָּן

וְנָתַן לָנוּ אֶת הַשַּׁבָּת

וְקֵרְבָנוּ לִפְנֵי הַר סִינַי

וְנָתַן לָנוּ אֶת הַתּוֹרָה

וְהִכְנִיסָנוּ לְאֶרֶץ יִשְׂרָאֵל

וּבָנָה לָנוּ אֶת בֵּית הַבְּחִירָה

לְכַפֵּר עַל כָּל עֲווֹנוֹתֵינוּ.

 SO WE COULD FIND ATONEMENT [THERE] FOR ALL OUR SINS
We stop singing but we do not stop praising. We want to make sure that
our appreciation is complete, so we list all of the gifts that we said would
have been enough each in isolation and string them together so that when
we reflect on it all in the aggregate we cannot *believe* our good fortune. Yet
we add something to this praise that is not in the original song. We conclude with our gratitude for the Temple "so we could find atonement for

רַבָּן גַּמְלִיאֵל Rabban Gamliel would say:
Anyone who does not say these three things on Pesaḥ
has not fulfilled his obligation,
and these are they:

PESAH, MATZA, AND BITTER HERBS.

The
PESAH
is what our ancestors would eat while the Temple stood:
and what does it recall?
It recalls the Holy One's
passing over (*Pasaḥ*) the houses of our ancestors in Egypt,
as it is said:
"You shall say: *Ex. 12*
'It is a Pesaḥ offering for the LORD,
for He passed over the houses of the Children of Israel in Egypt
while He struck the Egyptians,
but saved those in our homes' –
and the people bowed
and prostrated themselves.'"

---

made even greater because the listeners were provided with a visual aid.
Stories take on meaning when they have sensual resonance. We can see
them rather than purely imagine them. We can smell or taste them because
the storyteller understands that texture makes stories sing. The Paschal
lamb is a critical food object for Rabban Gamliel because had we not killed
the lamb – the god of Egypt – and painted our lintels with its blood, God
would not have passed over our homes. Because sheep had religious significance throughout Egypt, killing them was a way that those who committed

Continued on the next page.

רַבָּן גַּמְלִיאֵל הָיָה אוֹמֵר
כָּל שֶׁלֹא אָמַר שְׁלֹשָׁה דְבָרִים אֵלּוּ בַּפֶּסַח
לֹא יָצָא יְדֵי חוֹבָתוֹ
וְאֵלּוּ הֵן

פֶּסַח מַצָּה וּמָרוֹר

פֶּסַח

שֶׁהָיוּ אֲבוֹתֵינוּ אוֹכְלִים בִּזְמַן שֶׁבֵּית הַמִּקְדָּשׁ הָיָה קַיָּם
עַל שׁוּם מָה
עַל שׁוּם שֶׁפָּסַח הַקָּדוֹשׁ בָּרוּךְ הוּא
עַל בָּתֵּי אֲבוֹתֵינוּ בְּמִצְרַיִם
שֶׁנֶּאֱמַר

שמות יב

וַאֲמַרְתֶּם זֶבַח־פֶּסַח הוּא לַיהוה
אֲשֶׁר פָּסַח עַל־בָּתֵּי בְנֵי־יִשְׂרָאֵל בְּמִצְרַיִם
בְּנָגְפּוֹ אֶת־מִצְרַיִם
וְאֶת־בָּתֵּינוּ הִצִּיל
וַיִּקֹּד הָעָם וַיִּשְׁתַּחֲווּ:

RABBAN GAMLIEL WOULD SAY

Rabban Gamliel is very stringent in his view. If we tell a story but leave out three props, it is as if we had not told a story at all, even if we were up all night sharing details. But he is right. Think for a moment of a great story

The matzot are now lifted:

THIS MATZA

that we eat:
what does it recall?
It recalls the dough of our ancestors,
which did not have time to rise
before the King, King of kings, the Holy One,
Blessed Be He,
revealed Himself and redeemed them,
as it is said:
"They baked the dough   *Ex. 12*
that they had brought out of Egypt
into unleavened cakes, for it had not risen,
for they were cast out of Egypt
and could not delay,
and they made no provision for the way."

---

their bread to fully rise, thus leaving us matza as an unlikely gift for the ages. In this depiction, matza is a happy accident of redemption. And yet, matza is an unlikely food to take when you travel since it breaks so easily. Why would we care what snacks they took on the way out of Egypt, an unimportant detail in the majestic story of redemption?

Food has always been important in marking defining biblical moments, from the meal Abraham served strangers who were really angels to the drinking party where Esther revealed her identity and plight. Joseph's brothers threw him into a pit and then ate a meal, and later Yitro insisted that his daughters bring Moses home to break bread. Manna supplies us with heavenly sustenance in the wilderness while the people openly pine for meat. Famine, the absence of food, is a driver of travel throughout Genesis. Food details add texture to stories by adding taste. They enhance the credibility of our narratives by engaging us in a basic human need that we experience just as they did: hunger. The matza is a symbolic food, not

Continued on the next page.

The מצות *are now lifted:*

מַצָּה זוֹ

שֶׁאָנוּ אוֹכְלִים

עַל שׁוּם מָה

עַל שׁוּם שֶׁלֹּא הִסְפִּיק בְּצֵקָם שֶׁל אֲבוֹתֵינוּ לְהַחֲמִיץ

עַד שֶׁנִּגְלָה עֲלֵיהֶם מֶלֶךְ מַלְכֵי הַמְּלָכִים

הַקָּדוֹשׁ בָּרוּךְ הוּא, וּגְאָלָם

שֶׁנֶּאֱמַר

שמות יב

וַיֹּאפוּ אֶת־הַבָּצֵק אֲשֶׁר הוֹצִיאוּ מִמִּצְרַיִם

עֻגֹת מַצּוֹת, כִּי לֹא חָמֵץ

כִּי־גֹרְשׁוּ מִמִּצְרַיִם, וְלֹא יָכְלוּ לְהִתְמַהְמֵהַּ

וְגַם־צֵדָה לֹא־עָשׂוּ לָהֶם:

---

to leave no longer had the choice (for more, see "The Paschal Lamb and Impossible Possibilities" at the back of the book). The Egyptians would not break bread with the Hebrews because they were shepherds. All the more so would they cease tolerating them if they knew that the Hebrews killed their gods and ate them as a sacrifice to their own God. The lamb is a food of commitment. The matza is a food of expediency. The bitter herbs are a food of enslavement.

Name a few foods and their symbolism to you or to your family.
What food is critical to your personal or family narrative?

MATZA
If the Israelites made no provisions for the journey, then what is matza exactly? We thought it *was* their provision for the trip. They needed to leave in haste, when the opportunity arose, so they did not have time for

The bitter herbs are now lifted:

THESE BITTER HERBS
that we eat:
what do they recall?
They recall the bitterness
that the Egyptians imposed
on the lives of our ancestors in Egypt,
as it is said:
"They embittered their lives with hard labor,   *Ex. 1*
with clay and with bricks
and with all field labors, with all the work
with which they enslaved them –
hard labor."

BITTER HERBS

Watch carefully as the text weaves together symbolic food and the biblical text introduced through the posing of a question. There is no assumption that the symbolism behind the food is self-evident. This is empathic food. "What do they recall?" asks us to think as we taste the bitterness, if we can relive bitterness, even one we did not experience personally, through the bitterness that we do experience personally through eating. If this is what your mouth feels like, imagine the bitterness of hard labor, which our ancestors experienced with the totality of their being, the way that we consume food or even use the word consume to describe that which preoccupies us, holds onto us, and does not let us go.

Name another food whose unpleasantness takes you – through the power of association – to a bad place. What is your personal "bitter herb"?

List synonyms for "bitterness" and think of an instance in your own life for which bitterness is an apt description. Now think of someone you know who may be in a bitter place. What helped you move on? What can you do this Passover to help remove some of their bitterness?

The bitter herbs are now lifted:

מָרוֹר זֶה

שֶׁאָנוּ אוֹכְלִים

עַל שׁוּם מָה

עַל שׁוּם שֶׁמֵּרְרוּ הַמִּצְרִים אֶת חַיֵּי אֲבוֹתֵינוּ בְּמִצְרָיִם

שֶׁנֶּאֱמַר

וַיְמָרֲרוּ אֶת־חַיֵּיהֶם בַּעֲבֹדָה קָשָׁה

בְּחֹמֶר וּבִלְבֵנִים

וּבְכָל־עֲבֹדָה בַּשָּׂדֶה

אֵת כָּל־עֲבֹדָתָם אֲשֶׁר־עָבְדוּ בָהֶם בְּפָרֶךְ:

שמות א

---

because of the little time it took to bake but because of the flatness that resulted. The flatness of this bread was emblematic of the flatness of their lives as slaves. It was their regular food. That which is flat is not self-determining and full of color and vibrancy. This was the food of disempowerment. They ate it on the way to Sinai, a mountain, a place of elevation and contours where they would own the "high" and transcendent life ahead of them.

The Shabbat after Passover, we look at the contours of the *halla* cover, and it is high and rounded. We are grateful for the height after days of matzaeating. There is something sad about the matza lying flat on the table, as if it speaks to those who are about to eat it with an apology: I am sorry for providing so little by way of satisfaction. This is what slavery felt like – a lack of anticipation, a sameness without the height that speaks of elevation.

 Identify foods that make you feel bloated and those that make you feel lean.

What emotions besides hunger drive you to eat?

Put feeding the homeless or hungry within the framework of other hungers. Why does being charitable with food matter?

בְּכָל דּוֹר וָדוֹר

GENERATION BY GENERATION,

each person must see himself
as if he himself had come out of Egypt,

Pesaḥim
116b

as it is said:
> "And you shall tell your child
> on that day,
> 'Because of this
> the LORD acted for me
> when I came out of Egypt.'"
> It was not only our ancestors
> whom the Holy One redeemed;
> He redeemed us too along with them,

Ex. 13

as it is said:
> "He took us out of there,
> to bring us to the land
> He promised our ancestors
> and to give it to us."

Deut. 6

---

able point of view precisely because it is subjective. It is not trying to be everyone, only itself. The second verse from Deuteronomy is written about "us," adding a sense of community to the "me." Stories about the collective are powerful in a different way because they offer a sense of belonging. A "we" means each of us is not alone in the world. We created and own a story together. Juxtaposing these verses helps us vary the perspective of our story.

Observe yourself in conversation tonight and over this Passover. How many times do you use "I" or "me" versus "we"?

What is more compelling for you, a story about one person or a story about a group?

בְּכָל דּוֹר וָדוֹר

פסחים קטז:

חַיָּב אָדָם לִרְאוֹת אֶת עַצְמוֹ כְּאִלּוּ הוּא יָצָא מִמִּצְרַיִם

שֶׁנֶּאֱמַר

שמות יג

וְהִגַּדְתָּ לְבִנְךָ
בַּיּוֹם הַהוּא

לֵאמֹר
בַּעֲבוּר זֶה
עָשָׂה יהוה לִי בְּצֵאתִי מִמִּצְרָיִם:
לֹא אֶת אֲבוֹתֵינוּ בִּלְבָד גָּאַל הַקָּדוֹשׁ בָּרוּךְ הוּא
אֶלָּא אַף אוֹתָנוּ גָּאַל עִמָּהֶם

שֶׁנֶּאֱמַר

דברים ו

וְאוֹתָנוּ הוֹצִיא מִשָּׁם
לְמַעַן הָבִיא אֹתָנוּ
לָתֶת לָנוּ אֶת־הָאָרֶץ
אֲשֶׁר נִשְׁבַּע לַאֲבֹתֵינוּ:

GENERATION BY GENERATION

This famous expression of historic reenactment emerges from two biblical verses. The first, in Exodus 13, is written in the first-person: "because of this the LORD acted for *me*." Imagine telling the Exodus story in the first-person because that is what the verse asks us to do. Tell this as if it were your story and it will become your story. The first-person is such a powerful perspective because although we know that stories told in the first-person cannot account for as much knowledge and perspective as an omniscient narrator, we also find the first-person a credible and reli-

The matzot are covered and the cup is raised.

לְפִיכָךְ Therefore it is our duty
to thank, praise, laud, glorify,
exalt, honor, bless,
raise high, and acclaim
the One who has performed all these miracles
for our ancestors and for us;
who has brought us out from slavery to freedom,
from sorrow to joy, from grief to celebration;
from darkness to great light
and from enslavement to redemption;
and so we shall sing a new song before Him.

HALLELUYA!

The cup is put down.

THEREFORE IT IS OUR DUTY TO THANK

Because it is our duty to thank, praise, laud, and glorify, we begin that blessed task with the first two passages of Hallel, a pastiche of psalms collected and placed together to maximize our capacity to honor God with exalted words. We reserve the recitation of Hallel for Rosh Ḥodesh and holidays to make our praise distinct and not prosaic and expected. The Talmud contains a fascinating argument between Rabbi Yossei and Mar (Shabbat 118b). Rabbi Yossei wishes he could be counted among those who say Hallel every day, reflecting an ongoing sense of wonder at God's munificence. With each act of daily praise, Rabbi Yossei was expanding his experience of the universe and God's role in it, as the poet Rainer Maria Rilke wrote, "I live my life in widening circles that reach out across the world." But, the Talmud records, one who recites Hallel every day is actually a blasphemer. This is not because one cannot live in a daily state of enchantment, but because the Talmud understands that special, holy words fast become banal and pedestrian unless we guard and treasure them. We must mark unusual occasions with our additional praises. We need to put some language in reserve and take it out for times that warrant

Continued on the next page.

The מצות *are covered and the cup is raised.*

לְפִיכָךְ אֲנַחְנוּ חַיָּבִים
לְהוֹדוֹת, לְהַלֵּל, לְשַׁבֵּחַ, לְפָאֵר
לְרוֹמֵם, לְהַדֵּר, לְבָרֵךְ, לְעַלֵּה וּלְקַלֵּס
לְמִי שֶׁעָשָׂה לַאֲבוֹתֵינוּ וְלָנוּ אֶת כָּל הַנִּסִים הָאֵלֶּה
הוֹצִיאָנוּ מֵעַבְדוּת לְחֵרוּת
מִיָּגוֹן לְשִׂמְחָה, מֵאֵבֶל לְיוֹם טוֹב
וּמֵאֲפֵלָה לְאוֹר גָּדוֹל
וּמִשִּׁעְבּוּד לִגְאֻלָּה
וְנֹאמַר לְפָנָיו שִׁירָה חֲדָשָׁה
הַלְלוּיָהּ.

The cup is put down.

THEREFORE

The word *"lefikhakh"* is a conjunctive adverb that signals to the reader to pay attention to what has come before it because it is critical to what will come after it. It is a connector. There is a connection that must be noted. In the Haggada this word presents a powerful sense of condition. Because God did so much for us, we, therefore, have almost no choice but to thank. This impulse of gratitude – the conditional sense that receiving leads to thanking – is shockingly not universal. The Haggada makes sure that the impulse is deeply lodged within us by creating natural breaks throughout the text to express praise, inducing us to spill over this habit of goodness into all of Passover and all of the year.

Since we pause once again to express gratitude, take a few moments for people around the table to thank God for something that has happened between last Passover and this Passover. Try to be as specific as possible.

הַלְלוּיָהּ HALLELUYA!

Ps. 113

Servants of the Lord, give praise; praise the name of the Lord.

Blessed be the name of the Lord now and for evermore.

From the rising of the sun to its setting,

may the Lord's name be praised.

High is the Lord above all nations;

His glory is above the heavens.

Who is like the Lord our God, who sits enthroned so high,

yet turns so low to see the heavens and the earth?

He raises the poor from the dust

and the needy from the refuse heap,

giving them a place alongside princes, the princes of His people.

He makes the woman in a childless house

a happy mother of children.

HALLELUYA!

בְּצֵאת When Israel came out of Egypt,

Ps. 114

the house of Jacob from a people of foreign tongue,

Judah became His sanctuary, Israel His dominion.

The sea saw and fled; the Jordan turned back.

The mountains skipped like rams, the hills like lambs.

Why was it, sea, that you fled? Jordan, why did you turn back?

Why, mountains, did you skip like rams, and you, hills, like lambs?

It was at the presence of the Lord, creator of the earth,

at the presence of the God of Jacob,

who turned the rock into a pool of water, flint into a flowing spring.

If you regularly praise family and friends, how do you make your words authentically different for special occasions?

Think of expressions we use all of the time, like "I'm sorry," "I love you," or "Thank you very much." Together, come up with alternatives to these which may sound more sincere if only because they are used less frequently.

הַלְלוּיָהּ

הַלְלוּ עַבְדֵי יהוה, הַלְלוּ אֶת־שֵׁם יהוה:

יְהִי שֵׁם יהוה מְבֹרָךְ, מֵעַתָּה וְעַד־עוֹלָם:

מִמִּזְרַח־שֶׁמֶשׁ עַד־מְבוֹאוֹ, מְהֻלָּל שֵׁם יהוה:

רָם עַל־כָּל־גּוֹיִם יהוה, עַל הַשָּׁמַיִם כְּבוֹדוֹ:

מִי כַּיהוה אֱלֹהֵינוּ, הַמַּגְבִּיהִי לָשָׁבֶת:

הַמַּשְׁפִּילִי לִרְאוֹת, בַּשָּׁמַיִם וּבָאָרֶץ:

מְקִימִי מֵעָפָר דָּל, מֵאַשְׁפֹּת יָרִים אֶבְיוֹן:

לְהוֹשִׁיבִי עִם־נְדִיבִים, עִם נְדִיבֵי עַמּוֹ:

מוֹשִׁיבִי עֲקֶרֶת הַבַּיִת, אֵם־הַבָּנִים שְׂמֵחָה

הַלְלוּיָהּ:

בְּצֵאת יִשְׂרָאֵל מִמִּצְרָיִם, בֵּית יַעֲקֹב מֵעַם לֹעֵז:

הָיְתָה יְהוּדָה לְקָדְשׁוֹ, יִשְׂרָאֵל מַמְשְׁלוֹתָיו:

הַיָּם רָאָה וַיָּנֹס, הַיַּרְדֵּן יִסֹּב לְאָחוֹר:

הֶהָרִים רָקְדוּ כְאֵילִים, גְּבָעוֹת כִּבְנֵי־צֹאן:

מַה־לְּךָ הַיָּם כִּי תָנוּס, הַיַּרְדֵּן תִּסֹּב לְאָחוֹר:

הֶהָרִים תִּרְקְדוּ כְאֵילִים, גְּבָעוֹת כִּבְנֵי־צֹאן:

מִלִּפְנֵי אָדוֹן חוּלִי אָרֶץ, מִלִּפְנֵי אֱלוֹהַּ יַעֲקֹב:

הַהֹפְכִי הַצּוּר אֲגַם־מָיִם, חַלָּמִישׁ לְמַעְיְנוֹ־מָיִם:

---

it, or else risk the flattening of our emotions. If everything is wondrous all the time then even that which is truly distinctive will lose its patina of glory.

The cup is raised.

בָּרוּךְ Blessed are You, LORD our God,
King of the Universe,
who has redeemed us
and redeemed our ancestors from Egypt,
and brought us to this night
to eat matza and bitter herbs.
So may the LORD our God
bring us in peace
to other seasons and festivals
that are coming to us,
happy in the building of Your city
and rejoicing in Your service;
and there we shall eat of sacrifices
and Pesah offerings
[*On Motza'ei Shabbat:* of Pesah offerings and sacrifices],
of which the blood will reach
the side of Your altar to be accepted.
And we shall thank You
in a new song
for our redemption
and for our lives' salvation.
Blessed are You, LORD,
Redeemer of Israel.

Blessed are You, LORD our God,
King of the Universe,
who creates the fruit of the vine.

Drink while reclining to the left.

The cup is raised.

בָּרוּךְ אַתָּה יהוה אֱלֹהֵינוּ מֶלֶךְ הָעוֹלָם
אֲשֶׁר גְּאָלָנוּ, וְגָאַל אֶת אֲבוֹתֵינוּ מִמִּצְרַיִם
וְהִגִּיעָנוּ הַלַּיְלָה הַזֶּה, לֶאֱכָל בּוֹ מַצָּה וּמָרוֹר.
כֵּן יהוה אֱלֹהֵינוּ וֵאלֹהֵי אֲבוֹתֵינוּ
יַגִּיעֵנוּ לְמוֹעֲדִים וְלִרְגָלִים אֲחֵרִים
הַבָּאִים לִקְרָאתֵנוּ לְשָׁלוֹם
שְׂמֵחִים בְּבִנְיַן עִירֶךָ
וְשָׂשִׂים בַּעֲבוֹדָתֶךָ
וְנֹאכַל שָׁם
מִן הַזְּבָחִים וּמִן הַפְּסָחִים

/מוצאי שבת On: מִן הַפְּסָחִים וּמִן הַזְּבָחִים/

אֲשֶׁר יַגִּיעַ דָּמָם
עַל קִיר מִזְבַּחֲךָ לְרָצוֹן
וְנוֹדֶה לְךָ
שִׁיר חָדָשׁ
עַל גְּאֻלָּתֵנוּ וְעַל פְּדוּת נַפְשֵׁנוּ
בָּרוּךְ אַתָּה יהוה, גָּאַל יִשְׂרָאֵל.

בָּרוּךְ אַתָּה יהוה אֱלֹהֵינוּ מֶלֶךְ הָעוֹלָם
בּוֹרֵא פְּרִי הַגָּפֶן.

Drink while reclining to the left.

RAHTZA / WASHING

In preparation for the meal,
all participants wash their hands and recite the blessing:

בָּרוּךְ Blessed are You, LORD our God, King of the Universe,
who has made us holy through His commandments,
and has commanded us about washing hands.

MOTZI MATZA

The leader holds all three matzot and recites:

בָּרוּךְ Blessed are You, LORD our God, King of the Universe,
who brings forth bread from the earth.

The lowermost matza is replaced.

The leader recites the following blessing while holding the uppermost and middle matzot:

בָּרוּךְ Blessed are You, LORD our God, King of the Universe,
who has made us holy through His commandments,
and has commanded us to eat matza.

A piece of the uppermost matza, together with a piece of the middle matza,
is given to each member of the company.

Eat while reclining to the left.

MOTZI MATZA

Although matza on all other nights is eaten preceded by a *HaMotzi* blessing,
on this special night, we add a blessing unique to this food because it is a
mitzva to eat matza at the Seder and, according to Rabban Gamliel earlier,
we would not fulfill our Passover obligations were we not to both speak
about and consume the matza at the table. "On that night you should eat
matzot" (Ex. 12:8). The rabbis highlight an inconsistency about whether
you must eat matza for six days (Ex. 12:15) or seven days (Deut. 16:8), but
all agree that the Bible mandates the eating of matza on the first night. This
mitzva is not only about when you eat matza but also about the quantity
that you eat. The Talmud debated the minimum volume of food that needs
to be consumed to render the mitzva of eating complete. Many people are
particular on Passover to eat required *"shiurim,"* or technical measurements
of the symbolic foods at the Seder. This is not the work of technocrats who
merely want to satisfy requirements. For example, the Mishna (Pesahim

Continued on the next page.

רחצה

In preparation for the meal,
all participants wash their hands and recite the blessing:

בָּרוּךְ אַתָּה יהוה אֱלֹהֵינוּ מֶלֶךְ הָעוֹלָם
אֲשֶׁר קִדְּשָׁנוּ בְּמִצְוֹתָיו
וְצִוָּנוּ עַל נְטִילַת יָדַיִם.

מוציא מצה

The leader holds all three ‎מצות and recites:

בָּרוּךְ אַתָּה יהוה אֱלֹהֵינוּ מֶלֶךְ הָעוֹלָם
הַמּוֹצִיא לֶחֶם מִן הָאָרֶץ.

The lowermost ‎מצה is replaced.

The leader recites the following blessing while holding the uppermost and middle ‎מצות:

בָּרוּךְ אַתָּה יהוה אֱלֹהֵינוּ מֶלֶךְ הָעוֹלָם
אֲשֶׁר קִדְּשָׁנוּ בְּמִצְוֹתָיו
וְצִוָּנוּ עַל אֲכִילַת מַצָּה.

A piece of the uppermost ‎מצה, together with a piece of the middle ‎מצה,
is given to each member of the company.
Eat while reclining to the left.

RAḤTZA / WASHING

If our table is an altar, then our food is a gift to God as well as ourselves. We wash our hands to purify them the way the priests did when they performed divine service in the holy Temple (Ex. 30:17). Even when we no longer had a Temple, we carried that practice forward with us, perhaps in preparation for the time when the Temple will be rebuilt. Washing ritually before we eat helps us bring greater mindfulness and intention to our eating. It helps us sanctify and appreciate the abundance in front of us.

If you really thought of your table as an altar, what would change?
In what ways is your table a sanctified space now?

MAROR / BITTER HERBS

The maror is dipped in the ḥaroset before it is eaten.

בָּרוּךְ Blessed are You, LORD our God,
King of the Universe,
who has made us holy
through His commandments,
and has commanded us to eat bitter herbs.

---

are dry. Bitter foods ironically often stimulate the appetite, clear the palate, and intensify the flavor of other food tastes. There seems to be an important message in that for us, particularly for those who have the custom of putting a dab of *ḥaroset* on the maror we eat. Bitterness is important because it clears the way for sweetness and intensifies it, but only if we do not let the bitter taste linger but wipe it away with that which can take it away. There are so many people who live embittered, maror lives because they have become poisoned by anger. It reduces them, making them immobile, paralyzing them from feeling happiness. Instead of merely tasting the maror, they live and breathe it. It goes into the mouth and gets inhaled by the nose and is then constantly exhaled in the language they use to describe their lives. *Ḥizkuni*, the thirteenth-century exegete Rabbi Hezekiah ben Manoah, commented – based on a midrash – that when Jacob described his life retrospectively to Pharaoh, he said, "Few and bitter have been the years of my life" (Gen. 47:9). As a consequence of not being able to see the many ways in which his life was redeemed, according to *Ḥizkuni*, his years were reduced by the exact number of words he uttered in his brief life report. In other words, when you become bitter you shorten your years, if not in duration then at least in quality. Make sure your maror has a little *ḥaroset*, because a spoonful of sugar really does help the medicine go down.

Now think of a bittersweet moment. Break down the bitter and sweet components of it.

What is one sweet thing you can do to break down some bitterness in your life right now?

מָרוֹר

The מרור *is dipped in the* חרוסת *before it is eaten.*

בָּרוּךְ אַתָּה יהוה אֱלֹהֵינוּ מֶלֶךְ הָעוֹלָם
אֲשֶׁר קִדְּשָׁנוּ בְּמִצְוֹתָיו
וְצִוָּנוּ עַל אֲכִילַת מָרוֹר.

10:1) concludes that a waiter at a Seder who reclines and eats an olive-size volume of matza has fulfilled the obligation. This minimum measurement is critical in establishing what constitutes a normal act of eating. Can you really say that you have eaten enough matza to reenact the scene of the ancient Israelites leaving Egypt in haste if you have eaten just a small bite? If we want you to consume history literally, we need to know that you have made an effort to do so. Your appetite this evening is for re-creation rather than the pleasure of your taste buds. It would, therefore, be inappropriate to stop when you so desire. Without the experiential aspect of eating matza in sufficient quantity, would you really be reliving history or merely nibbling at our past?

 Name a food that you eat with great gusto, to the point that it's hard to stop.

Name a food that feels repulsive to you, even in the smallest amount.

Why should the quantity of what we eat matter in the experience of the Seder?

 MAROR / BITTER HERBS

It is hard to imagine that we make a blessing on food that most people dislike. One opinion in the Talmud posits that you do not make a blessing on food that is repulsive to you. A horseradish root may just fit into that category if we were having an evening of culinary delights. But since this is an evening of historic reenactment, the fact that you dislike what you are eating actually proves that the food did help you re-create the experience of bitterness. In the world of taste, food is generally grouped into four categories: salty, sour, sweet, and bitter. Some add pungent and astringent, foods that are flaming in heat because of the spices used and those which

KOREKH / WRAPPING

Maror is sandwiched between two pieces of matza taken from the lowermost matza.

זֵכֶר In memory of the Temple, in the tradition of Hillel. This is what Hillel would do when the Temple still stood: he would wrap [the Pesaḥ offering] up with matza and bitter herbs and eat them together, to fulfill what is said: "You shall eat it with matza and bitter herbs."

Ex. 12

Eat while reclining to the left.

SHULḤAN OREKH / TABLE SETTING

The festive meal is now eaten.

SHULḤAN OREKH / TABLE SETTING

In Jewish law, we refer to one of our most influential codes of halakha as the *Shulḥan Arukh*, "a set table." It was composed in the sixteenth century by Rabbi Joseph Karo, a legalist and mystic who died in the Land of Israel. He called his book *A Set Table* because it set out to order Jewish law into manageable categories that could then be studied and practiced in a more accessible way than was previously available. When we think of a set table, few of us are taken to this particular image. Instead we think literally of a beautiful table at the pristine moment before human beings enter the picture. The silverware is polished and carefully placed. The crystal wine glasses sparkle. The plates offer us a silent invitation to fill them. Nothing is yet distinguished by the subjective tastes of those who will soon select food for the plates. Every place is set, measured, and even. If you read manuals for table setting, this task in aristocratic homes often took several hours. Cutlery was placed with fork tines all at the same height and knife and spoon handles even at their bottoms, all measured with a table ruler. But you don't have to be royal to have a beautifully set table. The beauty in it is not only in the objects but in the symmetry. This is in sharp contrast to matza-breaking and storytelling, which is a very messy, non-linear business. Some have the custom to read *Maggid*, the story part of the Haggada, in a separate room, sometimes even decorated in ancient style, and then move to the set table to enhance the drama of the evening and to accentuate the story while still preserving the dignity and beauty of the set table,

Continued on the next page.

כורך

מרור is sandwiched between two pieces of מצה taken from the lowermost מצה.

זֵכֶר לַמִּקְדָּשׁ כְּהִלֵּל.
כֵּן עָשָׂה הִלֵּל בִּזְמַן שֶׁבֵּית הַמִּקְדָּשׁ הָיָה קַיָּם
הָיָה כּוֹרֵךְ פֶּסַח, מַצָּה וּמָרוֹר, וְאוֹכֵל בְּיַחַד
לְקַיֵּם מַה שֶׁנֶּאֱמַר: עַל־מַצּוֹת וּמְרֹרִים יֹאכְלֻהוּ:

שמות יב

Eat while reclining to the left.

שלחן עורך

The festive meal is now eaten.

KOREKH / WRAPPING

This is a confusing sandwich and a culinary conundrum. In Exodus 12, we learn that Hillel's ritual food was actually the condiments of the Paschal lamb. When we left on that night of wonder, we had to eat the Paschal lamb at twilight together with matza and maror. Yet here, in addition to the biblical citation, we eat this sandwich to commemorate the Temple. Which is it – a memory sandwich of the Exodus night or a scrap of matza and herbs to recall a destroyed Temple? When the Temple still stood, people could still make the exact sandwich that the ancient Israelites would once have eaten on their very first Passover, as was Hillel's practice. Although we have already fulfilled the food requirements of matza and maror by this time, when we eat them together, we recall not only the first time that this was done but the way that we were able to relive this event with greater precision when the Temple existed. It is as if a part of our very memory is impaired or compromised so that we mourn not only the loss of the Temple but the subsequent losses caused by its loss, like the failure to reenact the story through a ritual that is missing its key ingredient. If we had the Temple, Hillel reminds us at this juncture, we would be that much closer to reliving the memory of Passover. We need one to achieve the other.

What do you find gets in the way of memory-making?
Think of a powerful food or taste memory. Is there an "ingredient" missing that you cannot easily obtain now?

TZAFUN / HIDDEN

At the end of the meal, the remaining piece of the middle matza which had been hidden earlier (the Afikoman), is eaten.

BAREKH / BLESSING

The third cup of wine is poured.

שִׁיר הַמַּעֲלוֹת A song of ascents.   Ps. 126
When the Lord brought back the exiles of Zion
we were like people who dream.
Then were our mouths filled with laughter,
and our tongues with songs of joy.
Then was it said among the nations,
"The Lord has done great things for them."
The Lord did do great things for us and we rejoiced.
Bring back our exiles, Lord, like streams in a dry land.
May those who sowed in tears, reap in joy.
May one who goes out weeping, carrying a bag of seed,
come back with songs of joy, carrying his sheaves.

---

significance as well. In mystical literature, we speak of hidden light – "*or ganuz*" – and thirty-six hidden pious ones – the "*lamed-vav tzaddikim*." Biblical verses are decoded for secret meanings to reveal wisdom for only those who delve into their profundity. The *afikoman* tells us that although this evening is one of revelation – we tell our story loudly, proudly, and transparently – within every great story, there are hidden treasures, nuggets of meaning that lie concealed beneath surface events, miracles within miracles, secrets within secrets. We invite everyone to look hard for what is not immediately apparent and visible in this story of redemption and in every story that can take place on multiple levels of understanding.

Name your best AFIKOMAN *hiding or finding place.*
If you give or receive presents, what was your best AFIKOMAN *present?*
Why should we reward someone who finds the AFIKOMAN?

BAREKH / BLESSING

Too often, this section of the Haggada, the Grace After Meals, gets no explication, as if no comments are necessary on a text we say daily, even

Continued on the next page.

צפון

At the end of the meal, the remaining piece of the middle מצה
which had been hidden earlier (the אפיקומן), is eaten.

ברך

The third cup of wine is poured.

תהלים קכו

שִׁיר הַמַּעֲלוֹת, בְּשׁוּב יהוה אֶת־שִׁיבַת צִיּוֹן, הָיִינוּ כְּחֹלְמִים:
אָז יִמָּלֵא שְׂחוֹק פִּינוּ וּלְשׁוֹנֵנוּ רִנָּה
אָז יֹאמְרוּ בַגּוֹיִם הִגְדִּיל יהוה לַעֲשׂוֹת עִם־אֵלֶּה:
הִגְדִּיל יהוה לַעֲשׂוֹת עִמָּנוּ, הָיִינוּ שְׂמֵחִים:
שׁוּבָה יהוה אֶת־שְׁבִיתֵנוּ, כַּאֲפִיקִים בַּנֶּגֶב:
הַזֹּרְעִים בְּדִמְעָה, בְּרִנָּה יִקְצֹרוּ:
הָלוֹךְ יֵלֵךְ וּבָכֹה נֹשֵׂא מֶשֶׁךְ־הַזָּרַע
בֹּא־יָבֹא בְרִנָּה נֹשֵׂא אֲלֻמֹּתָיו:

---

highlighting another contradiction: the way in which chaos and order together are critical for redemption.

Think of the most beautiful set table you have ever seen. What was the secret of its appeal?

What is one thing you can do to make your Passover table more beautiful and orderly?

Why should we eat both a symbolic meal and a proper dinner on this night, especially if the hour is late and we're not feeling particularly hungry?

TZAFUN / HIDDEN

During our storytelling, we do not have time to hide the matza and find it. We need to focus on the story and its intricacies. Then we have to eat our ritual foods and our proper meal and only then do we have time to look for the hidden *afikoman*, the dessert or last course of our festive meal. *Tzafun* is the Aramaic word for hidden; our matza dessert is an enigma wrapped in a mystery. For many, this is the fun part of the evening, often because it is associated with giving and receiving presents, but it has deep mystical

Some say:

תְּהִלַּת My mouth shall speak the praise of God,   *Ps. 145*
and all creatures shall bless His holy name for ever and all time.
We will bless God now and for ever. Halleluya!   *Ps. 115*
Thank the Lord for He is good: His loving-kindness is for ever.   *Ps. 136*
Who can tell of the Lord's mighty acts   *Ps. 106*
and make all His praise be heard?

ZIMMUN / INVITATION

When three or more men say Birkat HaMazon together, the following zimmun is said.
When three or more women say Birkat HaMazon, substitute "Friends" for "Gentlemen."
The leader should ask permission from those with precedence to lead the Birkat HaMazon.

Leader   Gentlemen, let us say grace.

Others   May the name of the Lord be blessed from now and for ever.   *Ps. 113*

Leader   May the name of the Lord be blessed from now and for ever.
With your permission, (my father and teacher / my mother and
            teacher / the Kohanim present / our teacher the rabbi /
            the master of this house / the mistress of this house)
my masters and teachers,
let us bless (*in a minyan:* our God,) the One
from whose food we have eaten.

Others   Blessed be (*in a minyan:* our God,) the One
from whose food we have eaten, and by whose goodness we live.

        People present who have not taken part in the meal say:
        *Blessed be (*in a minyan:* our God,) the One
        whose name is continually blessed for ever and all time.

Leader   Blessed be (*in a minyan:* our God,) the One
from whose food we have eaten, and by whose goodness we live.
Blessed be He, and blessed be His name.

---

these blessings have such an integral role in the Haggada because they give
purpose and an end point to our exile and redemption:

We thank You, Lord our God, for having granted as a heritage to our
ancestors a desirable, good, and spacious land; for bringing us out, Lord

Continued on the next page.

תהלים קמה
תהלים קטו
תהלים קלו
תהלים קו
תהלים קיג

Some say:

תְּהִלַּת יהוה יְדַבֶּר פִּי וִיבָרֵךְ כָּל־בָּשָׂר שֵׁם קָדְשׁוֹ, לְעוֹלָם וָעֶד:

וַאֲנַחְנוּ נְבָרֵךְ יָהּ מֵעַתָּה וְעַד־עוֹלָם, הַלְלוּיָהּ:

הוֹדוּ לַיהוה כִּי־טוֹב, כִּי לְעוֹלָם חַסְדּוֹ:

מִי יְמַלֵּל גְּבוּרוֹת יהוה, יַשְׁמִיעַ כָּל־תְּהִלָּתוֹ:

סדר הזימון

When three or more men say ברכת המזון together, the following זימון is said.
When three or more women say ברכת המזון, substitute רְבוֹתַי for חֲבֵרוֹתַי.
The leader should ask permission from those with precedence to lead the ברכת המזון.

Leader   רַבּוֹתַי, נְבָרֵךְ.

Others   יְהִי שֵׁם יהוה מְבֹרָךְ מֵעַתָּה וְעַד־עוֹלָם:

Leader   יְהִי שֵׁם יהוה מְבֹרָךְ מֵעַתָּה וְעַד־עוֹלָם:

בִּרְשׁוּת (אָבִי מוֹרִי / אִמִּי מוֹרָתִי / כֹּהֲנִים / מוֹרֵנוּ הָרַב /
בַּעַל הַבַּיִת הַזֶּה / בַּעֲלַת הַבַּיִת הַזֶּה)

מָרָנָן וְרַבָּנָן וְרַבּוֹתַי

נְבָרֵךְ (במניין: אֱלֹהֵינוּ) שֶׁאָכַלְנוּ מִשֶּׁלוֹ.

Others   בָּרוּךְ (במניין: אֱלֹהֵינוּ) שֶׁאָכַלְנוּ מִשֶּׁלוֹ וּבְטוּבוֹ חָיִינוּ.

*People present who have not taken part in the meal say:

*בָּרוּךְ (במניין: אֱלֹהֵינוּ) וּמְבֹרָךְ שְׁמוֹ תָּמִיד לְעוֹלָם וָעֶד.

Leader   בָּרוּךְ (במניין: אֱלֹהֵינוּ) שֶׁאָכַלְנוּ מִשֶּׁלוֹ וּבְטוּבוֹ חָיִינוּ.

בָּרוּךְ הוּא וּבָרוּךְ שְׁמוֹ.

---

though most of it is as old as our Talmud. But precisely the opposite is
the case. Because of its familiarity, its meaning doubles in importance. It
is *Birkat HaMazon* which truly establishes the connection between God,
Israel, and our people by confirming the significance of each in our lives
and then weaving them all together. Lines like this help us understand why

BLESSING OF NOURISHMENT

בָּרוּךְ Blessed are You, LORD our God, King of the Universe,
who in His goodness feeds the whole world
with grace, kindness and compassion.
He gives food to all living things, for His kindness is for ever.
Because of His continual great goodness,
we have never lacked food,
nor may we ever lack it, for the sake of His great name.
For He is God who feeds and sustains all, does good to all,
and prepares food for all creatures He has created.
Blessed are You, LORD, who feeds all.

BLESSING OF LAND

נוֹדֶה We thank You, LORD our God,
for having granted as a heritage to our ancestors
a desirable, good and spacious land;
for bringing us out, LORD our God, from the land of Egypt,
freeing us from the house of slavery;
for Your covenant which You sealed in our flesh;
for Your Torah which You taught us;
for Your laws which You made known to us;
for the life, grace and kindness You have bestowed on us;
and for the food by which You continually feed and sustain us,
every day, every season, every hour.

Because tonight our meal is not an ordinary meal, the grace we say after
meals should not be an ordinary grace. Why is this night different from all
other nights? Because even that which is familiar is still holy, holier than
ever on this night. Let us elevate these passages of blessing and read them
slowly and with more focus and intention.

What is your favorite paragraph in BIRKAT HAMAZON?
*As you say the word "*BARUKH*" – blessed – again and again, highlight its meaning and say it as if you really feel blessed.*

ברכת הזן

בָּרוּךְ אַתָּה יהוה אֱלֹהֵינוּ מֶלֶךְ הָעוֹלָם
הַזָּן אֶת הָעוֹלָם כֻּלּוֹ בְּטוּבוֹ בְּחֵן בְּחֶסֶד וּבְרַחֲמִים
הוּא נוֹתֵן לֶחֶם לְכָל בָּשָׂר כִּי לְעוֹלָם חַסְדּוֹ.
וּבְטוּבוֹ הַגָּדוֹל, תָּמִיד לֹא חָסַר לָנוּ
וְאַל יֶחְסַר לָנוּ מָזוֹן לְעוֹלָם וָעֶד
בַּעֲבוּר שְׁמוֹ הַגָּדוֹל.
כִּי הוּא אֵל זָן וּמְפַרְנֵס לַכֹּל וּמֵטִיב לַכֹּל
וּמֵכִין מָזוֹן לְכָל בְּרִיּוֹתָיו אֲשֶׁר בָּרָא.
בָּרוּךְ אַתָּה יהוה, הַזָּן אֶת הַכֹּל.

ברכת הארץ

נוֹדֶה לְּךָ יהוה אֱלֹהֵינוּ
עַל שֶׁהִנְחַלְתָּ לַאֲבוֹתֵינוּ

אֶרֶץ חֶמְדָּה טוֹבָה וּרְחָבָה
וְעַל שֶׁהוֹצֵאתָנוּ יהוה אֱלֹהֵינוּ מֵאֶרֶץ מִצְרַיִם
וּפְדִיתָנוּ מִבֵּית עֲבָדִים
וְעַל בְּרִיתְךָ שֶׁחָתַמְתָּ בִּבְשָׂרֵנוּ
וְעַל תּוֹרָתְךָ שֶׁלִּמַּדְתָּנוּ
וְעַל חֻקֶּיךָ שֶׁהוֹדַעְתָּנוּ
וְעַל חַיִּים חֵן וָחֶסֶד שֶׁחוֹנַנְתָּנוּ
וְעַל אֲכִילַת מָזוֹן שָׁאַתָּה זָן וּמְפַרְנֵס אוֹתָנוּ תָּמִיד
בְּכָל יוֹם וּבְכָל עֵת וּבְכָל שָׁעָה.

---

our God, from the land of Egypt, freeing us from the house of slavery;
for Your covenant which You sealed in our flesh; for Your Torah which
You taught us.

For all this, LORD our God,
we thank and bless You.
May Your name be blessed continually
by the mouth of all that lives, for ever and all time –
for so it is written:
"You will eat and be satisfied, then you shall bless the LORD your   *Deut. 8*
God for the good land He has given you." Blessed are You, LORD,
for the land and for the food.

BLESSING FOR JERUSALEM
רַחֵם נָא Have compassion, please, LORD our God,
on Israel Your people,
on Jerusalem Your city,
on Zion the dwelling place of Your glory,
on the royal house of David Your anointed,
and on the great and holy House that bears Your name.
Our God, our Father,
tend us, feed us, sustain us and support us,
relieve us and send us relief,
LORD our God, swiftly from all our troubles.
Please, LORD our God, do not make us dependent
on the gifts or loans of other people,
but only on Your full, open, holy, and generous hand
so that we may suffer neither shame nor humiliation
for ever and all time.

> *On Shabbat, say:*
> רְצֵה Favor and strengthen us, LORD our God, through Your command-
> ments, especially through the commandment of the seventh day, this great
> and holy Sabbath. For it is, for You, a great and holy day. On it we cease
> work and rest in love in accord with Your will's commandment. May it be
> Your will, LORD our God, to grant us rest without distress, grief, or lament
> on our day of rest. May You show us the consolation of Zion Your city,
> and the rebuilding of Jerusalem Your holy city, for You are the master of
> salvation and consolation.

וְעַל הַכֹּל, יהוה אֱלֹהֵינוּ
אֲנַחְנוּ מוֹדִים לָךְ וּמְבָרְכִים אוֹתָךְ
יִתְבָּרַךְ שִׁמְךָ בְּפִי כָּל חַי תָּמִיד לְעוֹלָם וָעֶד

דברים ח

כַּכָּתוּב: וְאָכַלְתָּ וְשָׂבָעְתָּ, וּבֵרַכְתָּ אֶת־יהוה אֱלֹהֶיךָ
עַל־הָאָרֶץ הַטֹּבָה אֲשֶׁר נָתַן־לָךְ:
בָּרוּךְ אַתָּה יהוה, עַל הָאָרֶץ וְעַל הַמָּזוֹן.

בְּרְכַּת יְרוּשָׁלַיִם

רַחֶם נָא יהוה אֱלֹהֵינוּ
עַל יִשְׂרָאֵל עַמֶּךָ

וְעַל יְרוּשָׁלַיִם עִירֶךָ
וְעַל צִיּוֹן מִשְׁכַּן כְּבוֹדֶךָ
וְעַל מַלְכוּת בֵּית דָּוִד מְשִׁיחֶךָ
וְעַל הַבַּיִת הַגָּדוֹל וְהַקָּדוֹשׁ שֶׁנִּקְרָא שִׁמְךָ עָלָיו.
אֱלֹהֵינוּ, אָבִינוּ, רְעֵנוּ, זוּנֵנוּ, פַּרְנְסֵנוּ וְכַלְכְּלֵנוּ
וְהַרְוִיחֵנוּ, וְהַרְוַח לָנוּ יהוה אֱלֹהֵינוּ מְהֵרָה מִכָּל צָרוֹתֵינוּ.
וְנָא אַל תַּצְרִיכֵנוּ, יהוה אֱלֹהֵינוּ
לֹא לִידֵי מַתְּנַת בָּשָׂר וָדָם וְלֹא לִידֵי הַלְוָאָתָם
כִּי אִם לְיָדְךָ הַמְּלֵאָה, הַפְּתוּחָה, הַקְּדוֹשָׁה וְהָרְחָבָה
שֶׁלֹּא נֵבוֹשׁ וְלֹא נִכָּלֵם לְעוֹלָם וָעֶד.

On שבת, say:

רְצֵה וְהַחֲלִיצֵנוּ, יהוה אֱלֹהֵינוּ, בְּמִצְוֹתֶיךָ וּבְמִצְוַת יוֹם הַשְּׁבִיעִי
הַשַּׁבָּת הַגָּדוֹל וְהַקָּדוֹשׁ הַזֶּה, כִּי יוֹם זֶה גָּדוֹל וְקָדוֹשׁ הוּא
לְפָנֶיךָ, לִשְׁבָּת בּוֹ וְלָנוּחַ בּוֹ בְּאַהֲבָה כְּמִצְוַת רְצוֹנֶךָ. וּבִרְצוֹנְךָ הָנִיחַ לָנוּ,
יהוה אֱלֹהֵינוּ, שֶׁלֹּא תְהֵא צָרָה וְיָגוֹן וַאֲנָחָה בְּיוֹם מְנוּחָתֵנוּ. וְהַרְאֵנוּ, יהוה
אֱלֹהֵינוּ, בְּנֶחָמַת צִיּוֹן עִירֶךָ וּבְבִנְיַן יְרוּשָׁלַיִם עִיר קָדְשֶׁךָ, כִּי אַתָּה הוּא
בַּעַל הַיְשׁוּעוֹת וּבַעַל הַנֶּחָמוֹת.

אֱלֹהֵינוּ Our God and God of our ancestors,
may there rise, come, reach, appear, be favored, heard, regarded,
and remembered before You, our recollection and remembrance,
as well as the remembrance of our ancestors,
and of the Messiah son of David Your servant,
and of Jerusalem Your holy city,
and of all Your people the house of Israel –
for deliverance and well-being, grace, loving-kindness and
compassion, life and peace, on this day of the Festival of Matzot.
On it remember us, LORD our God, for good;
recollect us for blessing, and deliver us for life.
In accord with Your promise of salvation and compassion,
spare us and be gracious to us;
have compassion on us and deliver us,
for our eyes are turned to You because You are God,
gracious and compassionate.

And may Jerusalem the holy city be rebuilt soon, in our time.
Blessed are You, LORD, who in His compassion
will rebuild Jerusalem. Amen.

BLESSING OF GOD'S GOODNESS
בָּרוּךְ Blessed are You, LORD our God, King of the Universe –
God our father, our king, our sovereign,
our creator, our redeemer, our maker,
our Holy One, the Holy One of Jacob.
He is our shepherd, Israel's shepherd,
the good king who does good to all.
Every day He has done, is doing, and will do good to us.
He has acted, is acting,
and will always act kindly toward us for ever,
granting us grace, kindness and compassion, relief and rescue,
prosperity, blessing, redemption and comfort,
sustenance and support, compassion, life, peace and all good
things, and of all good things may He never let us lack.

אֱלֹהֵינוּ וֵאלֹהֵי אֲבוֹתֵינוּ

יַעֲלֶה וְיָבוֹא וְיַגִּיעַ, וְיֵרָאֶה וְיֵרָצֶה וְיִשָּׁמַע, וְיִפָּקֵד
דַּ: וְיִזָּכֵר זִכְרוֹנֵנוּ וּפִקְדוֹנֵנוּ, וְזִכְרוֹן אֲבוֹתֵינוּ

וְזִכְרוֹן מָשִׁיחַ בֶּן דָּוִד עַבְדֶּךָ

וְזִכְרוֹן יְרוּשָׁלַיִם עִיר קָדְשֶׁךָ

וְזִכְרוֹן כָּל עַמְּךָ בֵּית יִשְׂרָאֵל

לְפָנֶיךָ, לִפְלֵיטָה לְטוֹבָה, לְחֵן וּלְחֶסֶד וּלְרַחֲמִים
לְחַיִּים וּלְשָׁלוֹם בְּיוֹם חַג הַמַּצּוֹת הַזֶּה.

זָכְרֵנוּ יְהוָה אֱלֹהֵינוּ בּוֹ לְטוֹבָה וּפָקְדֵנוּ בּוֹ לִבְרָכָה
וְהוֹשִׁיעֵנוּ בּוֹ לְחַיִּים.

וּבִדְבַר יְשׁוּעָה וְרַחֲמִים, חוּס וְחָנֵּנוּ וְרַחֵם עָלֵינוּ, וְהוֹשִׁיעֵנוּ
כִּי אֵלֶיךָ עֵינֵינוּ, כִּי אֵל חַנּוּן וְרַחוּם אָתָּה.

וּבְנֵה יְרוּשָׁלַיִם עִיר הַקֹּדֶשׁ בִּמְהֵרָה בְיָמֵינוּ.

בָּרוּךְ אַתָּה יְהוָה, בּוֹנֵה בְרַחֲמָיו יְרוּשָׁלַיִם, אָמֵן.

ברכת הטוב והמטיב

בָּרוּךְ אַתָּה יְהוָה אֱלֹהֵינוּ מֶלֶךְ הָעוֹלָם
דַּ: הָאֵל אָבִינוּ, מַלְכֵּנוּ, אַדִּירֵנוּ

בּוֹרְאֵנוּ, גּוֹאֲלֵנוּ, יוֹצְרֵנוּ, קְדוֹשֵׁנוּ, קְדוֹשׁ יַעֲקֹב

רוֹעֵנוּ, רוֹעֵה יִשְׂרָאֵל, הַמֶּלֶךְ הַטּוֹב וְהַמֵּיטִיב לַכֹּל
שֶׁבְּכָל יוֹם וָיוֹם

הוּא הֵיטִיב, הוּא מֵיטִיב, הוּא יֵיטִיב לָנוּ

הוּא גְמָלָנוּ, הוּא גוֹמְלֵנוּ, הוּא יִגְמְלֵנוּ לָעַד

לְחֵן וּלְחֶסֶד וּלְרַחֲמִים, וּלְרֶוַח, הַצָּלָה וְהַצְלָחָה

בְּרָכָה וִישׁוּעָה, נֶחָמָה, פַּרְנָסָה וְכַלְכָּלָה

וְרַחֲמִים וְחַיִּים וְשָׁלוֹם וְכָל טוֹב, וּמִכָּל טוּב לְעוֹלָם אַל יְחַסְּרֵנוּ.

ADDITIONAL REQUESTS

הָרַחֲמָן May the Compassionate One
reign over us for ever and all time.

May the Compassionate One be blessed
in heaven and on earth.

May the Compassionate One be praised
from generation to generation, be glorified by us to all eternity,
and honored among us for ever and all time.

May the Compassionate One
grant us an honorable livelihood.

May the Compassionate One
break the yoke from our neck and lead us upright to our land.

May the Compassionate One
send us many blessings to this house
and this table at which we have eaten.

May the Compassionate One
send us Elijah the prophet –
may he be remembered for good –
to bring us good tidings of salvation and consolation.

May the Compassionate One
bless the State of Israel, first flowering of our redemption.

May the Compassionate One
bless the members of Israel's Defense Forces,
who stand guard over our land.

A guest says:

יְהִי רָצוֹן May it be Your will that the master of this house shall not suffer
shame in this world, nor humiliation in the World to Come. May all he
owns prosper greatly, and may his and our possessions be successful and
close to hand. Let not the Accuser hold sway over his deeds or ours, and
may no thought of sin, iniquity, or transgression enter him or us from
now and for evermore.

בקשות נוספות

הָרַחֲמָן הוּא יִמְלֹךְ עָלֵינוּ לְעוֹלָם וָעֶד.

הָרַחֲמָן הוּא יִתְבָּרַךְ בַּשָּׁמַיִם וּבָאָרֶץ.

הָרַחֲמָן הוּא יִשְׁתַּבַּח לְדוֹר דּוֹרִים
וְיִתְפָּאַר בָּנוּ לָעַד וּלְנֵצַח נְצָחִים
וְיִתְהַדַּר בָּנוּ לָעַד וּלְעוֹלְמֵי עוֹלָמִים.

הָרַחֲמָן הוּא יְפַרְנְסֵנוּ בְּכָבוֹד.

הָרַחֲמָן הוּא יִשְׁבֹּר עֻלֵּנוּ מֵעַל צַוָּארֵנוּ
וְהוּא יוֹלִיכֵנוּ קוֹמְמִיּוּת לְאַרְצֵנוּ.

הָרַחֲמָן הוּא יִשְׁלַח לָנוּ בְּרָכָה מְרֻבָּה בַּבַּיִת הַזֶּה
וְעַל שֻׁלְחָן זֶה שֶׁאָכַלְנוּ עָלָיו.

הָרַחֲמָן הוּא יִשְׁלַח לָנוּ אֶת אֵלִיָּהוּ הַנָּבִיא זָכוּר לַטּוֹב
וִיבַשֶּׂר לָנוּ בְּשׂוֹרוֹת טוֹבוֹת יְשׁוּעוֹת וְנֶחָמוֹת.

הָרַחֲמָן הוּא יְבָרֵךְ אֶת מְדִינַת יִשְׂרָאֵל
רֵאשִׁית צְמִיחַת גְּאֻלָּתֵנוּ.

הָרַחֲמָן הוּא יְבָרֵךְ אֶת חַיָּלֵי צְבָא הַהֲגָנָה לְיִשְׂרָאֵל
הָעוֹמְדִים עַל מִשְׁמַר אַרְצֵנוּ.

A guest says:

יְהִי רָצוֹן שֶׁלֹּא יֵבוֹשׁ בַּעַל הַבַּיִת בָּעוֹלָם הַזֶּה, וְלֹא יִכָּלֵם לָעוֹלָם
הַבָּא, וְיַצְלַח מְאֹד בְּכָל נְכָסָיו, וְיִהְיוּ נְכָסָיו וּנְכָסֵינוּ מֻצְלָחִים וּקְרוֹבִים
לָעִיר, וְאַל יִשְׁלֹט שָׂטָן לֹא בְּמַעֲשֵׂה יָדָיו וְלֹא בְּמַעֲשֵׂה יָדֵינוּ. וְאַל
יִזְדַּקֵּר לֹא לְפָנָיו וְלֹא לְפָנֵינוּ שׁוּם דְּבַר הִרְהוּר חֵטְא, עֲבֵירָה וְעָוֹן,
מֵעַתָּה וְעַד עוֹלָם.

הָרַחֲמָן May the Compassionate One bless –

When eating at one's own table, say (include the words in parentheses that apply):
me, (my wife / husband / my father, my teacher / my mother,
my teacher / my children) and all that is mine,

A guest at someone else's table says (include the words in parentheses that apply):
the master of this house, him (and his wife, the mistress of this
house / and his children) and all that is his,

Children at their parents' table say (include the words in parentheses that apply):
my father, my teacher (master of this house), and my mother, my
teacher (mistress of this house), them, their household, their
children, and all that is theirs.

For all other guests, add:
and all the diners here,

אוֹתָנוּ – together with us and all that is ours. Just as our forefathers
Abraham, Isaac, and Jacob were blessed in all, from all, with all,
so may He bless all of us together with a complete blessing,
and let us say: Amen.

בַּמָּרוֹם On high, may grace be invoked for them and for us,
as a safeguard of peace.
May we receive a blessing from the LORD
and a just reward from the God of our salvation,
and may we find grace and good favor in the eyes of God and man.

On Shabbat: May the Compassionate One let us inherit the time
that will be entirely Shabbat and rest for life everlasting.

May the Compassionate One let us inherit the day that is all good.

---

of Shabbat, the Messiah's arrival, and peace – is this unusual request for
scholars: "May the Compassionate One let us inherit the day that is all
good. The everlasting day, the day when the righteous will sit down with
crowns on their heads, benefiting from the divine glory, and may our portion be with them." We transition from Shabbat to asking God to bring

Continued on the next page.

הָרַחֲמָן הוּא יְבָרֵךְ

When eating at one's own table, say (include the words in parentheses that apply):

אוֹתִי (וְאֶת אִשְׁתִּי / וְאֶת בַּעֲלִי / וְאֶת אָבִי מוֹרִי / וְאֶת אִמִּי מוֹרָתִי / וְאֶת זַרְעִי)
וְאֶת כָּל אֲשֶׁר לִי.

A guest at someone else's table says (include the words in parentheses that apply):

אֶת בַּעַל הַבַּיִת הַזֶּה, אוֹתוֹ (וְאֶת אִשְׁתּוֹ בַּעֲלַת הַבַּיִת הַזֶּה /
וְאֶת זַרְעוֹ) וְאֶת כָּל אֲשֶׁר לוֹ.

Children at their parents' table say (include the words in parentheses that apply):

אֶת אָבִי מוֹרִי (בַּעַל הַבַּיִת הַזֶּה), וְאֶת אִמִּי מוֹרָתִי (בַּעֲלַת הַבַּיִת הַזֶּה)
אוֹתָם וְאֶת בֵּיתָם וְאֶת זַרְעָם וְאֶת כָּל אֲשֶׁר לָהֶם

For all other guests, add:

וְאֶת כָּל הַמְסֻבִּין כָּאן

אוֹתָנוּ וְאֶת כָּל אֲשֶׁר לָנוּ כְּמוֹ שֶׁנִּתְבָּרְכוּ אֲבוֹתֵינוּ
אַבְרָהָם יִצְחָק וְיַעֲקֹב, בַּכֹּל, מִכֹּל, כֹּל, כֵּן
יְבָרֵךְ אוֹתָנוּ כֻּלָּנוּ יַחַד בִּבְרָכָה שְׁלֵמָה, וְנֹאמַר אָמֵן.

בַּמָּרוֹם יְלַמְּדוּ עֲלֵיהֶם וְעָלֵינוּ זְכוּת
שֶׁתְּהֵא לְמִשְׁמֶרֶת שָׁלוֹם
וְנִשָּׂא בְרָכָה מֵאֵת יהוה וּצְדָקָה מֵאֱלֹהֵי יִשְׁעֵנוּ
וְנִמְצָא חֵן וְשֵׂכֶל טוֹב בְּעֵינֵי אֱלֹהִים וְאָדָם.

בשבת: הָרַחֲמָן הוּא יַנְחִילֵנוּ יוֹם שֶׁכֻּלּוֹ שַׁבָּת וּמְנוּחָה לְחַיֵּי הָעוֹלָמִים.

הָרַחֲמָן הוּא יַנְחִילֵנוּ יוֹם שֶׁכֻּלּוֹ טוֹב.

LET US INHERIT THE DAY THAT IS ALL GOOD

There is a *HaRaḥaman* included in the Grace After Meals for Passover that
rarely appears outside the Haggada. Nestled into the *"HaRaḥamans"* – the
requests we make of God to bless our hosts, ourselves, and be worthy

הָרַחֲמָן May the Compassionate One make us worthy
of the Messianic Age and life in the World to Come.
He is a tower of salvation to His king,   *II Sam. 22*
showing kindness to His anointed,
to David and his descendants for ever.
He who makes peace in His high places,
may He make peace for us and all Israel,
and let us say: Amen.

For at this festival, in houses that keep proper religious usage, they first of all honor the slaves with a dinner prepared as if for the master; and only afterward is the table set again for the head of the household. So then the chief slave came in to announce the time of dinner and to summon the masters to the table. (*Saturnalia* 1:24:22–23)

This small blessing now makes much more sense. It is said in contrast to a banquet holiday when slaves became a focus of the celebrations. The *HaRaḥaman* draws attention to the fact that our holiday was not merely a ruse for a day. On Passover, our slaves were "crowned" with lasting freedom, and for us, this freedom is not directed to temporal hedonistic pleasures, but to provide us with the time and energy to strive for righteousness and ensure that slavery is not mocked but ultimately eliminated. In fact, the proclamation of the Jubilee year stresses that it take effect everywhere; any lapse would create a general diminution of freedom: "And you shall proclaim liberty (*dror*) *throughout* the land to *all* its inhabitants" (Lev. 25:10). Everywhere and everyone must experience it for it to be real. The Talmud compares "*dror*" to "a man who dwells in any dwelling and moves merchandise anywhere is the country." In other words, freedom is not only a psychic feeling of liberty, but the space to roam without limit and to conduct and control one's business transactions. No doubt, this definition reflects the constraints on movement that were generally felt in this period.

Think of ways that you treat those who work for you. How can you show them greater and lasting respect?

How can you use this Passover to equalize the playing field for those who are "enslaved" by poverty, homelessness, or hunger?

הָרַחֲמָן הוּא יְזַכֵּנוּ לִימוֹת הַמָּשִׁיחַ וּלְחַיֵּי הָעוֹלָם הַבָּא

מִגְדּוֹל יְשׁוּעוֹת מַלְכּוֹ וְעֹשֶׂה-חֶסֶד לִמְשִׁיחוֹ

לְדָוִד וּלְזַרְעוֹ עַד-עוֹלָם:

עֹשֶׂה שָׁלוֹם בִּמְרוֹמָיו הוּא

יַעֲשֶׂה שָׁלוֹם עָלֵינוּ וְעַל כָּל יִשְׂרָאֵל וְאִמְרוּ אָמֵן.

---

about a time which is like an everlasting Shabbat. A salient feature of this time will be that *tzaddikim* will sit in true pleasure taking in God's glory and – if worthy – we may sit with them. Why not ask for this on any day of the week and not Passover specifically? The key lies in the crowns. In Rosh HaShana 8b, there is a debate about the status of slaves who are supposed to be freed between Rosh HaShana and Yom Kippur of the Jubilee year, yet the shofar that is the clarion call of their freedom has not yet been blown. The Talmud inquires about their status:

> From Rosh HaShana until Yom Kippur, Hebrew slaves were not released [to return home] but they were also not enslaved anymore to their masters. Rather, they would eat, drink, and rejoice and would wear crowns on their heads. Once Yom Kippur arrived, the court would sound the shofar and they would return to their homes.

In the ancient world, a crown was an external sign of freedom. The Romans had a holiday called Saturnalia, where slaves and free men and women would exchange or place crowns on each other, signifying a change of roles. This holiday is mentioned in the Mishna and the ensuing discussion in Avoda Zara 8a as to whether Jews were allowed to conduct business transactions on this day and dates it to eight days before the equinox. Saturnalia was celebrated until the third or fourth century in honor of the Roman agricultural god Saturn. The holiday was celebrated with carnival-like activities, a sacrifice at the Temple of Saturn, and public feasting just before the winter solstice. Part of the festivities included masters serving their slaves or dining together or the slaves dining first, reversing convention as a social equalizer that signals joy. The Latin writer Macrobius describes this aspect of the holiday and is a major source for information about Saturnalia:

יִרְאוּ Fear the Lᴏʀᴅ, you His holy ones; *Ps. 34*
those who fear Him lack nothing.
Young lions may grow weak and hungry,
but those who seek the Lᴏʀᴅ lack no good thing.
Thank the Lᴏʀᴅ for He is good: His loving-kindness is for ever. *Ps. 118*
You open Your hand and satisfy the desire of every living thing. *Ps. 145*
Blessed is the person who trusts in the Lᴏʀᴅ, *Jer. 17*
whose trust is in the Lᴏʀᴅ alone.
Once I was young, and now I am old, *Ps. 37*
yet I have never watched a righteous man forsaken
or his children begging for bread.
The Lᴏʀᴅ will give His people strength. *Ps. 29*
The Lᴏʀᴅ will bless His people with peace.

> Blessed are You, Lᴏʀᴅ our God, King of the Universe,
> who creates the fruit of the vine.

Drink while reclining to the left.

A cup of wine is now poured in honor of Elijah, and the door is opened.

שְׁפֹךְ POUR OUT Your wrath *Ps. 79*
upon the nations that do not know You,
and on regimes that have not called upon Your name.
For Jacob is devoured; they have laid his places waste.
Pour out Your great anger upon them, *Ps. 69*
and let Your blazing fury overtake them.
Pursue them in Your fury and destroy them *Lam. 3*
from under the heavens of the Lᴏʀᴅ.

---

this passage, we say to ourselves and others that we will not remain neutral
and ask God not to remain neutral when others suffer. We recite a verse
that asks God to spill divine wrath as a way of also placing the burden of
this anger on God and taking it away from us. We may judge too harshly or
misunderstand the motives behind an action. We ask that God, rather than
human beings, bring about ultimate justice. In fact, it is remarkable that we

Continued on the next page.

תהלים לד

יְראוּ אֶת־יהוה קְדֹשָׁיו כִּי־אֵין מַחְסוֹר לִירֵאָיו:
כְּפִירִים רָשׁוּ וְרָעֵבוּ וְדֹרְשֵׁי יהוה לֹא־יַחְסְרוּ כָל־טוֹב:

תהלים קיח

הוֹדוּ לַיהוה כִּי־טוֹב כִּי לְעוֹלָם חַסְדּוֹ:

תהלים קמה

פּוֹתֵחַ אֶת־יָדֶךָ וּמַשְׂבִּיעַ לְכָל־חַי רָצוֹן:

ירמיה יז

בָּרוּךְ הַגֶּבֶר אֲשֶׁר יִבְטַח בַּיהוה וְהָיָה יהוה מִבְטַחוֹ:

תהלים לז

נַעַר הָיִיתִי גַּם־זָקַנְתִּי וְלֹא־רָאִיתִי צַדִּיק נֶעֱזָב וְזַרְעוֹ מְבַקֶּשׁ־לָחֶם:

תהלים כט

יהוה עֹז לְעַמּוֹ יִתֵּן יהוה יְבָרֵךְ אֶת־עַמּוֹ בַשָּׁלוֹם:

בָּרוּךְ אַתָּה יהוה אֱלֹהֵינוּ מֶלֶךְ הָעוֹלָם, בּוֹרֵא פְּרִי הַגָּפֶן.

Drink while reclining to the left.

A cup of wine is now poured in honor of Elijah, and the door is opened.

תהלים עט

שְׁפֹךְ חֲמָתְךָ אֶל־הַגּוֹיִם אֲשֶׁר לֹא־יְדָעוּךָ
וְעַל מַמְלָכוֹת אֲשֶׁר בְּשִׁמְךָ לֹא קָרָאוּ:
כִּי אָכַל אֶת־יַעֲקֹב, וְאֶת־נָוֵהוּ הֵשַׁמּוּ:

תהלים סט

שְׁפָךְ־עֲלֵיהֶם זַעְמֶךָ וַחֲרוֹן אַפְּךָ יַשִּׂיגֵם:

איכה ג

תִּרְדֹּף בְּאַף וְתַשְׁמִידֵם מִתַּחַת שְׁמֵי יהוה:

POUR OUT YOUR WRATH UPON THE NATIONS

Some people find this so offensive that they change the language to "Pour out Your love," as if there is no anger to spill over (this is explored in depth in "Pour Out Your Wrath, Pour Out Your Love" in the essay section of this book). While well-meaning, these individuals may be offending those who have suffered profoundly as the victims of hate crimes, the kind of hatred that should generate outrage. Elie Wiesel wrote: "I swore never to be silent whenever and wherever human beings must endure suffering and humiliation. We must take sides. Neutrality helps the oppressor, never the victim. Silence encourages the tormentor, never the tormented." In reciting

HALLEL / PRAISING

The fourth cup of wine is poured, and Hallel is completed.

לֹא לָנוּ Not to us, LORD, not to us,   *Ps. 115*
   but to Your name give glory,
   for Your love, for Your faithfulness.
Why should the nations say, "Where now is their God?"
Our God is in heaven; whatever He wills He does.
Their idols are silver and gold, made by human hands.
They have mouths but cannot speak; eyes but cannot see.
They have ears but cannot hear; noses but cannot smell.
They have hands but cannot feel; feet but cannot walk.
No sound comes from their throat.
Those who make them become like them;
   so will all who trust in them.
Israel, trust in the LORD – He is their help and their shield.
House of Aaron, trust in the LORD –
He is their help and their shield.
You who fear the LORD trust in the LORD –
He is their help and their shield.

---

morning and the songs seem long and the hour is late, this latter part of the Seder is too often neglected, but ironically, this is where our truest joy and gratitude are offered. We accomplish this through a weaving of prayer. Once we tell the story, we cannot help but immerse ourselves in God's praises.

We say Hallel on special occasions, using Psalms 113–118 to mark sacred convocations of time. This section is called the "Lesser Hallel" and is followed in the Haggada by the "Greater Hallel," Psalm 136, ostensibly called this not because of its length but because of the frequent repetition of God's name in the latter psalm. The notion that God's steadfast love endures forever forms the spine of this prayer and its refrain. It is as if all of the examples given as we read down the laundry list of God's love cement and serve as testimony to the way in which God is loyal and loving.

Psalms 113–118 are sometimes referred to as "*Hallel HaMitzri*," the Egyptian Hallel, because its recitation is so closely aligned with the celebration

Continued on the next page.

הלל

The fourth cup of wine is poured, and הלל *is completed.*

לֹא לָנוּ יְהוה לֹא לָנוּ

כִּי־לְשִׁמְךָ תֵּן כָּבוֹד

עַל־חַסְדְּךָ עַל־אֲמִתֶּךָ:

לָמָּה יֹאמְרוּ הַגּוֹיִם אַיֵּה־נָא אֱלֹהֵיהֶם:

וֵאלֹהֵינוּ בַשָּׁמָיִם, כֹּל אֲשֶׁר־חָפֵץ עָשָׂה:

עֲצַבֵּיהֶם כֶּסֶף וְזָהָב, מַעֲשֵׂה יְדֵי אָדָם:

פֶּה־לָהֶם וְלֹא יְדַבֵּרוּ, עֵינַיִם לָהֶם וְלֹא יִרְאוּ:

אָזְנַיִם לָהֶם וְלֹא יִשְׁמָעוּ, אַף לָהֶם וְלֹא יְרִיחוּן:

יְדֵיהֶם וְלֹא יְמִישׁוּן, רַגְלֵיהֶם וְלֹא יְהַלֵּכוּ, לֹא־יֶהְגּוּ בִּגְרוֹנָם:

כְּמוֹהֶם יִהְיוּ עֹשֵׂיהֶם, כֹּל אֲשֶׁר־בֹּטֵחַ בָּהֶם:

יִשְׂרָאֵל בְּטַח בַּיהוה, עֶזְרָם וּמָגִנָּם הוּא:

בֵּית אַהֲרֹן בִּטְחוּ בַיהוה, עֶזְרָם וּמָגִנָּם הוּא:

יִרְאֵי יְהוה בִּטְחוּ בַיהוה, עֶזְרָם וּמָגִנָּם הוּא:

---

limit our anger in this whole story to a tame collection of three verses that seek more to validate the emotional cost of victimhood than to express violence. Great stories conjure multiple emotions. We take a moment before continuing our joy with the recitation of Hallel to acknowledge the painful side of this story and the emotional consequences of suffering.

Think of a personal story where joy is commingled with anger. What place have you reserved in your emotional landscape for both these feelings?

If you could add something to this section, what would it be?

HALLEL / PRAISING
Many Jews do not realize that the Seder has a second half or, if they realize it, they may just mumble through it because it is not the story but the emotional aftermath of the story. Because Hallel is read in synagogue the next

יהוה זְכָרָנוּ The LORD remembers us and will bless us.
He will bless the house of Israel.
He will bless the house of Aaron.
He will bless those who fear the LORD,
small and great alike.
May the LORD give you increase: you and your children.
May you be blessed by the LORD, maker of heaven and earth.
The heavens are the LORD's,
but the earth He has given over to mankind.
It is not the dead who praise the LORD,
nor those who go down to the silent grave.
But we will bless the LORD, now and for ever.

HALLELUYA!

give you increase, you and your children." In Psalm 116, the voice is one of individual pain and loss which finds healing and compassion in God: "I was overcome by trouble and sorrow. Then I called on the name of the LORD." Limiting prayer to one voice would be limiting prayer altogether since it speaks to the multiplicity of our needs as a collective and also as a personal outreach to heaven. When the petitioner asks, "How can I repay You?" the question gets to the heart of what prayer "accomplishes." Rabbi A. J. Heschel preferred the word indebtedness to gratitude because, in the words of one scholar: "the latter can be interpreted as a mere feeling, the former unequivocally conveys a sense of duty toward one's benefactor." In Heschel's own words: "The soul is endowed with a sense of indebtedness, and wonder, awe, and fear unlock that sense of indebtedness." Gratitude is not enough on this night. What obligations are attendant upon us toward God and others as a result of redemption? "The world is such that in its face one senses owingness rather than ownership."

Perhaps this explains why Hallel transitions into a meditation of being a servant of God: "Truly, God, I am Your servant … the son of Your maid-servant. You set me free from my chains. To You I shall bring a thanks-giving offering." I will serve You because You freed me. Often this is sung in a beautiful minor key musically suggesting the notion of a soulful

Continued on the next page.

יהוה זְכָרָנוּ יְבָרֵךְ
יְבָרֵךְ אֶת־בֵּית יִשְׂרָאֵל, יְבָרֵךְ אֶת־בֵּית אַהֲרֹן:
יְבָרֵךְ יִרְאֵי יהוה, הַקְּטַנִּים עִם־הַגְּדֹלִים:
יֹסֵף יהוה עֲלֵיכֶם, עֲלֵיכֶם וְעַל־בְּנֵיכֶם:
בְּרוּכִים אַתֶּם לַיהוה, עֹשֵׂה שָׁמַיִם וָאָרֶץ:
הַשָּׁמַיִם שָׁמַיִם לַיהוה, וְהָאָרֶץ נָתַן לִבְנֵי־אָדָם:
לֹא הַמֵּתִים יְהַלְלוּ־יָהּ, וְלֹא כָּל־יֹרְדֵי דוּמָה:
וַאֲנַחְנוּ נְבָרֵךְ יָהּ, מֵעַתָּה וְעַד־עוֹלָם

הַלְלוּיָהּ:

of Passover. There is a talmudic view that it was first uttered when the Israelites crossed the Reed Sea (Pesaḥim 117a). The Talmud emphasizes five
themes of Hallel that are central to the Passover experience, thus explaining why these passages were excerpted from Psalms for the occasion: the
Exodus, the splitting of the Reed Sea, the revelation at Sinai, the revival
of the dead, and the problems preceding redemption (Pesaḥim 118a). This
trajectory of experience is lyrically expressed in these psalms, making them
a good choice for a platform of praise on this night.

Here we continue with the midsection of Hallel and begin again with
two separate psalms, broken up into four passages. The first two are written
in the first-person plural: "Our God is in heaven" and "The LORD remembers us and will bless us" (Psalm 115) and the last two are in the first-person
singular: "I love the LORD, for He hears my voice, my pleas" and "How can
I repay the LORD for all His goodness to me?" (Psalm 116). These passages
do not raise tensions between the plural and singular voice in prayer but
legitimize the way that we move back and forth between them, expressing
ourselves sometimes in community and sometimes in the space of our in-
dividuality, without the presumption that our views and worries are shared.
Thematically, this also makes sense when looking carefully at the words.
We refer to the houses of Israel and of Aaron in Psalm 115 and ask that God
bless us as a community with protection and growth: "May the LORD

Ps. 116

אָהַבְתִּי I love the Lord,
for He hears my voice, my pleas.
He turns His ear to me whenever I call.
The bonds of death encompassed me,
the anguish of the grave came upon me,
I was overcome by trouble and sorrow.
Then I called on the name of the Lord: "Lord, I pray, save my life."
Gracious is the Lord, and righteous; our God is full of compassion.
The Lord protects the simple-hearted.
When I was brought low, He saved me.
My soul, be at peace once more, for the Lord has been good to you.
For You have rescued me from death,
my eyes from weeping, my feet from stumbling.
I shall walk in the presence of the Lord in the land of the living.
I had faith, even when I said, "I am greatly afflicted,"
even when I said rashly, "All men are liars."

מָה־אָשִׁיב How can I repay the Lord for all His goodness to me?
I will lift the cup of salvation and call on the name of the Lord.
I will fulfill my vows to the Lord in the presence of all His people.
Grievous in the Lord's sight is the death of His devoted ones.
Truly, Lord, I am Your servant;
I am Your servant, the son of Your maidservant.
You set me free from my chains.
To You I shall bring a thanksgiving offering
and call on the Lord by name.
I will fulfill my vows to the Lord in the presence of all His people,
in the courts of the House of the Lord, in your midst, Jerusalem.

HALLELUYA!

What is your favorite line of Hallel?
If you could pay the debt of redemption back to God, what would you do?
What's stopping you from doing it?

אָהַבְתִּי

כִּי־יִשְׁמַע יהוה, אֶת־קוֹלִי תַּחֲנוּנָי:

כִּי־הִטָּה אָזְנוֹ לִי, וּבְיָמַי אֶקְרָא:

אֲפָפוּנִי חֶבְלֵי־מָוֶת, וּמְצָרֵי שְׁאוֹל מְצָאוּנִי, צָרָה וְיָגוֹן אֶמְצָא:

וּבְשֵׁם־יהוה אֶקְרָא, אָנָּה יהוה מַלְּטָה נַפְשִׁי:

חַנּוּן יהוה וְצַדִּיק, וֵאלֹהֵינוּ מְרַחֵם:

שֹׁמֵר פְּתָאיִם יהוה, דַּלּוֹתִי וְלִי יְהוֹשִׁיעַ:

שׁוּבִי נַפְשִׁי לִמְנוּחָיְכִי, כִּי־יהוה גָּמַל עָלָיְכִי:

כִּי חִלַּצְתָּ נַפְשִׁי מִמָּוֶת, אֶת־עֵינִי מִן־דִּמְעָה, אֶת־רַגְלִי מִדֶּחִי:

אֶתְהַלֵּךְ לִפְנֵי יהוה, בְּאַרְצוֹת הַחַיִּים:

הֶאֱמַנְתִּי כִּי אֲדַבֵּר, אֲנִי עָנִיתִי מְאֹד:

אֲנִי אָמַרְתִּי בְחָפְזִי, כָּל־הָאָדָם כֹּזֵב:

מָה־אָשִׁיב לַיהוה, כָּל־תַּגְמוּלוֹהִי עָלָי:

כּוֹס־יְשׁוּעוֹת אֶשָּׂא, וּבְשֵׁם יהוה אֶקְרָא:

נְדָרַי לַיהוה אֲשַׁלֵּם, נֶגְדָה־נָּא לְכָל־עַמּוֹ:

יָקָר בְּעֵינֵי יהוה, הַמָּוְתָה לַחֲסִידָיו:

אָנָּה יהוה כִּי־אֲנִי עַבְדֶּךָ, אֲנִי־עַבְדְּךָ בֶּן־אֲמָתֶךָ, פִּתַּחְתָּ לְמוֹסֵרָי:

לְךָ־אֶזְבַּח זֶבַח תּוֹדָה, וּבְשֵׁם יהוה אֶקְרָא:

נְדָרַי לַיהוה אֲשַׁלֵּם, נֶגְדָה־נָּא לְכָל־עַמּוֹ:

בְּחַצְרוֹת בֵּית יהוה, בְּתוֹכֵכִי יְרוּשָׁלָיִם

הַלְלוּיָהּ:

---

indebtedness. Again to quote Heschel: "Man's sin is in his failure to live what he is. Being the master of the earth, man forgets that he is the servant of God."

הַלְלוּ Praise the LORD, all nations; acclaim Him, all you peoples;   *Ps. 117*
for His loving-kindness to us is strong,
and the LORD's faithfulness is everlasting.

HALLELUYA!

הוֹדוּ Thank the LORD for He is good,   *Ps. 118*
HIS LOVING-KINDNESS IS FOR EVER.

Let Israel say
HIS LOVING-KINDNESS IS FOR EVER.

Let the house of Aaron say
HIS LOVING-KINDNESS IS FOR EVER.

Let those who fear the LORD say
HIS LOVING-KINDNESS IS FOR EVER.

מִן־הַמֵּצַר In my distress I called on the LORD.
The LORD answered me and set me free.
The LORD is with me; I will not be afraid.
What can man do to me?
The LORD is with me. He is my helper.
I will see the downfall of my enemies.
It is better to take refuge in the LORD than to trust in man.
It is better to take refuge in the LORD than to trust in princes.

---

been enough, as the song goes, God brought us out of persecution with *love*, healing us as He redeemed us.

This psalm in relation to DAYEINU *is like a call-and-response song. To mimic it and understand it, have a child say three praises to a parent and a parent say three back. This technique can also be used between partners, husband and wife, or friends. We read this psalm later in the Seder evening, but what we miss when we don't read the psalm together with* DAYEINU *is that our emotions of gratitude toward God are responded to with love by God.*

הַלְלוּ אֶת־יהוה כָּל־גּוֹיִם, שַׁבְּחוּהוּ כָּל־הָאֻמִּים:
כִּי גָבַר עָלֵינוּ חַסְדּוֹ, וֶאֱמֶת־יהוה לְעוֹלָם

הַלְלוּיָהּ:

כִּי לְעוֹלָם חַסְדּוֹ:	הוֹדוּ לַיהוה כִּי־טוֹב
כִּי לְעוֹלָם חַסְדּוֹ:	יֹאמַר־נָא יִשְׂרָאֵל
כִּי לְעוֹלָם חַסְדּוֹ:	יֹאמְרוּ־נָא בֵית־אַהֲרֹן
כִּי לְעוֹלָם חַסְדּוֹ:	יֹאמְרוּ־נָא יִרְאֵי יהוה

מִן־הַמֵּצַר קָרָאתִי יָּהּ, עָנָנִי בַמֶּרְחָב יָהּ:
יהוה לִי לֹא אִירָא, מַה־יַּעֲשֶׂה לִי אָדָם:
יהוה לִי בְּעֹזְרָי, וַאֲנִי אֶרְאֶה בְשֹׂנְאָי:
טוֹב לַחֲסוֹת בַּיהוה, מִבְּטֹחַ בָּאָדָם:
טוֹב לַחֲסוֹת בַּיהוה, מִבְּטֹחַ בִּנְדִיבִים:

HIS LOVING-KINDNESS IS FOR EVER

The Exodus motif of oppression and redemption is stamped all over the Book of Psalms. In particular, the image of God bringing us as a collective or bringing singular individuals out of difficulty (*lehotzi*) is integral to the deeply felt supplications contained on its pages (see, for example, Psalms 18:20, 25:15, 43:3). Like *Dayeinu*, the famous exposition of the Exodus in Psalm 136 follows a similar repeated pattern of expressing an action and then the feeling attendant with it. *Dayeinu* is an expression of *our* emotions. When we recollect history, we are filled with gratitude. With each verse of the song, our gratitude grows. Psalm 136 is an expression of *God's* emotions when He brought us out of Egypt; God was filled with love. That love grew and grew over time. While bringing us out of Egypt would have

The nations all surrounded me,
but in the Lord's name I drove them off.
They surrounded me on every side,
but in the Lord's name I drove them off.
They surrounded me like bees,
they attacked me as fire attacks brushwood,
but in the Lord's name I drove them off.
They thrust so hard against me, I nearly fell,
but the Lord came to my help.
The Lord is my strength and my song;
He has become my salvation.
Sounds of song and salvation resound in the tents of the righteous:
"The Lord's right hand has done mighty deeds.
The Lord's right hand is lifted high.
The Lord's right hand has done mighty deeds."
I will not die but live, and tell what the Lord has done.
The Lord has chastened me severely,
but He has not given me over to death.
Open for me the gates of righteousness
that I may enter them and thank the Lord.
This is the gateway to the Lord;
through it, the righteous shall enter.

אוֹדְךָ I will thank You,
for You answered me, and became my salvation.
I will thank You, for You answered me, and became my salvation.

The stone the builders rejected has become the main cornerstone.
The stone the builders rejected has become the main cornerstone.

This is the Lord's doing. It is wondrous in our eyes.
This is the Lord's doing. It is wondrous in our eyes.

This is the day the Lord has made. Let us rejoice and be glad in it.
This is the day the Lord has made. Let us rejoice and be glad in it.

כָּל־גּוֹיִם סְבָבוּנִי

בְּשֵׁם יהוה כִּי אֲמִילַם:

סַבּוּנִי גַם־סְבָבוּנִי

בְּשֵׁם יהוה כִּי אֲמִילַם:

סַבּוּנִי כִדְבֹרִים, דֹּעֲכוּ כְּאֵשׁ קוֹצִים

בְּשֵׁם יהוה כִּי אֲמִילַם:

דָּחֹה דְחִיתַנִי לִנְפֹּל, וַיהוה עֲזָרָנִי:

עָזִּי וְזִמְרָת יָהּ, וַיְהִי־לִי לִישׁוּעָה:

קוֹל רִנָּה וִישׁוּעָה בְּאָהֳלֵי צַדִּיקִים

יְמִין יהוה עֹשָׂה חָיִל:

יְמִין יהוה רוֹמֵמָה

יְמִין יהוה עֹשָׂה חָיִל:

לֹא־אָמוּת כִּי־אֶחְיֶה, וַאֲסַפֵּר מַעֲשֵׂי יָהּ:

יַסֹּר יִסְּרַנִּי יָּהּ, וְלַמָּוֶת לֹא נְתָנָנִי:

פִּתְחוּ־לִי שַׁעֲרֵי־צֶדֶק

אָבֹא־בָם אוֹדֶה יָהּ:

זֶה־הַשַּׁעַר לַיהוה, צַדִּיקִים יָבֹאוּ בוֹ:

אוֹדְךָ כִּי עֲנִיתָנִי, וַתְּהִי־לִי לִישׁוּעָה:

אוֹדְךָ כִּי עֲנִיתָנִי, וַתְּהִי־לִי לִישׁוּעָה:

אֶבֶן מָאֲסוּ הַבּוֹנִים, הָיְתָה לְרֹאשׁ פִּנָּה:

אֶבֶן מָאֲסוּ הַבּוֹנִים, הָיְתָה לְרֹאשׁ פִּנָּה:

מֵאֵת יהוה הָיְתָה זֹּאת, הִיא נִפְלָאת בְּעֵינֵינוּ:

מֵאֵת יהוה הָיְתָה זֹּאת, הִיא נִפְלָאת בְּעֵינֵינוּ:

זֶה־הַיּוֹם עָשָׂה יהוה, נָגִילָה וְנִשְׂמְחָה בוֹ:

זֶה־הַיּוֹם עָשָׂה יהוה, נָגִילָה וְנִשְׂמְחָה בוֹ:

אָנָּא LORD, PLEASE, SAVE US.
LORD, PLEASE, SAVE US.
LORD, PLEASE, GRANT US SUCCESS.
LORD, PLEASE, GRANT US SUCCESS.

בָּרוּךְ Blessed is one who comes in the name of the LORD;
we bless you from the House of the LORD.
Blessed is one who comes in the name of the LORD;
we bless you from the House of the LORD.

The LORD is God; He has given us light. Bind the festival offering
with thick cords [and bring it] to the horns of the altar.
The LORD is God; He has given us light. Bind the festival offering
with thick cords [and bring it] to the horns of the altar.

You are my God and I will thank You;
You are my God, I will exalt You.
You are my God and I will thank You;
You are my God, I will exalt You.

Thank the LORD for He is good,
His loving-kindness is for ever.
Thank the LORD for He is good,
His loving-kindness is for ever.

יְהַלְלוּךָ ALL YOUR WORKS WILL PRAISE YOU,
LORD our God, and Your devoted ones –
the righteous who do Your will,
together with all Your people the house of Israel –
will joyously thank, bless, praise, glorify, exalt, revere, sanctify,
and proclaim the sovereignty of Your name, our King.
For it is good to thank You
and fitting to sing psalms to Your name,
for from eternity to eternity You are God.

אָנָּא יהוה הוֹשִׁיעָה נָּא:

אָנָּא יהוה הוֹשִׁיעָה נָּא:

אָנָּא יהוה הַצְלִיחָה נָּא:

אָנָּא יהוה הַצְלִיחָה נָּא:

בָּרוּךְ הַבָּא בְּשֵׁם יהוה, בֵּרַכְנוּכֶם מִבֵּית יהוה:

בָּרוּךְ הַבָּא בְּשֵׁם יהוה, בֵּרַכְנוּכֶם מִבֵּית יהוה:

אֵל יהוה וַיָּאֶר לָנוּ, אִסְרוּ־חַג בַּעֲבֹתִים עַד־קַרְנוֹת הַמִּזְבֵּחַ:

אֵל יהוה וַיָּאֶר לָנוּ, אִסְרוּ־חַג בַּעֲבֹתִים עַד־קַרְנוֹת הַמִּזְבֵּחַ:

אֵלִי אַתָּה וְאוֹדֶךָּ, אֱלֹהַי אֲרוֹמְמֶךָּ:

אֵלִי אַתָּה וְאוֹדֶךָּ, אֱלֹהַי אֲרוֹמְמֶךָּ:

הוֹדוּ לַיהוה כִּי־טוֹב, כִּי לְעוֹלָם חַסְדּוֹ:

הוֹדוּ לַיהוה כִּי־טוֹב, כִּי לְעוֹלָם חַסְדּוֹ:

יְהַלְלוּךָ

יהוה אֱלֹהֵינוּ כָּל מַעֲשֶׂיךָ

וַחֲסִידֶיךָ צַדִּיקִים עוֹשֵׂי רְצוֹנֶךָ

וְכָל עַמְּךָ בֵּית יִשְׂרָאֵל

בְּרִנָּה יוֹדוּ וִיבָרְכוּ וִישַׁבְּחוּ

וִיפָאֲרוּ וִירוֹמְמוּ וְיַעֲרִיצוּ וְיַקְדִּישׁוּ

וְיַמְלִיכוּ אֶת שִׁמְךָ מַלְכֵּנוּ

כִּי לְךָ טוֹב לְהוֹדוֹת וּלְשִׁמְךָ נָאֶה לְזַמֵּר

כִּי מֵעוֹלָם וְעַד עוֹלָם אַתָּה אֵל.

הודו Thank the Lord, for He is good, His loving-kindness is for ever. Ps. 136
Thank the God of gods, His loving-kindness is for ever.
Thank the Lord of lords, His loving-kindness is for ever.
To the One who alone
works great wonders, His loving-kindness is for ever.
Who made the heavens with wisdom, His loving-kindness is for ever.
Who spread the earth upon the waters, His loving-kindness is for ever.
Who made the great lights, His loving-kindness is for ever.
The sun to rule by day, His loving-kindness is for ever.
The moon and the stars to rule by night; His loving-kindness is for ever.
Who struck Egypt
through their firstborn, His loving-kindness is for ever.
And brought out Israel from their midst, His loving-kindness is for ever.
With a strong hand
and outstretched arm, His loving-kindness is for ever.
Who split the Reed Sea into parts, His loving-kindness is for ever.
And made Israel pass through it, His loving-kindness is for ever.
Casting Pharaoh and his army
into the Reed Sea; His loving-kindness is for ever.
Who led His people
through the wilderness; His loving-kindness is for ever.
Who struck down great kings, His loving-kindness is for ever.
And slew mighty kings, His loving-kindness is for ever.
Sihon, king of the Amorites, His loving-kindness is for ever.
And Og, king of Bashan, His loving-kindness is for ever.
And gave their land as a heritage, His loving-kindness is for ever.
A heritage for His servant Israel; His loving-kindness is for ever.
Who remembered us in our lowly state, His loving-kindness is for ever.
And rescued us from our tormentors, His loving-kindness is for ever.
Who gives food to all flesh, His loving-kindness is for ever.
Give thanks to the God of heaven. His loving-kindness is for ever.

כִּי לְעוֹלָם חַסְדּוֹ:	הוֹדוּ לַיהוה כִּי־טוֹב
כִּי לְעוֹלָם חַסְדּוֹ:	הוֹדוּ לֵאלֹהֵי הָאֱלֹהִים
כִּי לְעוֹלָם חַסְדּוֹ:	הוֹדוּ לַאֲדֹנֵי הָאֲדֹנִים
כִּי לְעוֹלָם חַסְדּוֹ:	לְעֹשֵׂה נִפְלָאוֹת גְּדֹלוֹת לְבַדּוֹ
כִּי לְעוֹלָם חַסְדּוֹ:	לְעֹשֵׂה הַשָּׁמַיִם בִּתְבוּנָה
כִּי לְעוֹלָם חַסְדּוֹ:	לְרֹקַע הָאָרֶץ עַל־הַמָּיִם
כִּי לְעוֹלָם חַסְדּוֹ:	לְעֹשֵׂה אוֹרִים גְּדֹלִים
כִּי לְעוֹלָם חַסְדּוֹ:	אֶת־הַשֶּׁמֶשׁ לְמֶמְשֶׁלֶת בַּיּוֹם
כִּי לְעוֹלָם חַסְדּוֹ:	אֶת־הַיָּרֵחַ וְכוֹכָבִים לְמֶמְשְׁלוֹת בַּלָּיְלָה
כִּי לְעוֹלָם חַסְדּוֹ:	לְמַכֵּה מִצְרַיִם בִּבְכוֹרֵיהֶם
כִּי לְעוֹלָם חַסְדּוֹ:	וַיּוֹצֵא יִשְׂרָאֵל מִתּוֹכָם
כִּי לְעוֹלָם חַסְדּוֹ:	בְּיָד חֲזָקָה וּבִזְרוֹעַ נְטוּיָה
כִּי לְעוֹלָם חַסְדּוֹ:	לְגֹזֵר יַם־סוּף לִגְזָרִים
כִּי לְעוֹלָם חַסְדּוֹ:	וְהֶעֱבִיר יִשְׂרָאֵל בְּתוֹכוֹ
כִּי לְעוֹלָם חַסְדּוֹ:	וְנִעֵר פַּרְעֹה וְחֵילוֹ בְיַם־סוּף
כִּי לְעוֹלָם חַסְדּוֹ:	לְמוֹלִיךְ עַמּוֹ בַּמִּדְבָּר
כִּי לְעוֹלָם חַסְדּוֹ:	לְמַכֵּה מְלָכִים גְּדֹלִים
כִּי לְעוֹלָם חַסְדּוֹ:	וַיַּהֲרֹג מְלָכִים אַדִּירִים
כִּי לְעוֹלָם חַסְדּוֹ:	לְסִיחוֹן מֶלֶךְ הָאֱמֹרִי
כִּי לְעוֹלָם חַסְדּוֹ:	וּלְעוֹג מֶלֶךְ הַבָּשָׁן
כִּי לְעוֹלָם חַסְדּוֹ:	וְנָתַן אַרְצָם לְנַחֲלָה
כִּי לְעוֹלָם חַסְדּוֹ:	נַחֲלָה לְיִשְׂרָאֵל עַבְדּוֹ
כִּי לְעוֹלָם חַסְדּוֹ:	שֶׁבְּשִׁפְלֵנוּ זָכַר לָנוּ
כִּי לְעוֹלָם חַסְדּוֹ:	וַיִּפְרְקֵנוּ מִצָּרֵינוּ
כִּי לְעוֹלָם חַסְדּוֹ:	נֹתֵן לֶחֶם לְכָל־בָּשָׂר
כִּי לְעוֹלָם חַסְדּוֹ:	הוֹדוּ לְאֵל הַשָּׁמָיִם

THE SOUL

of all that lives shall bless Your name, Lord our God,
and the spirit of all flesh shall always glorify
and exalt Your remembrance, our King.
From eternity to eternity You are God.
Without You, we have no king, redeemer, or savior,
who liberates, rescues, sustains,
and shows compassion in every time of trouble and distress.
We have no king but You,
God of the first and last, God of all creatures,
master of all ages, extolled by a multitude of praises,
who guides His world with loving-kindness
and His creatures with compassion.
The Lord neither slumbers nor sleeps.
He rouses the sleepers and wakens the slumberers.
He makes the dumb speak, sets the bound free,
supports the fallen, and raises those bowed down.

Nishmat is a very old prayer and mentioned explicitly in connection with the Seder in the Talmud (Pesaḥim 118a). Rabbi Yoḥanan bar Nafḥa posited that it should be said after Hallel of the Seder, which has been common practice for at least one thousand years, most likely because it contains a direct reference to the Exodus:

> You redeemed us from Egypt, Lord our God, and freed us from the house of bondage. In famine You nourished us; in times of plenty You sustained us. You delivered us from the sword, saved us from the plague, and spared us from serious and lasting illness.

As we read this prayer and thank God, we refer to specific times when rescue and relief was our foremost need. At these times, too, we are amazed at our good fortune.

If your every breath could sing a praise of God, what would it be?
What aspect of nature most speaks to your appreciation of the way God operates in the universe?

נִשְׁמַת

כָּל חַי תְּבָרֵךְ אֶת שִׁמְךָ, יהוה אֱלֹהֵינוּ
וְרוּחַ כָּל בָּשָׂר תְּפָאֵר וּתְרוֹמֵם זִכְרְךָ מַלְכֵּנוּ תָּמִיד.
מִן הָעוֹלָם וְעַד הָעוֹלָם אַתָּה אֵל
וּמִבַּלְעָדֶיךָ אֵין לָנוּ מֶלֶךְ
גּוֹאֵל וּמוֹשִׁיעַ פּוֹדֶה וּמַצִּיל וּמְפַרְנֵס וּמְרַחֵם
בְּכָל עֵת צָרָה וְצוּקָה אֵין לָנוּ מֶלֶךְ אֶלָּא אָתָּה.
אֱלֹהֵי הָרִאשׁוֹנִים וְהָאַחֲרוֹנִים, אֱלוֹהַּ כָּל בְּרִיּוֹת
אֲדוֹן כָּל תּוֹלָדוֹת, הַמְהֻלָּל בְּרֹב הַתִּשְׁבָּחוֹת
הַמְנַהֵג עוֹלָמוֹ בְּחֶסֶד וּבְרִיּוֹתָיו בְּרַחֲמִים.
וַיהוה לֹא יָנוּם וְלֹא יִישָׁן
הַמְעוֹרֵר יְשֵׁנִים וְהַמֵּקִיץ נִרְדָּמִים
וְהַמֵּשִׂיחַ אִלְּמִים וְהַמַּתִּיר אֲסוּרִים
וְהַסּוֹמֵךְ נוֹפְלִים וְהַזּוֹקֵף כְּפוּפִים.

THE SOUL OF ALL THAT LIVES

Nishmat is one of our most touching prayers, read every Shabbat as a close to *Pesukei DeZimra*, our unit of psalms and songs that creates spiritual preparedness for the recitation of *Shema* and *Shemoneh Esreh*. It begins with the words "The soul of all that lives," which indicates what will likely follow. Everything animate sings God's praises, as we read:

> If our mouths were as full of song as the sea, and our tongue with jubilation as its myriad waves, if our lips were full of praise like the spacious heavens, and our eyes shone like the sun and moon, if our hands were outstretched like eagles of the sky, and our feet as swift as hinds – still we could not thank You enough.

There is a sense of escalated joy as the universe joins us in song, and it is easy to understand its central place in the Haggada. When we experience joy and gratitude, we also project those feelings onto all that is around us.

To You alone we give thanks:
If our mouths were as full of song as the sea,
and our tongue with jubilation as its myriad waves,
if our lips were full of praise like the spacious heavens,
and our eyes shone like the sun and moon,
if our hands were outstretched like eagles of the sky,
and our feet as swift as hinds –
still we could not thank You enough,
LORD our God and God of our ancestors, or bless Your name
for even one of the thousand thousands
and myriad myriads of favors
You did for our ancestors and for us.
You redeemed us from Egypt, LORD our God,
and freed us from the house of bondage.
In famine You nourished us; in times of plenty You sustained us.
You delivered us from the sword, saved us from the plague,
and spared us from serious and lasting illness.
Until now Your mercies have helped us.
Your love has not forsaken us.
May You, LORD our God, never abandon us.
Therefore the limbs You formed within us,
the spirit and soul You breathed into our nostrils,
and the tongue You placed in our mouth –
they will thank and bless, praise and glorify, exalt and esteem,
hallow and do homage to Your name, O our King.
For every mouth shall give thanks to You,
every tongue vow allegiance to You, every knee shall bend to You,
every upright body shall bow to You, all hearts shall fear You,
and our innermost being sing praises to Your name,
as is written:

> "All my bones shall say, 'LORD, who is like You?   *Ps. 35*
> You save the poor from one stronger than him,
> the poor and needy from one who would rob him.'"

‏לְךָ לְבַדְּךָ אֲנַחְנוּ מוֹדִים.‏

‏אִלּוּ פִינוּ מָלֵא שִׁירָה כַּיָּם‏

‏וּלְשׁוֹנֵנוּ רִנָּה כַּהֲמוֹן גַּלָּיו‏

‏וְשִׂפְתוֹתֵינוּ שֶׁבַח כְּמֶרְחֲבֵי רָקִיעַ‏

‏וְעֵינֵינוּ מְאִירוֹת כַּשֶּׁמֶשׁ וְכַיָּרֵחַ‏

‏וְיָדֵינוּ פְרוּשׂוֹת כְּנִשְׁרֵי שָׁמָיִם‏

‏וְרַגְלֵינוּ קַלּוֹת כָּאַיָּלוֹת‏

‏אֵין אֲנַחְנוּ מַסְפִּיקִים לְהוֹדוֹת לְךָ, יהוה אֱלֹהֵינוּ וֵאלֹהֵי אֲבוֹתֵינוּ‏

‏וּלְבָרֵךְ אֶת שְׁמֶךָ‏

‏עַל אַחַת מֵאֶלֶף אֶלֶף אַלְפֵי אֲלָפִים וְרִבֵּי רְבָבוֹת פְּעָמִים הַטּוֹבוֹת‏

‏שֶׁעָשִׂיתָ עִם אֲבוֹתֵינוּ וְעִמָּנוּ.‏

‏מִמִּצְרַיִם גְּאַלְתָּנוּ, יהוה אֱלֹהֵינוּ, וּמִבֵּית עֲבָדִים פְּדִיתָנוּ‏

‏בְּרָעָב זַנְתָּנוּ וּבְשָׂבָע כִּלְכַּלְתָּנוּ, מֵחֶרֶב הִצַּלְתָּנוּ וּמִדֶּבֶר מִלַּטְתָּנוּ‏

‏וּמֵחֳלָיִים רָעִים וְנֶאֱמָנִים דִּלִּיתָנוּ.‏

‏עַד הֵנָּה עֲזָרוּנוּ רַחֲמֶיךָ, וְלֹא עֲזָבוּנוּ חֲסָדֶיךָ‏

‏וְאַל תִּטְּשֵׁנוּ, יהוה אֱלֹהֵינוּ, לָנֶצַח.‏

‏עַל כֵּן אֵבָרִים שֶׁפִּלַּגְתָּ בָּנוּ‏

‏וְרוּחַ וּנְשָׁמָה שֶׁנָּפַחְתָּ בְּאַפֵּינוּ, וְלָשׁוֹן אֲשֶׁר שַׂמְתָּ בְּפִינוּ‏

‏הֵן הֵם יוֹדוּ וִיבָרְכוּ וִישַׁבְּחוּ וִיפָאֲרוּ‏

‏וִירוֹמְמוּ וְיַעֲרִיצוּ וְיַקְדִּישׁוּ וְיַמְלִיכוּ אֶת שִׁמְךָ מַלְכֵּנוּ‏

‏כִּי כָל פֶּה לְךָ יוֹדֶה וְכָל לָשׁוֹן לְךָ תִשָּׁבַע‏

‏וְכָל בֶּרֶךְ לְךָ תִכְרַע וְכָל קוֹמָה לְפָנֶיךָ תִשְׁתַּחֲוֶה‏

‏וְכָל לְבָבוֹת יִירָאוּךָ וְכָל קֶרֶב וּכְלָיוֹת יְזַמְּרוּ לִשְׁמֶךָ‏

‏כַּדָּבָר שֶׁכָּתוּב‏

‏תהלים לה‏

‏כָּל עַצְמֹתַי תֹּאמַרְנָה יהוה מִי כָמוֹךָ‏

‏מַצִּיל עָנִי מֵחָזָק מִמֶּנּוּ, וְעָנִי וְאֶבְיוֹן מִגֹּזְלוֹ:‏

Who is like You?
Who is equal to You?
Who can be compared to You?
O great, mighty, and awesome God, God Most High,
maker of heaven and earth.
We will laud, praise, and glorify You and bless Your holy name,
as it is said:

> "Of David. Bless the LORD, O my soul,   Ps. 103
> and all that is within me bless His holy name."

God – in Your absolute power,
Great – in the glory of Your name,
Mighty – for ever,
Awesome – in Your awe-inspiring deeds,
The King – who sits on a throne.
High and lofty
He inhabits eternity; exalted and holy is His name.
And it is written:

> Sing joyfully to the LORD, you righteous,   Ps. 33
> for praise from the upright is seemly.
>
> | By the mouth | of the upright | You shall be praised. |
> | By the words | of the righteous | You shall be blessed. |
> | By the tongue | of the devout | You shall be extolled, |
> | And in the midst | of the holy | You shall be sanctified. |

וּבְמַקְהֲלוֹת And in the assemblies
of tens of thousands of Your people, the house of Israel,
with joyous song shall Your name, our King,
be glorified in every generation.
For this is the duty of all creatures before You,
LORD our God and God of our ancestors:
to thank, praise, laud, glorify, exalt,
honor, bless, raise high, and acclaim –
even beyond all the words of song and praise
of David, son of Jesse, Your servant, Your anointed.

מִי יִדְמֶה לָּךְ וּמִי יִשְׁוֶה לָּךְ וּמִי יַעֲרָךְ לָךְ
הָאֵל הַגָּדוֹל, הַגִּבּוֹר וְהַנּוֹרָא
אֵל עֶלְיוֹן, קוֹנֵה שָׁמַיִם וָאָרֶץ.
נְהַלֶּלְךָ וּנְשַׁבֵּחֲךָ וּנְפָאֶרְךָ וּנְבָרֵךְ אֶת שֵׁם קָדְשֶׁךָ
כָּאָמוּר

תהלים קג
לְדָוִד, בָּרְכִי נַפְשִׁי אֶת־יהוה, וְכָל־קְרָבַי אֶת־שֵׁם קָדְשׁוֹ:
הָאֵל בְּתַעֲצוּמוֹת עֻזֶּךָ
הַגָּדוֹל בִּכְבוֹד שְׁמֶךָ
הַגִּבּוֹר לָנֶצַח וְהַנּוֹרָא בְּנוֹרְאוֹתֶיךָ
הַמֶּלֶךְ הַיּוֹשֵׁב עַל כִּסֵּא.
רָם וְנִשָּׂא
שׁוֹכֵן עַד מָרוֹם וְקָדוֹשׁ שְׁמוֹ
וְכָתוּב

תהלים לג
רַנְּנוּ צַדִּיקִים בַּיהוה, לַיְשָׁרִים נָאוָה תְהִלָּה:

בְּפִי	יְשָׁרִים	תִּתְהַלָּל
וּבְדִבְרֵי	צַדִּיקִים	תִּתְבָּרַךְ
וּבִלְשׁוֹן	חֲסִידִים	תִּתְרוֹמָם
וּבְקֶרֶב	קְדוֹשִׁים	תִּתְקַדָּשׁ

וּבְמַקְהֲלוֹת רִבְבוֹת עַמְּךָ בֵּית יִשְׂרָאֵל
בְּרִנָּה יִתְפָּאַר שִׁמְךָ מַלְכֵּנוּ בְּכָל דּוֹר וָדוֹר
שֶׁכֵּן חוֹבַת כָּל הַיְצוּרִים
לְפָנֶיךָ יהוה אֱלֹהֵינוּ וֵאלֹהֵי אֲבוֹתֵינוּ
לְהוֹדוֹת, לְהַלֵּל, לְשַׁבֵּחַ, לְפָאֵר, לְרוֹמֵם
לְהַדֵּר, לְבָרֵךְ, לְעַלֵּה וּלְקַלֵּס
עַל כָּל דִּבְרֵי שִׁירוֹת וְתִשְׁבָּחוֹת
דָּוִד בֶּן יִשַׁי, עַבְדְּךָ מְשִׁיחֶךָ.

יִשְׁתַּבַּח May Your name be praised for ever, our King,
the great and holy God, king in heaven and on earth.
For to You, LORD our God and God of our ancestors,
it is right to offer song and praise,
hymn and psalm, strength and dominion,
eternity, greatness and power,
song of praise and glory, holiness and kingship,
blessings and thanks, from now and for ever.
Blessed are You, LORD, God and King, exalted in praises,
God of thanksgivings, master of wonders,
who delights in hymns of song,
King, God, giver of life to the worlds.

Blessed are You, LORD our God, King of the Universe,
who creates the fruit of the vine.

Drink the fourth cup while reclining to the left.

---

that He secured with our ancestors and *therefore* understood that for the
relationship to continue, God had to redeem us. But bringing us out of
Egypt would not have been sufficient to actualize our purpose as a nation.
We needed a meaningful survival then as we need a meaningful survival
now. For that to happen, God had to free us, redeem us, and adopt us as
His people:

> I have heard the groaning of the Israelites, whom the Egyptians are
> enslaving, and I have remembered My covenant. *Therefore,* say to the
> Israelites: "I am the LORD, and I will **bring you out** from under the yoke
> of the Egyptians. I will **free you** from being slaves to them, and I will
> **redeem you** with an outstretched arm and with mighty acts of judgment.
> I will **take you** as My own people, and I will be your God. Then you will
> know that I am the LORD your God, who brought you out from under
> the yoke of the Egyptians.

Bringing us out, as represented by our first cup of wine, was a physical act
of removal. Without it, the story of our spiritual development could not
have started. Redeeming us – the infinitive *"lig'ol"* – did not merely have

Continued on the next page.

יִשְׁתַּבַּח שִׁמְךָ לָעַד מַלְכֵּנוּ
הָאֵל הַמֶּלֶךְ הַגָּדוֹל וְהַקָּדוֹשׁ בַּשָּׁמַיִם וּבָאָרֶץ
כִּי לְךָ נָאֶה, יהוה אֱלֹהֵינוּ וֵאלֹהֵי אֲבוֹתֵינוּ
שִׁיר וּשְׁבָחָה, הַלֵּל וְזִמְרָה
עֹז וּמֶמְשָׁלָה, נֶצַח, גְּדֻלָּה וּגְבוּרָה
תְּהִלָּה וְתִפְאֶרֶת, קְדֻשָּׁה וּמַלְכוּת
בְּרָכוֹת וְהוֹדָאוֹת, מֵעַתָּה וְעַד עוֹלָם.
בָּרוּךְ אַתָּה יהוה, אֵל מֶלֶךְ גָּדוֹל בַּתִּשְׁבָּחוֹת
אֵל הַהוֹדָאוֹת אֲדוֹן הַנִּפְלָאוֹת
הַבּוֹחֵר בְּשִׁירֵי זִמְרָה, מֶלֶךְ, אֵל, חֵי הָעוֹלָמִים.

בָּרוּךְ אַתָּה יהוה אֱלֹהֵינוּ מֶלֶךְ הָעוֹלָם, בּוֹרֵא פְּרִי הַגָּפֶן.

Drink the fourth cup while reclining to the left.

WHO CREATES THE FRUIT OF THE VINE

We have finally arrived at the culminating glass of wine. We have raised a toast four times to God, representing the four verbs used in Exodus 6:6–7 to describe the fact that God redeemed us. With each mention of our upcoming freedom, we say "I'll drink to that!" and then we do, leaning as they once did in ancient homes to signify that the cramped posture of the slave is no longer ours. What some readers miss, however, is that these verses not only communicate different verbs about our freedom, they represent a trajectory in our developing relationship with God that is only fully realized with the fourth cup. As we read the verses, the transformation becomes apparent, beginning with the first Hebrew word of verse 6: "*lakhen,*" therefore. Some scholars believe this word creates an oath on God's part connected to the last word in verse 5, "covenant." Similar usage of this term appears in Genesis 4:15, 30:15 and Numbers 16:11, 20:12 and in a host of other locations throughout the Prophets, signaling that an action performed by one person brings about a reaction by God or by another. Here God heard our pain, remembered the bond

בָּרוּךְ Blessed are You, LORD our God, King of the Universe,
for the vine and the fruit of the vine,
and for the produce of the field;
for the desirable, good, and spacious land that You willingly gave as
heritage to our ancestors, that they might eat of its fruit
and be satisfied with its goodness.
Have compassion, LORD our God,
on Israel Your people, on Jerusalem,
Your city, on Zion the home of Your glory,
on Your altar and Your Temple.
May You rebuild Jerusalem,
the holy city, swiftly in our time,
and may You bring us back there,
rejoicing in its rebuilding,
eating from its fruit, satisfied by its goodness,
and blessing You for it in holiness and purity.
(*On Shabbat:* Be pleased to refresh us on this Sabbath Day.)
Grant us joy on this Festival of Matzot.
For You, God, are good and do good to all
and we thank You for the land
and for the fruit of the vine.
Blessed are You, LORD,
for the land and for the fruit of the vine.

God "takes" us as His own, the word "*lakaḥ*" is used; in many places in the
Bible it appears as a term of marriage. Obligation and responsibility are
transformed to love and finally into a covenantal partnership. With this last
cup of wine, we both remember and celebrate the changes that happened
in our relationship with God that created profound intimacy.

*Think of an important relationship to you and use four verbs to describe it at
different stages.*

*Why do you think we should drink to each stage of our relationship with God?
How else might we have marked these stages?*

בָּרוּךְ אַתָּה יהוה אֱלֹהֵינוּ מֶלֶךְ הָעוֹלָם

עַל הַגֶּפֶן וְעַל פְּרִי הַגֶּפֶן

וְעַל תְּנוּבַת הַשָּׂדֶה

וְעַל אֶרֶץ חֶמְדָּה טוֹבָה וּרְחָבָה

שֶׁרָצִיתָ וְהִנְחַלְתָּ לַאֲבוֹתֵינוּ

לֶאֱכֹל מִפִּרְיָהּ וְלִשְׂבֹּעַ מִטּוּבָהּ.

רַחֶם נָא יהוה אֱלֹהֵינוּ עַל יִשְׂרָאֵל עַמֶּךָ

וְעַל יְרוּשָׁלַיִם עִירֶךָ

וְעַל צִיּוֹן מִשְׁכַּן כְּבוֹדֶךָ

וְעַל מִזְבְּחֶךָ וְעַל הֵיכָלֶךָ.

וּבְנֵה יְרוּשָׁלַיִם עִיר הַקֹּדֶשׁ בִּמְהֵרָה בְיָמֵינוּ

וְהַעֲלֵנוּ לְתוֹכָהּ וְשַׂמְּחֵנוּ בְּבִנְיָנָהּ

וְנֹאכַל מִפִּרְיָהּ וְנִשְׂבַּע מִטּוּבָהּ

וּנְבָרֶכְךָ עָלֶיהָ בִּקְדֻשָּׁה וּבְטָהֳרָה.

(בשבת: וּרְצֵה וְהַחֲלִיצֵנוּ בְּיוֹם הַשַּׁבָּת הַזֶּה)

וְשַׂמְּחֵנוּ בְּיוֹם חַג הַמַּצּוֹת הַזֶּה

כִּי אַתָּה יהוה טוֹב וּמֵטִיב לַכֹּל

וְנוֹדֶה לְךָ

עַל הָאָרֶץ וְעַל פְּרִי הַגֶּפֶן/ ארץ ישראל *If from* גַּפְנָהּ./

בָּרוּךְ אַתָּה יהוה

עַל הָאָרֶץ וְעַל פְּרִי הַגֶּפֶן/ ארץ ישראל *If from* גַּפְנָהּ./

---

the messianic overtones it has today. It was used in the Bible to suggest the
obligations of relatives toward the most vulnerable, as in Ruth's redeemer
who was obligated in levirate marriage to protect her and the inheritance
of her husband's family. Here God fulfills that role with us. Finally, when

Outside Israel, this poem is recited on the first night of the festival only.

וּבְכֵן וַיְהִי בַּחֲצִי הַלַּיְלָה AND SO – IT HAPPENED AT MIDNIGHT. *Ex. 12*

Many were the miracles You performed long ago   at night.
At the beginning of the watch   on this night,
You won [Abraham]'s battle, when [his men were] split,   and the night
                                                                IT HAPPENED AT MIDNIGHT.

You judged the king of Gerar in his dream   at night.
You put dread into [Laban] the Aramean's heart   that night.
And Israel struggled with an angel and overcame him   at night
                                                                IT HAPPENED AT MIDNIGHT.

You crushed the firstborns of Patros [Egypt] in the middle   of the night.
They could not find their strength, when they rose up
                                                 [against Israel]   at night.
You flung [Sisera] the commander of Haroshet
                                     off course with the stars   of night
                                                                IT HAPPENED AT MIDNIGHT.

---

with darkness, in our song, the night of the Exodus had the clarity of day-time. When day is not day and night is not night, everything about nature turns on its head. Embraced in the totality of a miracle, everything blazes brightly with the imprint of God's presence and offers hope that all future darkness will turn into light.

This sentiment is echoed in the Talmud in a passage that identifies Nisan as the month of many remarkable developments, particularly redemption:

Rabbi Yehoshua says, "In Nisan the world was created; in Nisan the patriarchs were born; in Nisan the patriarchs died; on Passover Isaac was born…in Nisan the Jewish people were redeemed from Egypt, and in Nisan in the future, the Jewish people will be redeemed." (Rosh HaShana 11a)

When one event happens in a particular month, it makes the time period or season feel auspicious or special. When multiple events contribute to this impression, the overall impact is almost anticipatory. We make things happen at times that feel open to change and possibility.

Outside ארץ ישראל, *this poem is recited on the first night of the festival only.*

שמות יב

וּבְכֵן וַיְהִי בַּחֲצִי הַלַּיְלָה

בַּלַּיְלָה	אָז רֹב נִסִּים הִפְלֵאתָ
הַלַּיְלָה	בְּרֹאשׁ אַשְׁמוּרוֹת זֶה
לַיְלָה	גֵּר צֶדֶק נִצַּחְתּוֹ, כְּנֶחֱלַק לוֹ

וַיְהִי בַּחֲצִי הַלַּיְלָה

הַלַּיְלָה	דַּנְתָּ מֶלֶךְ גְּרָר בַּחֲלוֹם
לַיְלָה	הִפְחַדְתָּ אֲרַמִּי בְּאֶמֶשׁ
לַיְלָה	וַיִּשְׂרָאֵל יָשַׂר לָאֵל, וַיּוּכַל לוֹ

וַיְהִי בַּחֲצִי הַלַּיְלָה

הַלַּיְלָה	זֶרַע בְּכוֹרֵי פַתְרוֹס מָחַצְתָּ בַּחֲצִי
בַּלַּיְלָה	חֵילָם לֹא מָצְאוּ בְּקוּמָם
לַיְלָה	טִיסַת נְגִיד חֲרֹשֶׁת סִלִּיתָ בְּכוֹכְבֵי

וַיְהִי בַּחֲצִי הַלַּיְלָה

 IT HAPPENED AT MIDNIGHT

This medieval poem was composed by a scholar known as Yannai who lived in Israel in the sixth or seventh century and probably authored more than two thousand poems in his lifetime. We only learned of his prolific output with the discovery of the Cairo Geniza that held fragments of his works. This poem was originally composed to be said during prayer services on the Shabbat before Passover, traditionally called *Shabbat HaGadol*, the Great Shabbat, because rabbis usually give a lengthy sermon or class in preparation for Passover. Today, the song is sung on the first night of Passover at the conclusion of the Seder. In acrostic form, the song records many events in Jewish history that we believe took place on the night of the fifteenth of Nisan, with each stanza ending with the word "*laila*" – night. More than the build-up we make of the exact stroke of midnight on New Year's Eve, Jews should mark this exact time of night for its resonances throughout our history. The stanza above transforms the insecurity of the night into the gloriousness of midday through the act of redemption. Unlike Elie Wiesel's *Night*, where each day of the Holocaust became overshadowed

[Sennacherib] the blasphemer thought to raise his hand
against the beloved [city]; but You dried up the bodies of his fallen   in the night.
You overthrew Bel, idol and pedestal together, in the dead   of night.
To [Daniel] the beloved man were revealed
                   the secrets of that vision   of the night
                 IT HAPPENED AT MIDNIGHT.

[Belshazzar], who drank himself merry from the holy vessels,
                   was killed on that same   night.
[Daniel] was brought out unharmed from the
          lions' den; he who had explained those terrors   of the night.
[Haman] the Agagite bore his hatred and wrote his orders   at night
                 IT HAPPENED AT MIDNIGHT.

You awakened Your might against him, disturbing
               [King Aḥashverosh's] sleep   at night.
You shall tread the winepress of [Seir],
              who asks anxiously, "What   of the night?"
You will cry out like the watchman, calling, "Morning is come,   and also night"
                 IT HAPPENED AT MIDNIGHT.

Draw near the day that will be neither day   nor night.
Highest One, make known that day is Yours   and also night.
Appoint watchmen [to guard] Your city all day long   and all night,
Light up like daylight the darkness   of night
                 IT HAPPENED AT MIDNIGHT.

Outside Israel, this poem is recited on the second night of the festival only.

וּבְכֵן וַאֲמַרְתֶּם זֶבַח פֶּסַח TELL [your children]: "THIS IS THE PESAḤ." *Ex. 12*

You showed Your immense power in wonders   on Pesaḥ;
to the head of all seasons You have raised up   Pesaḥ.
You revealed to [Abraham] the Ezraḥi what would come at midnight   on Pesaḥ.
       TELL [your children]: "THIS IS THE PESAḤ."

Exodus 12:27, repeating our job but also suggesting that this is a story we
will tell again and again, on Pesaḥ and over the Pesaḥ. The beginning of the
song is really a tribute to Abraham by seeing in this story of our patriarch
the microcosmic narrative of our nationhood. In the first stanza, Abraham
is referred to as *"Ezraḥi"* – a man of the East (Bava Batra 15a). He was first

Continued on the next page.

בַּלַּיְלָה	יָעַץ מְחָרֵף לְנוֹפֵף אִוּוּי, הוֹבַשְׁתָּ פְגָרָיו
לַיְלָה	כָּרַע בֵּל וּמַצָּבוֹ בְּאִישׁוֹן
לַיְלָה	לְאִישׁ חֲמוּדוֹת נִגְלָה רָז חֲזוֹת
וַיְהִי בַּחֲצִי הַלַּיְלָה	

בַּלַּיְלָה	מִשְׁתַּכֵּר בִּכְלֵי קֹדֶשׁ נֶהֱרַג בּוֹ
לַיְלָה	נוֹשַׁע מִבּוֹר אֲרָיוֹת, פּוֹתֵר בִּעֲתוּתֵי
בַּלַּיְלָה	שִׂנְאָה נָטַר אֲגָגִי, וְכָתַב סְפָרִים
וַיְהִי בַּחֲצִי הַלַּיְלָה	

לַיְלָה	עוֹרַרְתָּ נִצְחֲךָ עָלָיו בְּנֶדֶד שְׁנַת
מִלַּיְלָה	פּוּרָה תִדְרֹךְ לְשׁוֹמֵר מַה
לַיְלָה	צָרַח כַּשּׁוֹמֵר, וְשָׂח אָתָא בֹקֶר וְגַם
וַיְהִי בַּחֲצִי הַלַּיְלָה	

לַיְלָה	קָרֵב יוֹם אֲשֶׁר הוּא לֹא יוֹם וְלֹא
הַלַּיְלָה	רָם הוֹדַע כִּי לְךָ הַיּוֹם אַף לְךָ
הַלַּיְלָה	שׁוֹמְרִים הַפְקֵד לְעִירְךָ כָּל הַיּוֹם וְכָל
לַיְלָה	תָּאִיר כְּאוֹר יוֹם חֶשְׁכַּת
וַיְהִי בַּחֲצִי הַלַּיְלָה	

Outside ארץ ישראל, *this poem is recited on the second night of the festival only.*

שמות יב

וּבְכֵן וַאֲמַרְתֶּם זֶבַח פֶּסַח

בְּפֶסַח	אֹמֶץ גְּבוּרוֹתֶיךָ הִפְלֵאתָ
פֶּסַח	בְּרֹאשׁ כָּל מוֹעֲדוֹת נִשֵּׂאתָ
פֶּסַח	גִּלִּיתָ לְאֶזְרָחִי חֲצוֹת לֵיל
וַאֲמַרְתֶּם זֶבַח פֶּסַח	

TELL [YOUR CHILDREN]: "THIS IS THE PESAḤ"

"This is the Pesaḥ," we read in Exodus 12, but what are we doing when we say this? We were holding up the Paschal lamb, telling God that we did our job as commanded. We are repeating again and again the exact words of

You knocked at his doors in the heat of the day   on Pesaḥ;
he gave Your shining [messengers] unleavened cakes to eat   on Pesaḥ;
and he ran to the herd, hinting at the ox in the Torah reading   of Pesaḥ.
            TELL [your children]: "THIS IS THE PESAḤ."

The men of Sodom raged and burned in fire   on Pesaḥ.
Lot was saved; he baked matzot at the end   of Pesaḥ.
You swept bare the land of Mof and Nof [Egypt] in Your great rage   on Pesaḥ.
            TELL [your children]: "THIS IS THE PESAḤ."

The firstborns of [Egypt's] vigor You crushed, LORD,
                        on the night of guarding,   on Pesaḥ.
[But,] Mighty One, You passed over Your firstborn son
                        when You saw the blood   of the Pesaḥ,
allowing no destruction through my doors   on Pesaḥ.
            TELL [your children]: "THIS IS THE PESAḤ."

The walled city [of Jericho] was closed [for fear] when it was   Pesaḥ.
Midian was destroyed in the din, [after a dream of] Omer barley   on Pesaḥ.
The fat ones of [Assyria; of] Pul and Lud were burned away in fires   on Pesaḥ.
            TELL [your children]: "THIS IS THE PESAḤ."

This day [Sennacherib] halted at Nob [and laid siege] until the time   of Pesaḥ.
A hand wrote Babylonia's doom on the wall   at Pesaḥ:
the lamp was lit, the table was laid   on Pesaḥ.
            TELL [your children]: "THIS IS THE PESAḤ."

Hadassa gathered the people to fast three days   at Pesaḥ;
You crushed [Haman,] the head of that evil family,
                        on a gallows fifty cubits high   on Pesaḥ.
[Loss and widowhood –] You will bring these two
                in a moment to [Edom, which rules us now,]   on Pesaḥ.
Strengthen Your hand, raise Your right hand,
                        as on the night first sanctified   as Pesaḥ.
            TELL [your children]: "THIS IS THE PESAḤ."

---

by the welcome that Abraham gave to the three angels who visited him in
the guise of human travelers. The third stanza compares Sodom to Egypt,
both places of injustice that God destroyed through miracles. Lot is also

Continued on the next page.

בְּפֶסַח	דְּלָתָיו דָּפַקְתָּ כְּחֹם הַיּוֹם
בְּפֶסַח	הִסְעִיד נוֹצְצִים עֻגוֹת מַצּוֹת
פֶּסַח	וְאֶל הַבָּקָר, רָץ זֵכֶר לְשׁוֹר עֵרֶךְ
וַאֲמַרְתֶּם זֶבַח פֶּסַח	

בְּפֶסַח	זֹעֲמוּ סְדוֹמִים, וְלֹהֲטוּ בָּאֵשׁ
פֶּסַח	חֻלַּץ לוֹט מֵהֶם, וּמַצּוֹת אָפָה בְּקֵץ
בְּפֶסַח	טִאטֵאתָ אַדְמַת מֹף וְנֹף בְּעָבְרְךָ
וַאֲמַרְתֶּם זֶבַח פֶּסַח	

פֶּסַח	יָהּ, רֹאשׁ כָּל אוֹן מָחַצְתָּ בְּלֵיל שִׁמּוּר
פֶּסַח	כַּבִּיר, עַל בֵּן בְּכוֹר פָּסַחְתָּ בְּדַם
בְּפֶסַח	לְבִלְתִּי תֵּת מַשְׁחִית לָבֹא בִּפְתָחַי
וַאֲמַרְתֶּם זֶבַח פֶּסַח	

פֶּסַח	מְסֻגֶּרֶת סֻגְּרָה בְּעִתּוֹתֵי
פֶּסַח	נִשְׁמְדָה מִדְיָן בִּצְלִיל שְׂעוֹרֵי עֹמֶר
פֶּסַח	שֹׂרְפוּ מִשְׁמַנֵּי פּוּל וְלוּד, בִּיקַד יְקוֹד
וַאֲמַרְתֶּם זֶבַח פֶּסַח	

פֶּסַח	עוֹד הַיּוֹם בְּנֹב לַעֲמֹד, עַד גָּעָה עוֹנַת
בְּפֶסַח	פַּס יָד כָּתְבָה לְקַעֲקֵעַ צוּל
בְּפֶסַח	צָפֹה הַצָּפִית עָרוֹךְ הַשֻּׁלְחָן
וַאֲמַרְתֶּם זֶבַח פֶּסַח	

בְּפֶסַח	קָהָל כִּנְּסָה הֲדַסָּה, צוֹם לְשַׁלֵּשׁ
בְּפֶסַח	רֹאשׁ מִבֵּית רָשָׁע מָחַצְתָּ בְּעֵץ חֲמִשִּׁים
בְּפֶסַח	שְׁתֵּי אֵלֶּה, רֶגַע תָּבִיא לְעוּצִית
פֶּסַח	תָּעֹז יָדְךָ, תָּרוּם יְמִינֶךָ, כְּלֵיל הִתְקַדֶּשׁ חַג
וַאֲמַרְתֶּם זֶבַח פֶּסַח	

told that his future heirs would one day be enslaved and then a mass exodus would take place. The tribute to Abraham continues, as another aspect of Passover is emphasized, the importance of kindness to strangers, illustrated

כִּי לוֹ יָאֶה FOR HIM IT IS FITTING
Majestic in kingship, truly chosen: His legions say to Him:
"Yours and Yours; Yours, for it is Yours; Yours, only Yours;
Yours, LORD, is the Kingdom."   *1 Chron. 29*
FOR HIM IT IS FITTING, FOR HIM IT IS RIGHT.

Unmistakable in His kingship, truly glorious: His venerable ones say to Him:
"Yours and Yours; Yours, for it is Yours; Yours, only Yours;
Yours, LORD, is the kingdom."
FOR HIM IT IS FITTING, FOR HIM IT IS RIGHT.

Worthy of kingship, truly mighty: His officers say to Him:
"Yours and Yours; Yours, for it is Yours; Yours, only Yours;
Yours, LORD, is the kingdom."
FOR HIM IT IS FITTING, FOR HIM IT IS RIGHT.

One in kingship, truly omnipotent: His learned ones say to Him:
"Yours and Yours; Yours, for it is Yours; Yours, only Yours;
Yours, LORD, is the kingdom."
FOR HIM IT IS FITTING, FOR HIM IT IS RIGHT.

---

given its emphasis on kingship. The refrain – "For Him it is fitting, for Him
it is right" – also accords with the royal theme. Because all is under God's
dominion as Master of the universe, God can decide what is His and what
fate is fitting for us, His servants. The expression "Yours and Yours" that
is repeated confirms this ownership and capacity to choose and seems to
have its origins in I Chronicles 29:10–16, where King David, upon dedicat-
ing the Temple his son Solomon built, offers the following praise of God:

David praised the LORD in the presence of the whole assembly, saying,
"Praise be to You, O LORD, God of our father Israel, from everlasting to
everlasting. **Yours,** O LORD, is the greatness and the power and the glory
and the majesty and the splendor, for everything in heaven and earth
is Yours. **Yours,** O LORD, is the kingdom; You are exalted as head over
all. **Wealth and honor come from You; You are the ruler of all things.
In Your hands are strength and power to exalt and give strength to
all.** Now, our God, we give You thanks, and praise Your glorious name.
But who am I, and who are my people, that we should be able to give as

Continued on the next page.

דברי הימים
א׳ כט

כִּי לוֹ נָאֶה, כִּי לוֹ יָאֶה

אַדִּיר בִּמְלוּכָה   בָּחוּר כַּהֲלָכָה   גְּדוּדָיו יֹאמְרוּ לוֹ
לְךָ וּלְךָ, לְךָ כִּי לְךָ, לְךָ אַף לְךָ, לְךָ יהוה הַמַּמְלָכָה
כִּי לוֹ נָאֶה, כִּי לוֹ יָאֶה

דָּגוּל בִּמְלוּכָה   הָדוּר כַּהֲלָכָה   וָתִיקָיו יֹאמְרוּ לוֹ
לְךָ וּלְךָ, לְךָ כִּי לְךָ, לְךָ אַף לְךָ, לְךָ יהוה הַמַּמְלָכָה
כִּי לוֹ נָאֶה, כִּי לוֹ יָאֶה

זַכַּאי בִּמְלוּכָה   חָסִין כַּהֲלָכָה   טַפְסְרָיו יֹאמְרוּ לוֹ
לְךָ וּלְךָ, לְךָ כִּי לְךָ, לְךָ אַף לְךָ, לְךָ יהוה הַמַּמְלָכָה
כִּי לוֹ נָאֶה, כִּי לוֹ יָאֶה

יָחִיד בִּמְלוּכָה   כַּבִּיר כַּהֲלָכָה   לִמּוּדָיו יֹאמְרוּ לוֹ
לְךָ וּלְךָ, לְךָ כִּי לְךָ, לְךָ אַף לְךָ, לְךָ יהוה הַמַּמְלָכָה
כִּי לוֹ נָאֶה, כִּי לוֹ יָאֶה

mentioned in Genesis 19:3 as baking matzot. The fourth stanza focuses on Egypt itself and then the text jumps through history – Jericho and Assyria, Shushan and the lower parts of Babylonia – where we were the unexpected victors in battle, and uses the reference point of our Exodus to explain our triumph: "This is the Pesaḥ." What happened before happened then and will happen again. This is the song of our blessed survival and it all goes back to the object that represents the partnership between God's effort and our own efforts: the Pesaḥ.

FOR HIM IT IS FITTING

This song is also of medieval origin, likely composed in the twelfth or thirteenth century, as we have no earlier documentation for it. We also do not know its author. It references a chorus of angels singing to God. The first words, "Majestic in kingship," are mentioned in the Jerusalem Talmud (Y. Rosh HaShana 4:6) as a prayer of praise. Some believe that it was created by a circle of German pietists for the High Holy Days, which makes sense

King in His kingship, truly awesome: those surrounding Him say to Him:
"Yours and Yours; Yours, for it is Yours; Yours, only Yours;
Yours, LORD, is the kingdom."
FOR HIM IT IS FITTING, FOR HIM IT IS RIGHT.

Humble in kingship, truly the redeemer, His righteous ones say to Him:
"Yours and Yours; Yours, for it is Yours; Yours, only Yours;
Yours, LORD, is the kingdom."
FOR HIM IT IS FITTING, FOR HIM IT IS RIGHT.

Holy in kingship, truly compassionate, His angels say to Him:
"Yours and Yours; Yours, for it is Yours; Yours, only Yours;
Yours, LORD, is the kingdom."
FOR HIM IT IS FITTING, FOR HIM IT IS RIGHT.

Powerful in kingship, truly our support, His perfect ones say to Him:
"Yours and Yours; Yours, for it is Yours; Yours, only Yours;
Yours, LORD, is the kingdom."
FOR HIM IT IS FITTING, FOR HIM IT IS RIGHT.

NIRTZA / PARTING

חֲסַל סִדּוּר פֶּסַח The Pesaḥ service is finished,
as it was meant to be performed,
in accordance with all its rules and laws.
Just as we have been privileged to lay out its order,
so may we be privileged to perform it [in the Temple].
Pure One, dwelling in Your heaven,
raise up this people, too abundant to be counted.
Soon, lead the shoots of [Israel's] stock,
redeemed, into Zion with great joy.

THE PESAḤ SERVICE IS FINISHED

When are we ever finished with anything? Parenting? Working? Spiritual
and professional growth? A painting or poem? All endings are subjective,
but all endings should be noted. Think of a time that you finished something important and made a point of celebrating it.

Continued on the next page.

מֶלֶךְ בִּמְלוּכָה   נוֹרָא כַּהֲלָכָה   סְבִיבָיו יֹאמְרוּ לוֹ
לְךָ וּלְךָ, לְךָ כִּי לְךָ, לְךָ אַף לְךָ, לְךָ יהוה הַמַּמְלָכָה
כִּי לוֹ נָאֶה, כִּי לוֹ יָאֶה

עָנָו בִּמְלוּכָה   פּוֹדֶה כַּהֲלָכָה   צַדִּיקָיו יֹאמְרוּ לוֹ
לְךָ וּלְךָ, לְךָ כִּי לְךָ, לְךָ אַף לְךָ, לְךָ יהוה הַמַּמְלָכָה
כִּי לוֹ נָאֶה, כִּי לוֹ יָאֶה

קָדוֹשׁ בִּמְלוּכָה   רַחוּם כַּהֲלָכָה   שִׁנְאַנָּיו יֹאמְרוּ לוֹ
לְךָ וּלְךָ, לְךָ כִּי לְךָ, לְךָ אַף לְךָ, לְךָ יהוה הַמַּמְלָכָה
כִּי לוֹ נָאֶה, כִּי לוֹ יָאֶה

תַּקִּיף בִּמְלוּכָה   תּוֹמֵךְ כַּהֲלָכָה   תְּמִימָיו יֹאמְרוּ לוֹ
לְךָ וּלְךָ, לְךָ כִּי לְךָ, לְךָ אַף לְךָ, לְךָ יהוה הַמַּמְלָכָה
כִּי לוֹ נָאֶה, כִּי לוֹ יָאֶה

נרצה

חֲסַל סִדּוּר פֶּסַח כְּהִלְכָתוֹ, כְּכָל מִשְׁפָּטוֹ וְחֻקָּתוֹ
כַּאֲשֶׁר זָכִינוּ לְסַדֵּר אוֹתוֹ, כֵּן נִזְכֶּה לַעֲשׂוֹתוֹ
זָךְ שׁוֹכֵן מְעוֹנָה, קוֹמֵם קְהַל עֲדַת מִי מָנָה
קָרֵב נַהֵל נִטְעֵי כַנָּה, פְּדוּיִים לְצִיּוֹן בְּרִנָּה.

---

generously as this? Everything comes from You, and we have given You only what comes from Your hand. We are aliens and strangers in Your sight, as were all our forefathers. Our days on earth are like a shadow, without hope. O LORD our God, as for all this abundance that we have provided for building You a Temple for Your holy name, **it comes from Your hand, and all of it belongs to You.**

Even once a Temple is built, David assured God that it was God's house to do with as He pleased because all belongs to God. Perhaps the transference of this song to Passover addresses the concern that we not read this story as a human military triumph divorced from its spiritual power and animated and inspired by God.

NEXT YEAR
IN JERUSALEM REBUILT!

and our own sense of sacred purpose. We hope that as we sing this song, it bring us closer to each other as a people, one living whole, with Jerusalem as a shared heart.

With this song, we have completed the Exodus, beginning in Egypt and ending in Jerusalem – or at least only a year away from Jerusalem. These three potent words signal closure of the story, but they also raise interesting questions: If you live in Jerusalem, should you say "Next year in Jerusalem"? If you have no intention of going to Jerusalem, should you say this phrase anyway? On an existential and even practical level, we never really know what tomorrow will bring. We may be swept up from the four corners of the rabbinic earth in messianic fervor and be dropped into a golden Jerusalem, waiting for the return of its exiles with warm embrace in this holy city, the center of the very universe on ancient maps. These three words remind us to have faith in God and in a better future. We end our master story of Jewish peoplehood with a shared vision of a geographic and spiritual center: Jerusalem. Even if one lives there geographically, he or she may not live there spiritually. It is for this reason that the Talmud (Berakhot 30a) asks us to direct our prayers ever and ever closer to God in physical and mental proximity:

> If one is standing outside of Israel, he should turn his heart toward the Land of Israel, as it says, "And pray unto You toward their land" (I Kings 8:48). If he is standing in the Land of Israel he should turn his heart toward Jerusalem, as it says, "And they pray to the LORD toward the city You have chosen" (I Kings 8:44). If he is standing in Jerusalem, he should turn his heart toward the Temple, as it says, "If they pray toward this house" (II Chr. 6:26). If he stands in the Temple, he should turn his heart toward the Holy of Holies.

In medieval Spain, Judah Halevi captured this sentiment with his yearnings: "My heart is in the East but I am at the edge of the West." In our collective imagination, every Jewish heart is a resident of Jerusalem.

Think of a time when you were so elated that you broke into song.

לְשָׁנָה הַבָּאָה בִּירוּשָׁלַיִם הַבְּנוּיָה.

How odd it is that we end the order with *Nirtza*, as if we reached the close of a show and an image on a screen appeared with the words "The End." But this, too, is an important part of the way we order our universe. When we reach the end of an accomplishment, we pause and name it, allowing us to stop and look back and then look forward. We declare that we are finished, just as God made a declaration, "The heaven and the earth were finished, and all their array. On the seventh day God finished the work that He had been doing, and He ceased on the seventh day from the work that He had done" (Gen. 2:2). Multiple times are we told here that God, too, finished the world and noted that before Shabbat was introduced, the work of the week had to be done. We begin the Seder with the physical and emotional entrapment of slavery and imagine the rapture of freedom with all its attendant possibilities. And then we arrive and we let everyone know that we have arrived. We let ourselves know that we completed the Seder according to its laws and requirements. If we are asked multiple times in the Bible to pass this story forward, we must make note when we have executed that responsibility of continuity.

If this were not the ending of your Haggada, what end would you choose for this master story?

NEXT YEAR IN JERUSALEM

When we sing this song, let it ring. Let it fill up your lungs and then the entire space. When we sing it we acknowledge that leaving Egypt was not enough. We needed to arrive in the Promised Land to become who we were always meant to be. It is not only what you leave behind but where you are going that matters. And if we feel that perhaps we should not sing this loudly because it will not likely be true to our situation, this expression reminds us that the Jews never thought they would leave Egypt either. So much can happen in a year. We end on a note of possibility; since we do not know what tomorrow will bring, we pray that it brings us closer to holiness, closer to the center of our spiritual world, closer to our families

Some communities sing HaTikva.

כֹּל עוֹד As long as the Jewish spirit
is yearning deep in the heart,
With eyes turned toward the East,
looking toward Zion,

Then our hope –
the two-thousand-year-old hope –
will not be lost:
To be a free people in our land,
The land of Zion and Jerusalem.

---

powerful image of the valley of dry bones in chapter 37, where he claims that hope was lost. God brought Ezekiel to a valley of dry bones and said, "O mortal, will these bones live again?" to which the prophet replied, "O LORD, God, only You know." God then breathed life back into the bones and said to Ezekiel: "O mortal, these bones are the house of Israel. They say, 'Our bones are dried up, our hope is gone; we are doomed'" (37:11). God wanted us to see beyond the reality before us to a vision not yet seen. We will yet live. For us as Jews, hope is never lost.

THE LAND OF ZION AND JERUSALEM

The centrality of Israel represents the next chapter in our master narrative of Jewish peoplehood. For the many centuries that the Haggada has been read around the globe, it is only in the past century that it has been read in the State of Israel as opposed to the Land of Israel. While the Haggada contains passages from the Hebrew Bible and Mishna that were composed in Israel, the document is a product of exile and ends with a sense of yearning. Our yearning does not end because even with a politically autonomous state comes the responsibility of determining the Jewish identity of that state, an issue far from resolution today. Politics aside, it is important to meditate on the fact that we have a land at all. It conjures the emotions of Maimonides, who even in a code of law, took a moment to share the intensity of our feelings about the Holy Land: "Great sages would kiss the borders of the Land of Israel, kiss its stones and roll in its dust, as it says in Psalms: 'Behold, Your servants hold her stones dear and cherish her dust' (102:15)" (*Mishneh Torah*, Laws of Kings and Wars 5:10). Centuries later, the first prime minister of Israel, David Ben-Gurion, formulated a view of

Continued on the next page.

Some communities sing התקווה.

כָּל עוֹד בַּלֵּבָב פְּנִימָה

נֶפֶשׁ יְהוּדִי הוֹמִיָּה

וּלְפַאֲתֵי מִזְרָח, קָדִימָה

עַיִן לְצִיּוֹן צוֹפִיָּה

עוֹד לֹא אָבְדָה תִּקְוָתֵנוּ

הַתִּקְוָה בַּת שְׁנוֹת אַלְפַּיִם

לִהְיוֹת עַם חָפְשִׁי בְּאַרְצֵנוּ

אֶרֶץ צִיּוֹן וִירוּשָׁלָיִם.

HATIKVA

We started with a blessing. Let's end with a blessing – the blessing of being able to sing a national anthem that is all our own, something we never could have imagined as slaves in Egypt. Nothing says freedom quite like an anthem. Some have the custom to sing *HaTikva* at this juncture as an acknowledgment that there is a State of Israel with Jerusalem as its capital, where we can go next year or at any time. It is a beautiful custom that reflects another layer of our collective history: triumph. The point of the Exodus has been realized in our days because we have a home and a refuge for our people. *HaTikva* is based on a poem that Naphtali Herz Imber wrote in 1886. Imber was from Bohemia but immigrated to Palestine and, legend has it, he wrote the poem upon the establishment of Petaḥ Tikva during Ottoman rule. The poem seemed to make itself into an anthem, given its popularity with early Zionists, and was adopted as our anthem by the First Zionist Congress in 1897. Its words were revised several times, and although it served as the anthem upon the declaration of the State, it was actually not official until the Knesset amended it into law in 2004. The melody is attributed to Samuel Cohen, who based it on a musical theme found in Bedrich Smetana's "Moldau." It seems that Smetana may have himself borrowed aspects of the melody from Giuseppe Cenci's "La Mantovana," making the haunting tune more than four hundred years old.

OUR HOPE...WILL NOT BE LOST

"Our hope will not be lost" may be the way the artist responded to Ezekiel's

Outside Israel, the Omer is counted on the second night of the festival.

בָּרוּךְ Blessed are You, LORD our God, King of the Universe, who has made us holy through His commandments, and has commanded us about counting the Omer. Today is the first day of the Omer.

to our people. This anticipatory count that acknowledges the important connection between these two types of covenants is spelled out directly in Leviticus:

> From the day after the Sabbath, the day you brought the sheaf of the wave offering, count off seven full weeks. Count off fifty days up to the day after the seventh Sabbath, and then present an offering of new grain to the LORD. From wherever you live, bring two loaves made of two-tenths of an ephah of fine flour, baked with yeast, as a wave offering of first fruits to the LORD. (23:15–17)

Shavuot is a time when we celebrate receiving the Torah at Sinai, thus deepening our covenant further – the tripartite commitment to people, homeland, and Torah. Who we are. Where we are. And finally, what we are, the values we stand for until eternity.

We count the Omer carefully, by days and weeks. Mystics have a complex *sefira* count that reflects the perfection of character traits on each day following from a belief that human beings have forty-nine drives and tendencies that correspond to the forty-nine days of counting the Omer. The Israelites set out on the fifteenth of Nisan into the wilderness and got to Mount Sinai on the sixth of Sivan, and we mimic their physical journey with a parallel inner journey of the soul.

A beloved friend observes that in Genesis, when Abraham was about to die, the text uses an odd and bulky expression to reflect his age: "The days of the years of his life were..." (25:7). Upon hearing this, I thought of another example. This same expression is used again later when Jacob describes his age to Pharaoh upon their first meeting: "The days of the years of my life are" (47:9). In the first example, Abraham died old and contented. He had lived each of the days of the years of his life in mastery of a sacred mission. Jacob's count reflects the exact opposite, a bitter dissatisfaction that he had not achieved in his days what his ancestors had in theirs. Both patriarchs understood that achievement is not measured in years but by

Continued on the next page.

Outside ארץ ישראל, *the* עומר *is counted on the second night of the festival.*

בָּרוּךְ אַתָּה יהוה אֱלֹהֵינוּ מֶלֶךְ הָעוֹלָם
אֲשֶׁר קִדְּשָׁנוּ בְּמִצְוֹתָיו וְצִוָּנוּ עַל סְפִירַת הָעֹמֶר.
הַיּוֹם יוֹם אֶחָד בָּעֹמֶר.

Israel that was not only religious but also a center for Jewish accomplishments on the world stage: "For most Jews, Israel is Zion. Zion has a special meaning for our people everywhere. Ultimately, it is the meaning of home. Israel is the Jewish home. As such it is a haven. But it is also a functioning enterprise with a future to fulfill and to look forward to." Israel is not only a refuge: "We are a busy, forward-looking nation with much more work to accomplish. Israel cannot just be a refuge. If it is to survive as a valid nation, it has to be much, much more." Ben-Gurion could only have dreamed of the day that Israel would participate as a nation at the United Nations and at Eurovision, at the Olympics, and on the Nasdaq. Israel's Nobel Prizes and scientific accomplishments had yet to feature in Ben-Gurion's worldview, but the seeds of his thinking were already germinating into such a vision of what a Jewish State could become: "You cannot reach for the higher virtue without being an idealist. The Jews are chronic idealists which makes me humbly glad to belong to this people and to have shared in their noble epic."

As you sing this, name the emotions you experience. What word or line resonates most?

Anthems sometimes change and often come under criticism as not reflective of current political, natural, or national realities. If you could write your own national anthem for Israel today, what would it be about?

COUNTING THE OMER

On the second Seder night in the Diaspora and the first day of Ḥol HaMoed in Israel, we begin the forty-nine-day count between Passover and Shavuot. In sacrificial terms, we count between the Paschal lamb sacrifice that shows our collective commitment to Jewish peoplehood and the Omer, the barley sacrifice required on Shavuot based on our harvest in the Land of Israel. In counting, we bridge these two commitments and understand that a commitment to our people without our homeland is not complete; neither is a nationalistic commitment absent a commitment

אַדִּיר הוּא HE IS MAJESTIC
may He build His house soon,
soon, speedily in our days.
Build, O God,   build, O God,
build Your house soon.

He is chosen,	He is great,	He is unmistakable
He is glorious,	He is venerable,	He is worthy
He is kind,	He is pure,	He is One
He is mighty,	He is learned,	He is King
He is awesome,	He is elevated,	He is strong
He is Savior,	He is righteous,	He is holy
He is compassionate,	He is Almighty,	He is powerful

may He build His house soon,
soon, speedily in our days.
Build, O God,   build, O God,
BUILD YOUR HOUSE SOON.

Is there anything in life you are counting up to in anticipation right now?

What personal goal could you set for yourself this Passover that you could keep track of until Shavuot, reporting your results?

HE IS MAJESTIC

This gorgeous song balances adjectives about God with verbs: the being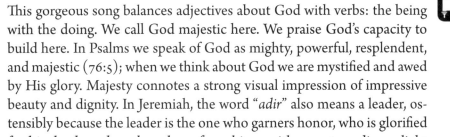
with the doing. We call God majestic here. We praise God's capacity to
build here. In Psalms we speak of God as mighty, powerful, resplendent,
and majestic (76:5); when we think about God we are mystified and awed
by His glory. Majesty connotes a strong visual impression of impressive
beauty and dignity. In Jeremiah, the word "*adir*" also means a leader, ostensibly because the leader is the one who garners honor, who is glorified
for his deeds and works, whose face shines with an extraordinary light
(30:21). When we call God "*adir*," we try – almost impossibly – to capture
these aspects of God and then twin them with what God does that makes
us revere Him. God builds a house. This is odd because if this special *piyut*,

Continued on the next page.

אַדִּיר הוּא
יִבְנֶה בֵיתוֹ בְּקָרוֹב
בִּמְהֵרָה בִּמְהֵרָה, בְּיָמֵינוּ בְּקָרוֹב
אֵל בְּנֵה   אֵל בְּנֵה   בְּנֵה בֵיתְךָ בְּקָרוֹב

דָּגוּל הוּא	גָּדוֹל הוּא	בָּחוּר הוּא
זַכַּאי הוּא	וָתִיק הוּא	הָדוּר הוּא
יָחִיד הוּא	טָהוֹר הוּא	חָסִיד הוּא
מֶלֶךְ הוּא	לָמוּד הוּא	כַּבִּיר הוּא
עִזּוּז הוּא	שַׂגִּיב הוּא	נוֹרָא הוּא
קָדוֹשׁ הוּא	צַדִּיק הוּא	פּוֹדֶה הוּא
תַּקִּיף הוּא	שַׁדַּי הוּא	רַחוּם הוּא

יִבְנֶה בֵיתוֹ בְּקָרוֹב
בִּמְהֵרָה בִּמְהֵרָה, בְּיָמֵינוּ בְּקָרוֹב
אֵל בְּנֵה   אֵל בְּנֵה
בְּנֵה בֵיתְךָ בְּקָרוֹב

---

our small, incremental accomplishments day in and day out, as Winston Churchill once said, "Everyone has his day and some days last longer than others." Some people manage to squeeze more out of a day because they bring more to it. *Yom yom.* Any spiritual or personal goal must be broken down into these daily rhythms of achievement. Any more and it becomes overwhelming. Any less and it dissolves into nothing. People in recovery programs are reminded again and again: one day at a time. A lifetime of abstinence sounds daunting. A day sounds manageable.

With *Sefira,* we remind ourselves that each and every day counts so we must actively count it, building up love and anticipation as we move from the time of liberation to the time of our spiritual maturation.

אֶחָד מִי יוֹדֵעַ WHO KNOWS ONE?
I know one:
our God is One, in heaven and on earth.

Who knows two?
I know two:
two Tablets of the Covenant;
but our God is One, in heaven and on earth.

This song probably comes to us from Germany in the seventeenth century. A tradition in this place and period was to wish someone leaving prayers "*bau gut*" – build well. We imitate God by being good builders ourselves, especially as this night asks us to build up in intensity and feeling our sense of God's extraordinary hand in our lives. The iconic tune (and hand motions) we use also helps us build in intensity the force and urgency of the song as we sing about building. We move through the adjectives from *aleph* onward, reinforcing the same message. With every letter, we praise God. With every letter, we find more subtle ways to notice the way God works in the world. We also have a chance to think about the kind of spaces we build today that are sacred enough to let God in.

WHO KNOWS ONE?

This song is more than five hundred years old and may have had its origins in Germany. It has versions in Yiddish, Hebrew, and English, in addition to many other languages. Its history may not be clear, but its message certainly is. In the call-and-response style in which it is often sung, it asks each participant to be the "I" in the song. If this night long ago cemented our relationship with God – making us a nation under the Divine Presence – then each of us must reiterate that commitment personally. Who knows God, the One who originated all life and every created thing, who designed the universe through acts of separation as if to suggest that all living things were once ultimately one, originally connected to each other? God did, and we try, in bridging the abyss this night, to achieve closeness and intimacy with God through knowledge.

אֶחָד מִי יוֹדֵעַ

אֶחָד אֲנִי יוֹדֵעַ
אֶחָד אֱלֹהֵינוּ שֶׁבַּשָּׁמַיִם וּבָאָרֶץ

שְׁנַיִם מִי יוֹדֵעַ
שְׁנַיִם אֲנִי יוֹדֵעַ
שְׁנֵי לוּחוֹת הַבְּרִית
אֶחָד אֱלֹהֵינוּ שֶׁבַּשָּׁמַיִם וּבָאָרֶץ

---

prose poem, is about the Temple then it is we who built God's house in the days of old. It was the community of Israel with Moses at its head who built the *Mishkan*, the Tabernacle. King Solomon with his extensive labor forces built the Temple, which was destroyed in 586 BCE, and then rebuilt again in approximately 516 BCE; it stood until 70 CE, before the second destruction. Here we ask God to be the ultimate builder in creating the conditions by which we may once again rebuild this holy Sanctuary, no easy fate with the complex political cocktail of forces surrounding its location today. May the next Temple be built without violence. May it be built as a structure that celebrates our unity rather than be a source of Jewish divisiveness. May it be a gathering place for exiles and a place of solace for those seeking a spiritual anchor.

Alternatively, we may be thanking God for the very fact that God allowed the Divine Presence to occupy a space at all, as recorded initially in Exodus: "And let them make Me a sanctuary that I may dwell among them. Exactly as I show you … so shall you make it" (25:8–9). God gave us the exact specifications, offering us expert guidance in how to create a dwelling worthy of the divine. God created a presence at the heart of the Israelite camp, showing us His portability; God would travel with us and help us feel less alone, more protected, less remote, more intimate. The presence of God is not a given in our lives. Many spend a lifetime seeking God without direction or a sense of destination. The God of the Hebrew Bible gave us more.

Who knows three?
I know three:
three fathers,
two Tablets of the Covenant;
but our God is One, in heaven and on earth.

Who knows four?
I know four:
four mothers,
three fathers,
two Tablets of the Covenant;
but our God is One, in heaven and on earth.

Who knows five?
I know five:
five books of the Torah,
four mothers,
three fathers,
two Tablets of the Covenant;
but our God is One, in heaven and on earth.

Who knows six?
I know six:
six divisions of the Mishna,
five books of the Torah,
four mothers,
three fathers,
two Tablets of the Covenant;
but our God is One, in heaven and on earth.

שְׁלוֹשָׁה מִי יוֹדֵעַ
שְׁלוֹשָׁה אֲנִי יוֹדֵעַ
שְׁלוֹשָׁה אָבוֹת
שְׁנֵי לוּחוֹת הַבְּרִית
אֶחָד אֱלֹהֵינוּ שֶׁבַּשָּׁמַיִם וּבָאָרֶץ

אַרְבַּע מִי יוֹדֵעַ
אַרְבַּע אֲנִי יוֹדֵעַ
אַרְבַּע אִמָּהוֹת
שְׁלוֹשָׁה אָבוֹת   שְׁנֵי לוּחוֹת הַבְּרִית
אֶחָד אֱלֹהֵינוּ שֶׁבַּשָּׁמַיִם וּבָאָרֶץ

חֲמִשָּׁה מִי יוֹדֵעַ
חֲמִשָּׁה אֲנִי יוֹדֵעַ
חֲמִשָּׁה חֻמְשֵׁי תוֹרָה
אַרְבַּע אִמָּהוֹת   שְׁלוֹשָׁה אָבוֹת
שְׁנֵי לוּחוֹת הַבְּרִית
אֶחָד אֱלֹהֵינוּ שֶׁבַּשָּׁמַיִם וּבָאָרֶץ

שִׁשָּׁה מִי יוֹדֵעַ
שִׁשָּׁה אֲנִי יוֹדֵעַ
שִׁשָּׁה סִדְרֵי מִשְׁנָה
חֲמִשָּׁה חֻמְשֵׁי תוֹרָה   אַרְבַּע אִמָּהוֹת
שְׁלוֹשָׁה אָבוֹת
שְׁנֵי לוּחוֹת הַבְּרִית
אֶחָד אֱלֹהֵינוּ שֶׁבַּשָּׁמַיִם וּבָאָרֶץ

Who knows seven?
I know seven:
seven days from Sabbath to Sabbath,
six divisions of the Mishna,
five books of the Torah,
four mothers,
three fathers,
two Tablets of the Covenant;
but our God is One, in heaven and on earth.

Who knows eight?
I know eight:
eight days to a brit,
seven days from Sabbath to Sabbath,
six divisions of the Mishna,
five books of the Torah,
four mothers,
three fathers,
two Tablets of the Covenant;
but our God is One, in heaven and on earth.

Who knows nine?
I know nine:
nine months until birth, eight days to a brit,
seven days from Sabbath to Sabbath,
six divisions of the Mishna,
five books of the Torah,
four mothers,
three fathers,
two Tablets of the Covenant;
but our God is One, in heaven and on earth.

שִׁבְעָה מִי יוֹדֵעַ

שִׁבְעָה אֲנִי יוֹדֵעַ

שִׁבְעָה יְמֵי שַׁבְּתָא

שִׁשָּׁה סִדְרֵי מִשְׁנָה   חֲמִשָּׁה חֻמְשֵׁי תוֹרָה

אַרְבַּע אִמָּהוֹת   שְׁלוֹשָׁה אָבוֹת

שְׁנֵי לוּחוֹת הַבְּרִית

אֶחָד אֱלֹהֵינוּ שֶׁבַּשָּׁמַיִם וּבָאָרֶץ

שְׁמוֹנָה מִי יוֹדֵעַ

שְׁמוֹנָה אֲנִי יוֹדֵעַ

שְׁמוֹנָה יְמֵי מִילָה

שִׁבְעָה יְמֵי שַׁבְּתָא   שִׁשָּׁה סִדְרֵי מִשְׁנָה

חֲמִשָּׁה חֻמְשֵׁי תוֹרָה   אַרְבַּע אִמָּהוֹת

שְׁלוֹשָׁה אָבוֹת

שְׁנֵי לוּחוֹת הַבְּרִית

אֶחָד אֱלֹהֵינוּ שֶׁבַּשָּׁמַיִם וּבָאָרֶץ

תִּשְׁעָה מִי יוֹדֵעַ

תִּשְׁעָה אֲנִי יוֹדֵעַ

תִּשְׁעָה יַרְחֵי לֵדָה

שְׁמוֹנָה יְמֵי מִילָה   שִׁבְעָה יְמֵי שַׁבְּתָא

שִׁשָּׁה סִדְרֵי מִשְׁנָה   חֲמִשָּׁה חֻמְשֵׁי תוֹרָה

אַרְבַּע אִמָּהוֹת   שְׁלוֹשָׁה אָבוֹת

שְׁנֵי לוּחוֹת הַבְּרִית

אֶחָד אֱלֹהֵינוּ שֶׁבַּשָּׁמַיִם וּבָאָרֶץ

Who knows ten?
I know ten:
Ten Commandments,
nine months until birth, eight days to a brit,
seven days from Sabbath to Sabbath,
six divisions of the Mishna,
five books of the Torah,
four mothers, three fathers,
two Tablets of the Covenant;
but our God is One, in heaven and on earth.

Who knows eleven?
I know eleven:
eleven stars [in Joseph's dream],
Ten Commandments,
nine months until birth,
eight days to a brit,
seven days from Sabbath to Sabbath,
six divisions of the Mishna, five books of the Torah,
four mothers, three fathers,
two Tablets of the Covenant;
but our God is One, in heaven and on earth.

Who knows twelve?
I know twelve:
twelve tribes, eleven stars,
Ten Commandments,
nine months until birth,
eight days to a brit,
seven days from Sabbath to Sabbath,
six divisions of the Mishna, five books of the Torah,
four mothers, three fathers,
two Tablets of the Covenant;
but our God is One, in heaven and on earth.

עֲשָׂרָה מִי יוֹדֵעַ

עֲשָׂרָה אֲנִי יוֹדֵעַ

עֲשָׂרָה דִבְּרַיָא

תִּשְׁעָה יַרְחֵי לֵדָה   שְׁמוֹנָה יְמֵי מִילָה

שִׁבְעָה יְמֵי שַׁבַּתָּא   שִׁשָּׁה סִדְרֵי מִשְׁנָה

חֲמִשָּׁה חֻמְשֵׁי תוֹרָה   אַרְבַּע אִמָּהוֹת   שְׁלוֹשָׁה אָבוֹת

שְׁנֵי לוּחוֹת הַבְּרִית

אֶחָד אֱלֹהֵינוּ שֶׁבַּשָּׁמַיִם וּבָאָרֶץ

אַחַד עָשָׂר מִי יוֹדֵעַ

אַחַד עָשָׂר אֲנִי יוֹדֵעַ

אַחַד עָשָׂר כּוֹכְבַיָא

עֲשָׂרָה דִבְּרַיָא   תִּשְׁעָה יַרְחֵי לֵדָה

שְׁמוֹנָה יְמֵי מִילָה   שִׁבְעָה יְמֵי שַׁבַּתָּא

שִׁשָּׁה סִדְרֵי מִשְׁנָה   חֲמִשָּׁה חֻמְשֵׁי תוֹרָה

אַרְבַּע אִמָּהוֹת   שְׁלוֹשָׁה אָבוֹת   שְׁנֵי לוּחוֹת הַבְּרִית

אֶחָד אֱלֹהֵינוּ שֶׁבַּשָּׁמַיִם וּבָאָרֶץ

שְׁנֵים עָשָׂר מִי יוֹדֵעַ

שְׁנֵים עָשָׂר אֲנִי יוֹדֵעַ

שְׁנֵים עָשָׂר שִׁבְטַיָא

אַחַד עָשָׂר כּוֹכְבַיָא   עֲשָׂרָה דִבְּרַיָא

תִּשְׁעָה יַרְחֵי לֵדָה   שְׁמוֹנָה יְמֵי מִילָה

שִׁבְעָה יְמֵי שַׁבַּתָּא   שִׁשָּׁה סִדְרֵי מִשְׁנָה   חֲמִשָּׁה חֻמְשֵׁי תוֹרָה

אַרְבַּע אִמָּהוֹת   שְׁלוֹשָׁה אָבוֹת   שְׁנֵי לוּחוֹת הַבְּרִית

אֶחָד אֱלֹהֵינוּ שֶׁבַּשָּׁמַיִם וּבָאָרֶץ

Who knows thirteen?

I know thirteen:

thirteen attributes [of God's compassion],

twelve tribes,

eleven stars,

Ten Commandments,

nine months until birth,

eight days to a brit,

seven days from Sabbath to Sabbath,

six divisions of the Mishna,

five books of the Torah,

four mothers,

three fathers,

two Tablets of the Covenant;

BUT

OUR GOD

IS ONE,

IN HEAVEN AND ON EARTH.

שְׁלוֹשָׁה עָשָׂר מִי יוֹדֵעַ

שְׁלוֹשָׁה עָשָׂר אֲנִי יוֹדֵעַ

שְׁלוֹשָׁה עָשָׂר מִדַּיָּא

שְׁנֵים עָשָׂר שִׁבְטַיָּא

אַחַד עָשָׂר כּוֹכְבַיָּא

עֲשָׂרָה דִבְּרַיָּא

תִּשְׁעָה יַרְחֵי לֵדָה

שְׁמוֹנָה יְמֵי מִילָה

שִׁבְעָה יְמֵי שַׁבְּתָא

שִׁשָּׁה סִדְרֵי מִשְׁנָה

חֲמִשָּׁה חֻמְשֵׁי תוֹרָה

אַרְבַּע אִמָּהוֹת

שְׁלוֹשָׁה אָבוֹת

שְׁנֵי לוּחוֹת הַבְּרִית

אֶחָד

אֱלֹהֵינוּ

שֶׁבַּשָּׁמַיִם וּבָאָרֶץ

חַד גַּדְיָא ONE LITTLE GOAT

one little goat
my father bought for two zuzim;
one little goat, one little goat.

Along came a cat and ate the goat
my father bought for two zuzim;
one little goat, one little goat.

Then came a dog and bit the cat who ate the goat
my father bought for two zuzim;
one little goat, one little goat.

Then came a stick and hit the dog who bit the cat
who ate the goat
my father bought for two zuzim;
one little goat, one little goat.

Then came a fire and burned the stick that hit the dog
who bit the cat who ate the goat
my father bought for two zuzim;
one little goat, one little goat.

---

get the last laugh. We still survive to sing about our vulnerability. We are the one little goat who outdid the typical domestic enemies: the cat, the dog, the stick, the fire. And we even beat the larger, more threatening, harder, but looming enemies: the ox, the butcher, the Angel of Death, before finally God appears. Some name each animal as representing a different nation bound on our destruction, from the Assyrians to the Babylonians to the Crusaders and then more modern-day enemies. What starts the entire song moving is the two zuzim used to purchase the goat, referring to the two tablets given to us at Sinai. Because we were claimed and "purchased" for this covenant, God ultimately intervenes to make sure that we are protected and redeemed, and that is the message of Passover generally as we close the Seder. The song asks us not to fear the repetition of our hardest hours in history because God breaks the cycle of violence, and we endure. It also communicates a more personal message when we see ourselves as

Continued on the next page.

חַד גַּדְיָא חַד גַּדְיָא

דְּזַבִּן אַבָּא בִּתְרֵי זוּזֵי

חַד גַּדְיָא חַד גַּדְיָא

וַאֲתָא שׁוּנְרָא וְאָכְלָה לְגַדְיָא

דְּזַבִּן אַבָּא בִּתְרֵי זוּזֵי

חַד גַּדְיָא חַד גַּדְיָא

וַאֲתָא כַלְבָּא וְנָשַׁךְ לְשׁוּנְרָא דְּאָכְלָה לְגַדְיָא

דְּזַבִּן אַבָּא בִּתְרֵי זוּזֵי

חַד גַּדְיָא חַד גַּדְיָא

וַאֲתָא חֻטְרָא וְהִכָּה לְכַלְבָּא דְּנָשַׁךְ לְשׁוּנְרָא

דְּאָכְלָה לְגַדְיָא

דְּזַבִּן אַבָּא בִּתְרֵי זוּזֵי

חַד גַּדְיָא חַד גַּדְיָא

וַאֲתָא נוּרָא וְשָׂרַף לְחֻטְרָא דְּהִכָּה לְכַלְבָּא

דְּנָשַׁךְ לְשׁוּנְרָא דְּאָכְלָה לְגַדְיָא

דְּזַבִּן אַבָּא בִּתְרֵי זוּזֵי

חַד גַּדְיָא חַד גַּדְיָא

ONE LITTLE GOAT

Ḥad Gadya is a fanciful whimsy of a song, likely of medieval German origin. This type of folksong that introduces characters who each have a destructive relationship with the previous character creates an image of a creature who ultimately swallows all. While it is a song performed with a lot of enthusiasm, props, and sound effects, it hides a certain dark message. Are we – on this night of the Paschal lamb (which could be a goat, according to Exodus 12:5 – "you may take it from sheep or from goats") – suggesting that so many of our enemies have come to swallow us and obliterate us? We

Then came water and put out the fire that burned the stick
that hit the dog who bit the cat who ate the goat
my father bought for two zuzim;
one little goat, one little goat.

Then came an ox and drank the water that put out the fire
that burned the stick that hit the dog who bit the cat who ate the goat
my father bought for two zuzim;
one little goat, one little goat.

Then came a slaughterer and slew the ox who drank the water
that put out the fire that burned the stick that hit the dog
who bit the cat who ate the goat
my father bought for two zuzim;
one little goat, one little goat.

Then came the Angel of Death and slew the slaughterer
who slew the ox who drank the water that put out the fire
that burned the stick that hit the dog
who bit the cat who ate the goat
my father bought for two zuzim;
one little goat, one little goat.

Then came the Holy One
and slew the Angel of Death, who slew the slaughterer
who slew the ox who drank the water that put out the fire
that burned the stick that hit the dog
who bit the cat who ate the goat
my father bought for two zuzim;
ONE LITTLE GOAT, ONE LITTLE GOAT.

---

fragile in this world – that will live on, that will become the Paschal lamb
and symbolize our freedom for eternity. We never ask to turn into the ox
or the butcher to combat our enemies. We ask to stay small and humble
and for our humility to be the hallmark of our identity, along with the two
zuzim, the laws, that keep us holy.

וְאָתָא מַיָּא   וְכָבָה לְנוּרָא   דְּשָׂרַף לְחֻטְרָא   דְּהִכָּה לְכַלְבָּא
דְּנָשַׁךְ לְשׁוּנְרָא   דְּאָכְלָה לְגַדְיָא
דְּזַבִּן אַבָּא בִּתְרֵי זוּזֵי
חַד גַּדְיָא   חַד גַּדְיָא

וְאָתָא תוֹרָא   וְשָׁתָה לְמַיָּא   דְּכָבָה לְנוּרָא   דְּשָׂרַף לְחֻטְרָא
דְּהִכָּה לְכַלְבָּא   דְּנָשַׁךְ לְשׁוּנְרָא   דְּאָכְלָה לְגַדְיָא
דְּזַבִּן אַבָּא בִּתְרֵי זוּזֵי
חַד גַּדְיָא   חַד גַּדְיָא

וְאָתָא הַשּׁוֹחֵט   וְשָׁחַט לְתוֹרָא   דְּשָׁתָא לְמַיָּא   דְּכָבָה לְנוּרָא
דְּשָׂרַף לְחֻטְרָא   דְּהִכָּה לְכַלְבָּא   דְּנָשַׁךְ לְשׁוּנְרָא   דְּאָכְלָה לְגַדְיָא
דְּזַבִּן אַבָּא בִּתְרֵי זוּזֵי
חַד גַּדְיָא   חַד גַּדְיָא

וְאָתָא מַלְאַךְ הַמָּוֶת   וְשָׁחַט לְשׁוֹחֵט   דְּשָׁחַט לְתוֹרָא
דְּשָׁתָא לְמַיָּא   דְּכָבָה לְנוּרָא   דְּשָׂרַף לְחֻטְרָא
דְּהִכָּה לְכַלְבָּא   דְּנָשַׁךְ לְשׁוּנְרָא   דְּאָכְלָה לְגַדְיָא
דְּזַבִּן אַבָּא בִּתְרֵי זוּזֵי
חַד גַּדְיָא   חַד גַּדְיָא

וְאָתָא הַקָּדוֹשׁ בָּרוּךְ הוּא   וְשָׁחַט לְמַלְאַךְ הַמָּוֶת   דְּשָׁחַט לְשׁוֹחֵט
דְּשָׁחַט לְתוֹרָא   דְּשָׁתָא לְמַיָּא   דְּכָבָה לְנוּרָא   דְּשָׂרַף לְחֻטְרָא
דְּהִכָּה לְכַלְבָּא   דְּנָשַׁךְ לְשׁוּנְרָא   דְּאָכְלָה לְגַדְיָא
דְּזַבִּן אַבָּא בִּתְרֵי זוּזֵי
חַד גַּדְיָא   חַד גַּדְיָא

a vulnerable little goat facing difficult demons and walls ahead. It is the
little goat or lamb – the small, innocent symbol of all that is precious and